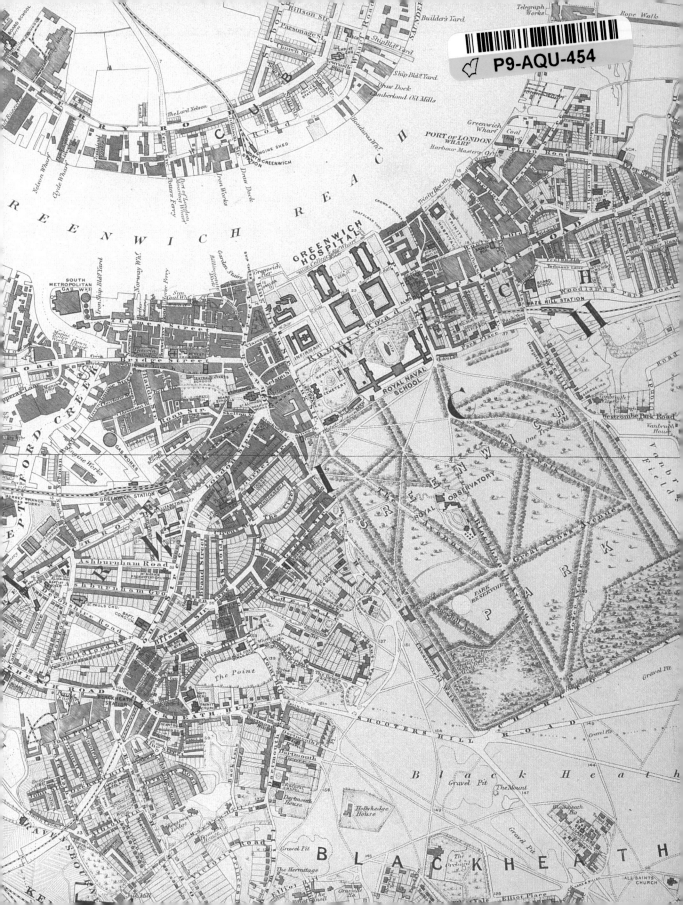

# THE STORY OF
# GREENWICH

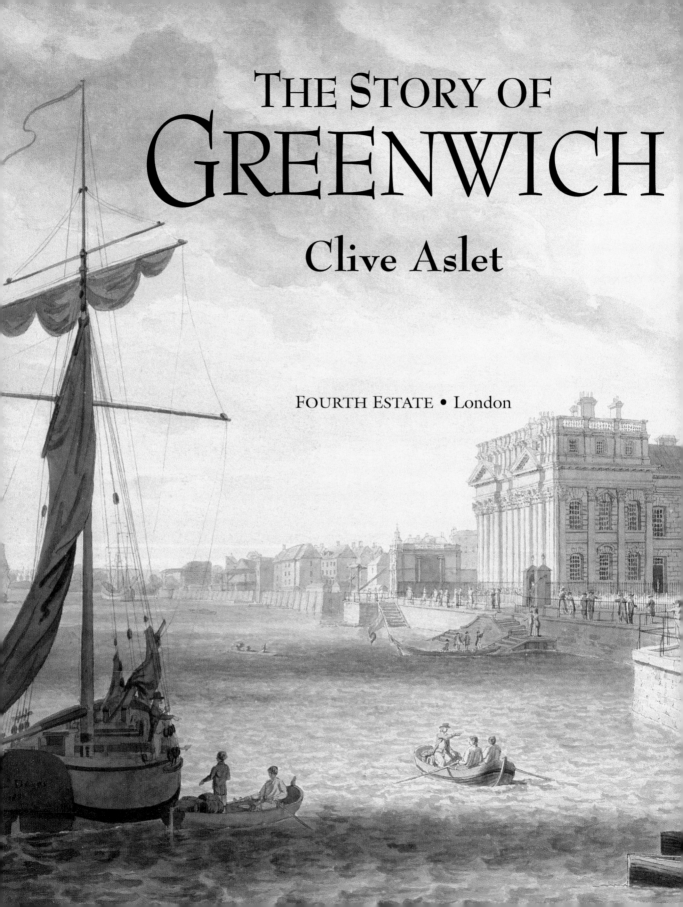

# THE STORY OF
# GREENWICH

## Clive Aslet

FOURTH ESTATE • London

*To Johnny*

I would like to thank the following for their help in making this book: Pieter van der Merwe, an historian as well as resident of Greenwich, who not only provided many insights but also read the manuscript; Julian Bowsher and other archaeologists in the Museum of London for help steering me through Greenwich's early history; the incomparable Lucy Pelz and Virginia Forrester, for additional research; Richard Ormond, director of the National Maritime Museum; and antiquarian, restaurateur and Greenwich resident, Dick Moy. Julian Watson and the staff of the Greenwich Local History Library have gone beyond the call of duty, as has Ralph Hyde, Keeper of Prints and Maps at the Guildhall Library. Mr Watson also read the manuscript. Juliet Brightmore's triumph in picture research speaks for itself. I owe a special debt to my editor Clive Priddle because he had the original idea for this book. But any errors in it are entirely my own.

First published in Great Britain in 1999 by
Fourth Estate Limited
6 Salem Road
London W2 4BU

Copyright © Clive Aslet 1999

1 3 5 7 9 10 8 6 4 2

The right of Clive Aslet to be identified as the author of this work has been asserted by him in accordance with the Copyright, Designs and Patents Act 1988.

A catalogue record for this book is available from the British Library.

ISBN 1-85702-825-2

Picture research by Juliet Brightmore
Designed by Robert Updegraff
Colour separations by ArtiColor, Verona
Printed in Italy by L.E.G.O., Vicenza

*Endpapers:* **Stanford's *Map of London*, 1886.**
*Half-title:* **Allegory of Britannia with Greenwich and the railway behind, c.1840.**
*Title pages:* **View of Greenwich Hospital, 1788, watercolour by Edward Dayes.**
*Overleaf:* **Greenwich Hospital from the River, c.1748, by Samuel Wale.**

# CONTENTS

The whole civilised world has heard of Greenwich. The very boot-blacks in the basement of Charing Cross Station know something of it. See?

from *The Secret Agent* by Joseph Conrad, 1907

# *Prologue*

Christmas Eve, 1805: Greenwich. It had been a filthy day, with a westerly gale blowing. As dusk fell, a crowd of men, many of them missing limbs, stood beside the river stairs of the Seamen's Hospital in Greenwich. These pensioners, buffeted by the wars against France, had been there all afternoon. So had an assembly of people from the little town that lay around the skirts of this great complex of buildings. With them were a troop of the Loyal Greenwich Volunteers, together with the River Fencibles (always 'very complete', it was later remembered, as regards both equipment and discipline). Lord Hood, the admiral who was now Governor of the Hospital, may have reflected on the dignity of the scene. The terrace on which they had assembled was surrounded by perhaps the most splendid parade of public architecture in Britain. The feet of the patiently waiting crowd stood on ground that had once belonged to the royal palace where Henry VIII and Elizabeth I were born.

They had been waiting for several hours, on that miserable afternoon. The light failed, then darkness closed in. The river was in darkness, on the opposite bank was darkness; they were wrapped in darkness. As the crowd shuffled to keep warm, rain lashing them, they may have felt that they were participating in another great moment in the country's history. For they were there to receive the body of Horatio Nelson back on to British soil, his death having shot through the celebrations after the British triumph at Trafalgar with national grief. But there was no sign of the yacht bearing the coffin. Hood concluded that it was not coming that day. He dismissed the guard and retired to his quarters, and the crowd melted away to glowing fires and dry clothes. By eight o'clock the pensioners – sea-hardened men, in the prime of life, despite their injuries – had warmed themselves with their Christmas double-ration of rum. The day's fruitless vigil perhaps inspired some of them to reminisce about Nelson.

After Trafalgar, Nelson's flagship the *Victory* had been patched up sufficiently to struggle home. It reached the south coast of England six weeks later, in early December. When the Prince of Wales, who had already been 'affected most extremely' by the news of Nelson's death, saw it from the Royal Pavilion at

Brighton, his emotionally susceptible nature suffered a new agony of soul. The *Victory* anchored in the Thames estuary. Nelson's remains, pickled from the cask of spirits where they had been preserved during the long sea voyage, were laid in a coffin made from the wood of the mainmast saved from the French ship *L'Orient*, which had blown up at the Battle of the Nile. *L'Orient's* mast had been fir. This coffin was in turn placed inside another one made of lead, appropriately lined with thick planks of British oak. Thus encased, Nelson's body was transferred from the *Victory* to Commissioner Grey's yacht to sail up the Thames to Greenwich. It was accompanied by his chaplain, Alexander Scott, and a hand-picked guard from the *Victory*, who would not be parted from their commander.

Bells tolled, then rang a muffled peal. Minute guns boomed out from Tilbury and Gravesend. As the weather worsened, the yacht struggled up the river. According to the *Naval Chronicle*, Lord Hood received the body 'with the greatest privacy'. This was something of an understatement. On that tempestuous Christmas Eve nobody at Greenwich had stayed on the waterfront to notice the yacht painfully beating its way up the Thames. At eight o'clock, when it anchored in front of the great riverfront gates, the terrace was deserted. The sailors from the *Victory* managed to land the coffin, weighing nearly four hundred-weight, and carry it to the top of the slime-covered steps. But they had to leave it there while someone went into the Hospital by another entrance to find the officer with the keys to the river gate. He came hurrying up to let them in, and the party proceeded to the Painted Hall. That was also found to be locked, so another search for the man with the keys began. Finally the body was carried into a little room off the Upper Hall used for storing documents and records. Here it was found that no one had remembered to arrange a stand for the coffin, so some of the sailors had to go back on to the yacht to bring the trestles that had supported it on deck. It was nearly Christmas Day before they were finished.

Greenwich was a doubly appropriate destination for the hero's body. For the previous five hundred years it had been associated with the pageantry of great state occasions, through its role as a royal palace; and it was as strongly allied with Britain's maritime expansion as it was possible to be. Furthermore, Nelson had known Greenwich when he was alive. In recent years he had not spent many days ashore in England, but on at least one occasion he stayed at Greenwich, as the guest of his old friend and former 'sea-daddy' Captain William Locker, who was Lieutenant-Governor of the Hospital. It was in October 1797, soon after Nelson had lost his arm, and he was taking opium every night for the pain. Crushed into the carriage that transported Nelson and his wife to Greenwich was Sir Gilbert Elliot, soon to become Lord Minto, who was suffering badly from gout. It cannot have been an entirely cheerful outing. Writing to his wife, Sir Gilbert reported that Nelson was 'impatient for the healing of his wound that he may go to sea again. He writes very tolerably with his left hand.'

Horatio Nelson, painted by Lemuel Abbott. This is one of several versions made from sketches for which the then Rear-Admiral sat at Greenwich in 1797.

At the Hospital, the Nelsons were received by Mrs Locker and her family in the drawing-room of their apartment. Part of the object of the visit was for the sea-hero to have his portrait painted by Lemuel Abbott. This took place in the panelled room that was Locker's personal sanctum. In after years Locker's daughter would recall how she helped Nelson 'on and off with his gold-laced coat before and after each sitting', according to her nephew Frederick Locker-Lampson. Two sketches were made of Nelson that October. From these were generated some forty derivative likenesses, as well as a mezzotint.

Locker had died in 1801, and now, in the last days of 1805, it was in the Record Room that Nelson's body was laid, while the walls of the Painted Hall were draped in black, and a dais, canopy and heavy curtains were erected. According to *Fairburn's Edition of the Funeral of Admiral Lord Nelson*, a contemporary report of the obsequies, the setting for the 'melancholy spectacle' was achieved 'with peculiar taste and elegance; and was beyond all precedent, mournfully grand and impressive'. The lying-in-state began after the New Year. The first mourners included the Princess of Wales, a usually boisterous figure who on this occasion, wrote Admiral Collingwood, 'remained several hours in contemplation and silent sorrow'. When she had gone a 'few persons of respectability' were admitted. Then, for three days, the British public was given the opportunity to pay its last respects to its hero. The queues of people wanting to file past the coffin stretched all the way back into London. 'During those three days the road from the metropolis to Greenwich was covered with carriages and foot-passengers of every description, as was also the river below the bridge with boats, filled with persons anxious for the sight. Greenwich was never so full of visitors since the memory of man.' It is estimated that ninety thousand people filed past the coffin – an enormous number. The entrances to the Hospital were guarded once again by Volunteers and River Fencibles. Cheering greeted the forty-six seamen and fourteen marines who had fought under Nelson on the *Victory*, when they jumped ashore from their brig. In that emotionally expressive age, 'every eye' watching the scene was so moved by the combined feelings of 'rapture and agony' that it shed tears.

Eventually, the funeral procession that followed the coffin to its final resting-place in St Paul's Cathedral would include most of the great figures of the age. It was so long that the vanguard had already arrived at St Paul's before the last peers and others had properly left the starting-point in Whitehall. But the departure of the coffin from Greenwich had been even more dramatic. 'No spectacle was ever so interesting, and none ever excited such an ardent curiosity among the public.' It took place on 8 January 1806. The night before had been squally, but the morning dawned bright and clear, and winter sunshine sparkled on the barges that were assembling to accompany Nelson's mortal remains. The leading barges were solemnly draped in black cloth, the one carrying Nelson in black velvet. Drums and trumpets sounded funeral music. All the state barges that could be mustered – the King's, the Lords Commissioners of the Admiralty's, the Lord Mayor's – manoeuvred into position. Five hundred pensioners, all of whom had served with Nelson, preceded the coffin as it left the Painted Hall. At three o'clock, the body was carried down the stairs from the terrace of the Hospital. Just at that moment the skies darkened and a violent hailstorm exploded over the river like grapeshot. The procession of barges stretched out for a mile, the oarsmen rowing bravely through the rain. At last it reached Whitehall steps. Four admirals gathered to hold up the canopy that would cover Nelson's coffin for the short journey to its overnight lodging in the Admiralty. And then the downpour stopped, the clouds parted and the sun burst forth. It seemed to be a piece of natural symbolism to complement the more florid attempts of the Lord Chamberlain's department, as though the gods of the watery element were angry at surrendering their hero.

The next day, which saw one of the most theatrically impressive ceremonies ever staged in Britain, belonged to London. But Greenwich, its history interwoven with the sea, kept the memory of it alive for longer. After the funeral, the famous funeral car, its prow imitating the *Victory* and its canopy supported by palm trees recalling the Battle of the Nile, was displayed in the vestibule to the Painted Hall. It stayed there until 1840, when it was found to have decayed so badly that it was broken up. By then a shrine of Nelson memorabilia had been established. The relics included the coat he had worn at the Battle of the Nile and a stocking worn at Tenerife in 1797. Prince Albert donated the coat and waistcoat which Nelson had worn at Trafalgar, complete with bullet hole, in 1845. In 1810 a sculpture depicting the death of Nelson was put into the colonnade pediments of the King William court of the Hospital. One of the most famous protagonists of that drama, Captain Thomas Hardy, lies not far away. Later a sea lord, a vice-admiral and a baronet, Hardy became Governor of the Hospital, his time being remembered for the change in pensioners' uniforms from outmoded knee breeches to trousers. He is buried in the Hospital mausoleum, alongside the modern Maritime Museum. Dr Beattie, the doctor who attended Nelson as he lay dying, joined Hardy as the physician to Greenwich Hospital, wearing the bullet that had killed Nelson as a brooch.

Nelson's funeral procession leaves the Royal Hospital for Seamen at Greenwich, 8 January 1806. The Admiral's body is contained in the barge flying the Union flag. The barges had spent all morning manoeuvring into position. Watercolour over etched outline by A. C. Pugin.

A. C. Pugin's aquatint of Nelson's lying-in-state at Greenwich Hospital. Nelson's devoted chaplain, Alexander Scott, stayed with the body throughout the lying-in-state. The crowds of people wanting to pay their respects stretched all the way from Greenwich to London.

It was a subject of national scandal when a thief, hiding behind one of the statues in the Painted Hall, wrenched the gold hilts off Nelson's dress swords (including the one that had lain on his coffin), forced the jewels from their scabbards and made off with such precious relics as Nelson's Order of the Bath and other decorations, along with his gold watch and seal. History repeated itself in 1950 when the gaudiest of all the decorations which Nelson was entitled to wear – and wear them he did – was stolen from the National Maritime Museum. This was the famous Chelengk, a diamond ornament given to Nelson by the Sultan of Turkey after the Battle of the Nile (it can be seen in the portrait by Lemuel Abbott). These thefts reflect the iconic status that Nelson occupies in the British mind. There is a certain pathos in the inability of those with custody of them to guard them securely. But by far the sorriest tale uniting Nelson's memory with Greenwich concerns the shabby figure whom a Major Gordon met in 1811 as she shepherded half a dozen school children through Greenwich Park. It was Nelson's destitute mistress, Emma Hamilton, with their daughter Horatia; it was

Horatia's birthday, and she was being taken to meet some of the heroes of Trafalgar in the Hospital as a treat.

Echoes of national history resonate through every corner of Greenwich. Its role in Nelson's funeral rites suggests that it has long been used to having the eyes of the whole country upon it. With the dawn of the new millennium, it will attract the attention not just of Britain but the world. It is more than just a borough in the suburbs of London, more than a collection of great buildings, more than a location where people of distinction have lived. It is one of very few places to have been endowed, both intentionally and by association, with a symbolic identity. Recently this has been recognised by the choice of Greenwich as the site of the Millennium Dome and as a UNESCO World Heritage Site. It reflects associations with British history, the history of the world – the history, it might almost be said, of time itself – which stretch back for hundreds if not thousands of years. This book sets out to trace them.

*'Ah! The Navy an't what it was!'* **Two Greenwich pensioners lament changing times in a coloured lithograph of 1828.**

# A DEAD STICK
# BURSTS INTO LEAF

AT THE TOP OF A STEEP HILL, about half a mile back from the River Thames, stands one of the oddities of English architecture: a gimcrack little building that nevertheless boasts turrets, very tall sash windows, all the appurtenances of the English Renaissance – as well as, on top of one of the turrets, a large red ball on a spike. This is the old Royal Observatory at Greenwich, where seventeenth-century astronomers sought to fathom the workings of the universe by means of long telescopes and pendulum clocks. They had the good fortune to work in a building which not only provided a clear view of the heavens, but enjoyed a celebrated panorama of London and the Thames. Visitors regularly exclaimed over it, perhaps finding these observations easier to comprehend than those of the Astronomers Royal. There is no better place to take a first look at Greenwich.

From the terrace, two millennia of history seem to roll out down the slope in front of you like a carpet. In the distance, London, the temples of Mammon, as one might conceive the modern skyscrapers, now overshadowing St Paul's Cathedral; to the left, Deptford, home to the Tudor navy, and the town of Greenwich, much of it little changed since the Regency; in the middle foreground, Charles II's park, the Queen's House that was completed for his mother Henrietta Maria, and beyond it, the baroque parade of what used to be the old Seamen's Hospital, was until recently the Royal Naval College and is now becoming a campus of the University of Greenwich. Above this rise the masts of the nineteenth-century tea-clipper the *Cutty Sark*, and then the eye sweeps across the Thames to the shiny transatlantic megaliths of Canary Wharf, on the promontory where Henry VIII's hunting dogs were maybe kennelled (hence its name, the Isle of Dogs). To the right bristle the spines, each a hundred metres tall, of the Millennium Dome, instantly identifiable from the windows of aeroplanes finding their way to Heathrow Airport along the Thames. And threading its way through the centre of this tapestry, the river, always the river, which has chosen this point to deviate in its passage to the sea by describing a great redundant loop around the Isle of Dogs. The river accounts for almost everything about the origins of Greenwich. Even today there is likely to be a cruise ship moored off Deptford Reach, just next to Greenwich, seeming a bulky and unsettling intrusion to eyes that have grown unaccustomed to a dynamic Thames.

The martyrdom of St Alfege, depicted in a twelfth-century window from Canterbury Cathedral. Alfege, Archbishop of Canterbury, was killed by Danish invaders at Greenwich. This shows him being taken prisoner after the sack of Canterbury.

17

Two thousand years ago, the view would not have contained any of these man-made features. But it would still have seemed pleasant enough to the people who took it in. For before them they could contemplate about as perfect a place for settlement as they might find. First there was the river. It did not look like the modern Thames, a relatively narrow belt whose width is defined by Victorian embankments. Then, it would have appeared more like a broad band of fraying cloth, much wider and shallower than the present river, as it wove its way between a mass of little islands. On either bank it was not obvious what belonged to the river and what did not. There were mudflats, reedbeds, then marshes. Behind the marshes rose clumps of trees, oaks, some of them centuries old. At the place that would become Greenwich a brook flowed into the broad river, carrying water from the higher ground. It was a landscape animated by wildlife. Wading birds with long beaks – spoonbills, herons, cranes – fished along the mudflats. They were joined by otters and watervole, while beavers busied themselves damming streams. Brown bears, wolves, elk, wild boar, badgers and red deer roamed among the trees and beside the water. Apart from the cries of the animals and birds, it would, for the most part, have been silent.

What made this scene so attractive to our ancestors? First the river itself. Dry land could only be traversed with difficulty: there were few roads, few horses, little to sustain the traveller on his journey. Water was the element that joined people and cities together, and provided access to a world beyond walking distance. It would retain this ascendancy until the eighteenth century. To traders such as the Celts the river, giving into the sea, provided the medium across which their goods could be transported and exchanged. The existence of a tributary river in the Ravensbourne meant that settlers could penetrate inland as well. Furthermore, Greenwich was one of the few places on this stretch of the Thames where a bed of gravel touched the river. This provided a firm beach on to which boats could be drawn up.

The river also offered food. It fairly teemed with fish. The eddies formed at the mouth of tributaries such as the Ravensbourne often formed little islands. It is likely that there was one here. The margins of these islands attracted shoals of little fish. This resource could be managed by the construction of fish weirs. And the river put more than fish on the menu. The birds that fed among the mudflats, reedbeds and marshes could be trapped and eaten. Nor was eating the only thing that this waterside life was good for. The fur of the beavers, otters and other creatures could be made into clothes. Weave together some of the osiers growing by the river and cover them with mud: this made a wall. Reeds could be worked into baskets. Even the grasses from the marsh might be plaited together to make cups.

Near the river there was secure dry ground. As we have seen, the land rises steeply to the bluff where the old Royal Observatory was built, and beyond it is the plateau of Blackheath. Not much more than gorse would have grown on the wretched, waterless soil of the heath itself. But round about there were woods, which had an obvious usefulness. Man had already been gathering berries, laying traps and felling trees for thousands of years. Some prehistoric individual was working in the woods one day, hacking at a tree with a piece of sharpened stone. It was a milky grey flint, ground and polished at the edge. Somehow it became lost in the undergrowth; perhaps he dropped it, or perhaps it flew out of his hand. It must have been a precious possession, to someone who had very few possessions of any kind, but he did not manage to recover it. There it lay, beside the Thames, until it was discovered earlier this century and put into the Museum of London.

By the time the Romans came, establishing a port out of what had previously been a scattering of homesteads, at a point where the river, more than usually broad, looked almost like a lake flowing around an archipelago of little islands – they would call their port Londinium – the woods at Greenwich would no longer have been virgin. Parts would have been coppiced: the practice by which trees are systematically cut down to the ground to provide a cluster of whippy young shoots that can be harvested. Woods were regarded as important assets, whether of an individual or a tribe, and their ownership was fiercely protected. The woodland could be cleared to provide farmland, and this would have been another attraction of the site. While cattle and pigs might roam among the watermeadows and marshes, wet conditions were impossible for sheep, which only thrive where the ground is reasonably dry. Altogether the conjunction of so many different types of habitat – mudflats, reed beds, marsh, woodland and pasture – would have made this elbow of the river seem eminently congenial to prospective settlers.

We do not know precisely when the enticing invitation offered by the landscape was accepted. Already the first Romans, making their way along the river, would have seen earthworks at Charlton, immediately east of Greenwich, protecting a scattering of huts from marauders; most evidence of this settlement was destroyed when sand was dug from the area in the eighteenth and nineteenth centuries. The Celts who lived there farmed, made pots and worked iron. The Greenwich Borough Museum at Plumstead now contains some of the humble debris of their lives, a rather sad assemblage of items such as flint flakes, clay-loom weights, brooches, bone pins, fragments of coarse pottery, coins bearing the head of the Emperor Claudius, on whose order an army of forty thousand men invaded Britain in AD 43. There are one or two farmsteads that we know about from the domestic debris that has been found, but they may not have been permanent dwellings. These huts had floors of trodden earth, and the inhabitants lived much as they would have done in the Iron Age five hundred years before. No doubt other such habitations existed, surrounded by fields and linked to each other by paths. If there was one at Greenwich, any trace of it has been lost as a result of the centuries of building work that have taken place there.

Probably the Roman presence made little difference to the lives of the families scattered about this area. Perhaps they now paid dues to a Roman tax collector rather than to a tribal overlord: beyond that, they won a meagre existence from the landscape as they always had done. But more people would have passed near to them. As they worked beside the river, they would have seen an increasing number of boats making their way up and down the river – the occasional tubby sea-going merchant ship, with its one square sail; numbers of flat-bottomed lighters and coastal ships from Rochester and Dover; probably some barges; canoes hollowed from tree trunks, as they would have been for centuries before. From the end of the first century, sailors would probably have been able to see, in the woods at Greenwich, a small temple or shrine.

At the time this shrine was constructed, London was recovering from its devastation by Queen Boudicca, who burnt it as part of the ultimately unsuccessful uprising of the Iceni tribe. The quays of the port were developing. Warehouses were being erected. Few Londoners were of Italian origin, but many of them had acquired the cosmopolitan tastes associated with the Empire – including, as the shrine suggests, some of their religious practices. Wine, olive oil and olives arrived in long-necked amphorae. The houses of the rich were furnished with pottery from Gaul, glass from Italy and silver and bronze tableware from around the Mediterranean. Most of the traffic was in goods from elsewhere in Britain: for example, the Kentish ragstone from which the walls were built. Some imports, though, came from far away; among the archaeological finds from the Greenwich temple is a fragment of ivory, which must have originated in Africa. The ships went away again, perhaps back to Rome, carrying lead, hunting dogs, oysters and slaves from the northern tribes.

The Romans also built roads. One of them was Watling Street, connecting the ports of Rochester and Dover with London. This road seems to have come over the brow of Shooters Hill, crossed what became the royal park and kissed the Thames at Greenwich, before marching onwards, straight as could be, to the ford at Westminster. At the point where Watling Street reached the river at Greenwich, there may have been a dock or even a ferry; certainly there was a ferry here in later centuries. (It is marked as a horse ferry on John Rocque's map of 1746, showing that it was intended for carts as well as people. It must have been part of a fairly important route running south from Old Ford, through the Isle of Dogs.) Traces of what could have been Watling Street were uncovered during the digging of a gas main in the 1960s. The conjunction of these modes of transport – road and river – made some form of development at Greenwich inevitable. If only we knew when the inevitable happened.

One of the coins found at the Romano-British temple, or shrine, that stood in Greenwich Park. The emperor is Flavius Julius Constans, son of Constantine the Great. The coin is dated AD 337. Flavius Julius Constans was murdered in AD 350.

Archaeology reveals rather more about the temple. It stood just off Watling Street, in what is now Greenwich Park. People may have thought that spirits lived in the woods here. The shrine stood all alone on the hill. At the beginning of this century, when its red mosaic pavement was discovered, archaeologists thought it was a villa; they even imagined that they had discovered the site of a lost settlement, known from descriptions of the Roman roads, as Noviomagus. More recent investigations suggest the villa theory to be false. The building was probably raised in this remote area to celebrate some cult. The men and women visiting it left their tribute in the form of hundreds of Roman coins that have since been unearthed. Since the earliest of these coins dates from about AD 70, it was probably around then that the structure was erected.

There was a statue in the shrine: an arm holding drapery is all that has been found of it. Unfortunately the inscriptions on the fragments of stone that have been discovered are mostly illegible. The letters *C V L A P*, or what appear to be such, might come from Aesculapius, the Roman god of medicine. If so, it records the origin of an association with health-giving properties that survived into the seventeenth century, when Queen Anne of Denmark wanted to take the waters here. Perhaps other buildings were grouped around the temple to service it. One would think so from the quantity of animal bones and mollusc shells, as well as rough pottery and other objects, that have been excavated.

In the course of the next two centuries, some of the Romans – or more likely British people with Roman habits – came to live in the vicinity of Greenwich. There is little evidence of them beyond a scattering of cremation sites. There was thought to be a building of some kind to the south-west of Blackheath, but when excavated, this was found to be a natural feature.

Inspecting the archaeological dig that revealed the temple in Greenwich Park, 1902. The bearded figure is probably the superintendent of the park, A. D. Webster.

When, towards the end of the fourth century AD, Rome began to lose its grip on the world, places like London were vulnerable to the general collapse. So bustling in the second century, so cosmopolitan in its tastes, London began to decline as a port, and then as a city. When the emperor pulled out his troops from England, it suffered further. Eventually, by the middle of the fifth century, the inhabitants abandoned it. There was no one from London to make the pilgrimage to the shrine at Greenwich. Watling Street grew over with weeds.

\* \* \*

The last of the Roman legions left Britain in 405. Afterwards, what used to be known as the Dark Ages are, for Greenwich, precisely that. There is little to illuminate whatever meagre existence was played out beside this curve of the Thames. Next to nothing, then, about life; but a little more is known about its concomitant, death.

Historically Greenwich is part of Kent, an area that came to be dominated by warrior families originating from the borders of what are now the Netherlands and Denmark. These were the Jutes. As a result, Kent acquired a character different from that of the Anglo-Saxon counties of England, including different laws of inheritance. There were probably no Jutes around Greenwich, however. Instead the twenty or so burial mounds that can still be seen in Greenwich Park almost centainly belonged to Saxons, the earliest dating from the seventh century. The men were put into the ground with their shields and spears. Some of these weapons were discovered when an antiquarian called the Rev. James Douglas excavated eighteen of these barrows in the late eighteenth century. Douglas also found what he took to be the decayed traces of wooden coffins, though no human bones. Clearly Greenwich was a centre of some sort, and the people who inhabited it were of sufficient power to be buried with pomp. There were fifty of the barrows in Douglas's time, so the settlement to which they were related must have

Saxon barrows in Greenwich Park, attracting the interest of Victorian visitors. Greenwich is a Saxon place-name, possibly meaning Green Market.

been of some size. Another group has been found in the grounds of the National Maritime Museum, along with two more at Deptford Broadway.

In Saxon place-names the suffix 'wich' usually signifies port but can also indicate the presence of a market. Green Market – it has rather a modern ring. Unfortunately the only evidence that it might have flourished as a market is a single fragment of Ipswich ware pottery, now in the Museum of London. Ipswich ware was turned out in what, by the standards of the time, was large volume. It was the sort of product sold at markets. But we have just the one piece.

There is a glimmer of light in 964 when King Edgar, who liked to call himself Emperor of Britain, granted the manor of Lewisham, including Greenwich, to St Peter's Abbey in Ghent. It used to be thought that the gift was made earlier, by Elstrudis, a daughter or niece of Alfred the Great, but the relevant document appears to have been forged. No doubt it was manufactured by one of the medieval abbots, anxious to safeguard his property by pretending a more ancient claim to it than he had. It may be that the English king retained a house at Greenwich, giving rise to later ambiguity over the manor's ownership.

The monks who arrived in the tenth century came during uncertain times. Since the eighth century long narrow boats, their square sails supplemented by oars – elegant vessels with their prows and ends turned up like Turkish slippers – had been snaking their way across the North Sea from Denmark, and up the estuaries and rivers of England. These were the Viking longships, full of salt-caked, ferocious raiders who seemed utterly without pity for the shore people whose livings they plundered. They must have been a terrifying sight to anyone who observed them making their swift, silent way along even quite small rivers. A shiver ran through the whole of Christendom when the monastery at Lindisfarne, rich in the culture of the Celts, was sacked by these ruthless men. From the middle of the ninth century, the Viking raids were part of life – as unpredictable and devastating as the sudden illnesses that carried off whole villages. The Vikings came continuously now. The monks from Ghent were not able to hold their possessions beside the Thames in peace and security very long. They were not well placed for the quiet life. The Viking fleets, fifty longships at a time, which came up the Thames did not sail away so quickly as before. They spent the winter there. They needed a harbour for their ships and an area of open ground where their warriors could camp. The river at Greenwich was broad, the channel deep; it was near to London, which they could terrorise; the waste of Blackheath lay at hand. So it was at Greenwich that they moored their ships.

In 1012 the Vikings came up the Thames to Greenwich and lay at anchor for three years. In the course of their campaign they besieged Canterbury. The town ran out of food after twenty days, and the Archbishop, who was called Alfege, sent messengers to remonstrate with them. It was no use. They set fire to the town, broke through the wall and, in the words of the eighteenth-century volume *Britannia*

*Sancta, or the Lives of the Most Celebrated British, English, Scottish and Irish Saints*, 'made a terrible slaughter of all they met, without distinction of either sex or age'. Alfege, by this time immured within the cathedral with his monks, ventured out, begging them to spare the 'poor harmless people'. Their response was to seize him by the throat, bind his hands and beat him up; 'which, in imitation of his Redeemer, he suffered with wonderful meekness and silence'. Alfege, it will be gathered, was a figure of extraordinary piety. Born into a noble family, he had turned his back on worldly possessions by entering a monastery. Even this was not enough for him, and he became an anchorite at Bath. So many people came to consult him there that they founded a monastery. St Andrew supposedly appeared in a dream to St Dunstan, the Archbishop of Canterbury, recommending Alfege to the see of Winchester, following the death of its bishop: 'thus was he forced out of his solitude.' When St Dunstan himself died, Alfege succeeded him. En route to Rome to receive his pall from the Pope, he was attacked by brigands – whereupon the town that the ruffians came from was consumed with flames until they relented, imploring Alfege to persuade God to stop burning their homes. The miserable ravaging of England by the Danes was, to this holy man, merely another opportunity to exercise his charity, 'as well in relieving and redeeming the English, whom these barbarous invaders had ruined or enslaved; as in preaching the word of life to the Danes, a great number of whom he converted to the faith of Christ'. His preaching did not, however, make much of an impression on the men who had captured Alfege at Canterbury.

They cared nothing for his piety and culture. They dragged him to Greenwich, locked him up in a damp cell infested with frogs and put his feet into irons. They began to feel differently after his intervention with God cured them of the 'violent torments in their bowels' that had beset them; but their offer to release him for a ransom of three thousand marks was spurned. His parishioners were too destitute to raise it. It caused the Danes to treat him more cruelly than ever. There was an attempt at rescuing him. A man appeared at the cell door one night, holding a flaming torch and quoting scriptures. Alfege followed him, hoping to escape over the streams and ditches of the marsh beside the Thames. The captors quickly realised he was gone and set off in pursuit. It was an unequal contest. Alfege stumbled along on feet that had been damaged by the manacles, and was unable to keep up. Finally he fell into a bog. The Danes seized him once again. They told him that

> either he must furnish them with the gold they demanded, or must die. He replied, that he had no other gold to bestow, but the gold of true wisdom, consisting in the knowledge and worship of the true and living God, which he was willing to impart to them: but if they continued obstinately to refuse this, he told them they would one day fare worse than Sodom; and that their Empire should not be long lived in England.

It was not the answer they wanted. They now had a grand prisoner who was useless to them. They held a council in their campaign hall, made of a great leather-sided tent; and afterwards they got to feasting. As the evening degenerated they began hurling abuse at Alfege. Words were followed by more substantial missiles, in the shape of bits of food. All of this Alfege suffered in his holy way, quoting scripture. This, however, only provoked the Danes to throw bones at him. Eventually an ox head was hurled in his direction, knocking him to the ground. One Dane, whom Alfege had baptised only the previous day, then split open his skull with an axe and, in the words of the Anglo-Saxon Chronicle, 'his holy soul was sent forth to God's kingdom'. By tradition, the murder is supposed to have take place on the site of the parish church.

The slaughter of an archbishop was an outrage, even by the brutal standards of the Danes. Apparently it so distressed Thurkill, commander of the Danes at Greenwich, who was an unwilling witness at the scene, that he changed sides, offering his services – and his forty-five ships – to the English King Ethelred. The

St Alfege is put to death by the Danes. Window from Canterbury Cathedral.

ships remained at Greenwich, and there must have been much local rejoicing when it was discovered that Sweyn, the Danish leader, had sailed to attack the Humber instead of the Thames. But he marched southwards, conquering all. Soon Ethelred had fled to the Isle of Wight, and thence to Normandy, aboard one of Thurkill's ships. And Greenwich continued as the centre of the Danish infestation. It took piles of Danegeld to persuade them to go.

It was not long before relics of the martyred Alfege were believed to have caused miracles. Probably he became credited with powers that were formerly the property of quite other kinds of deity. When a dead stick was sprinkled with his blood and fixed in the ground, it burst into leaf the next morning. Perhaps he was ascribed the powers that had previously been associated with the pagan temple in the woods at Greenwich. To this day the parish church of Greenwich is dedicated to St Alfege. Alfege was a local saint: this is the only church in Britain to bear his name.

To follow St Alfege's association with Greenwich further, we must spool history forward to the Middle Ages, when the parish church assumed a form that we can recognise. This was the old church. It probably incorporated parts of a Saxon building which would have stood there when St Alfege was slain. Few representations of the Tudor structure exist but it can be pictured from various references in documents. There was an image of 'Saint Alphey' in the choir, with another of the Virgin Mary. The vicar, Edmond Russell, wished to be buried in front of it in 1486, and one parishioner left 6s 8d to put a light before it in 1509. This church was Gothic, three aisles wide and of no great distinction. It was sometimes enriched with gifts, such as the 'standying cuppe of sylver and gylte' weighing twenty-four ounces that any bride who was married in the church could have carried before her in the wedding procession. It would have been filled with wine and blessed in memory of the marriage at Cana.

Like many medieval structures, the church of St Alfege was built more on faith than engineering science. The digging of graves in the nave of the church, too near the pillars, had weakened such foundations as it possessed, and they were probably not up to much anyway. On a stormy November night in 1710 one of the pillars of the nave gave way and a large part of the roof came crashing down. Except for the tower at the west, the old fabric was deemed too rotten to repair, and whatever had not collapsed was demolished. Greenwich now had no church, and no money to build another one. A petition was sent to Parliament, painting the destitution of the parish in lurid colours (see page 123). It was a good moment to present it. Only the previous month Tories had come into government, and they prided themselves on being the Church of England party. The labour of rebuilding the City churches destroyed in the Great Fire of London had been almost completed, but the coal tax that had been imposed to finance the work was still in place, producing a revenue that had yet to be ear-

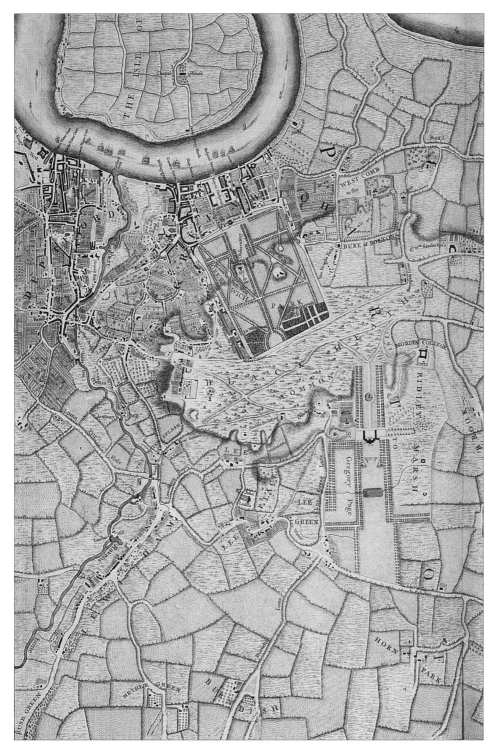

Greenwich and Blackheath, from the *Survey of London* published by John Rocque in 1746. Greenwich Hospital stands on the outside bend of the river, with the park planted by Charles II, with geometrical avenues, behind it. At this date Greenwich and Blackheath were surrounded by country houses, such as Sir Gregory Page's Wricklemarsh estate, shown south-east of the park.

marked for another use. Non-conformism was on the march in the new suburbs. With all this behind it, the Greenwich petition persuaded Parliament not just to rebuild St Alfege's but to construct a total of fifty new churches throughout London. Appropriately the first of these was the one that had set this great work in motion, St Alfege's. Its architect was one of the Surveyors to the Commission which Parliament established, Nicholas Hawksmoor.

Hawksmoor spent a career in the shadow of other men's glory: he assisted Wren and Vanbrugh, but one official position after another – including the Surveyorship of Greenwich Hospital – went to other architects. 'Poor Hawksmoor,' wrote Vanbrugh in 1721, 'what a Barbarous Age have his fine, ingenious, parts fallen into. What wou'd monsr. Colbert in France have given for such a man?' Disappointment showed clearly in his features: disappointment and the dyspeptic temperament that was provoked by an illness referred to as gout. At Greenwich, however, he had one of relatively few opportunities to shine by himself.

**Bust of Nicholas Hawksmoor by Sir Henry Cheere.**

And he did so. Few parish churches in England can rival St Alfege's for the drama of its east portico – a composition on a giant scale, inspired by Alberti's portico, part triumphal arch and part temple front, on the church of S. Andrea in Mantua. The interior was remarkable for its absence of supporting columns, allowing a free view of the altar and pulpit. The giant scale of the portico is continued in two pairs of Corinthian columns in the chancel, supporting the coffered vault of the apse.

By this date, it was nothing new for an English church to be built in a classical style, as all kinds of religious buildings had been throughout Europe since the Renaissance. But the grand classical manner, so obviously intended to emulate the grandeur of Ancient Rome, has a special if ironic appropriateness in a church dedicated to a saint whose miraculous powers, as we have seen, may partly have been borrowed from the pagan deities lurking in the woods at Greenwich – among them the god or gods in whose honour the vanished shrine in Greenwich Park was erected.

*Opposite:* **Lithograph of St Alfege's Church, Greenwich, viewed from Stockwell Street. The church was built by Nicholas Hawksmoor in 1711, with the steeple added by John James in 1730. Stockwell Street takes its name from the wells where stock was watered.**

29

Ad ripas Grenovica tuas, hic THAMESIS unda
Alluit Angligenum Regalia tecta Monarchæ,
Quæ situs quæ forma, decusq, virentia septa,
Concelebrant totum longe latèq per orbem,
Behould, by Prospect with what Art.
Fairre Greenwich Castle, pleasantly.
A House of Banquet, neare & part;
Of Thames, and London how they ly.

# LA MAISON DE GRENEVWYC

G REENWICH HAS ALWAYS been cosmopolitan. Its position on the Thames has made it the home of sailors and merchants, people who travelled far through their professional bond with the sea, foreigners who first touched English land at Greenwich, or thereabouts, and stayed there. The longest association in its history, in terms of ownership, has been with the Abbey of St Peter in Ghent. This began, as we have seen, as an outright gift, at a time when the common allegiance to Christendom was stronger than a sense of English nationhood. As England came to cohere as a state, the monarch – a succession of monarchs – managed to weaken the foreign abbot's hold on Greenwich, perfectly lawful though it was, until it fell from his grasp altogether. Being rather more than a bauble, it was picked up, put in the royal pocket, treasured and polished until it sparkled as one of the most splendid palaces and royal building sites in the land.

Before then, the connection with Ghent, beginning in 964, had been a long one. The abbots retained the manor of Lewisham, of which Greenwich was part, for four and a half centuries. Their principal interest in it, materially, must have been the rents and manorial dues that it generated. But Greenwich also had a strategic importance, as a natural harbour from which an attack on London could have been launched. This was not lost on William the Conqueror to whom it must have been particularly important to protect the Flemish holdings around Greenwich, because of his need to keep in with Flanders. But this close royal interest may have given rise to the ambiguity that allowed later sovereigns to push the abbots out of their inheritance.

Far away in Ghent, the abbots had difficulty in keeping possession of their property. They also suffered the unpopularity that is usually the lot of absentee landlords, and with reason. In the thirteenth century the abbots, or their representatives, flouted the law of the land by inflicting an illegal toll of a penny-halfpenny on woolcarts that crossed the king's highway on the way to the quay. The local people, of course, hated these imposts, and whipped up all sorts of ill feeling towards the foreign monks. It was said that the large number of foreigners living in this strategic site on the Thames imperilled national security. This gave Edward

Greenwich Castle, in a drawing by Wenceslaus Hollar dated 1637. The castle was originally built by Humphrey Duke of Gloucester and was for many years known as Duke Humphrey's Tower.

31

*Opposite:* **The Peasants' Revolt, 1381. As on other occasions, Blackheath provided a convenient open space for the rabble led by Wat Tyler and Jack Straw to assemble, before descending on London. In the twentieth century there was local controversy as to whether Tyler or Anne Boleyn should lend his or her name to a road; it was typical of the area's radical tradition that Tyler won.**

III an excuse to take the abbey's lands into his own custody, supposedly as a defensive measure during the Hundred Years War against France. Around Christmas time, in the year 1366, two attendants, a pipe of salted beef, eight bacons and three barrels of beer set off for Flanders. With them went the then prior. He never came back.

Without a prior, the monks struggled on, disheartened and increasingly lax, until their possessions, along with those of other foreign monasteries, were confiscated by Henry V in 1414. The end for the monks had been a long time in coming. For Greenwich, it was a beginning.

There was by now a big house by the river at Greenwich: it is not known exactly when, or by whom, it was built, though in the twelfth century it was already being referred to as old. It stood roughly on the site of the palace that would later be built by the Tudors, and established this location by the strand of the Thames as somewhere to live. A description comes from the end of the fourteenth century, when the abbot of St Peter's, Ghent, realising that the Flemish presence at Greenwich was at its last gasp, dispatched an agent called Gille Delaporte to report on what could be salvaged from the decline. The answer put an end to any hope of reasserting Flemish rights, since the reply to every question of ownership came back like a litany: 'On dit que le Roy les a tous.' People say that the king owns everything. 'La maison de Grenevwyc' was found to be well maintained, with a gatehouse roofed with tiles towards the fields. The only person who lived there, however, was a concierge, Henry Brioul, who had only one eye. How forlorn it sounds! The mood of the abbot in Ghent when he read the report must also have been melancholy.

At the beginning of the fourteenth century, the monks at Greenwich had used their buildings to the full, dispensing hospitality to travellers such as the prior of Salisbury (an item for stabling his horses appears in the accounts). They continued to hold courts there. But long before the abbots of Ghent gave up their claim of ownership the residential parts of the house at Greenwich had been let to tenants. The nature of these tenants gives a flavour of the status of Greenwich during the Middle Ages. There were the Rokesleys from Kent, descended from a goldsmith and mayor of London, who was big in the wool trade; Nicholas Brembre, a London grocer who had ridden out against Wat Tyler's rebels and been knighted for it; and John Norbury, who had been Henry IV's treasurer: a former soldier, rich enough to lend the king large sums of money. It may have been his interests in the shipping of wool that drew his attention to Greenwich, after the monks had departed. Norbury spent money on the buildings at Greenwich, as well as establishing a monastery of 'black monks alien' (as the antiquarian John Weever described them in 1631: 'alien' meaning 'foreign') at Lewisham. He must have lived in some style, since Henry IV seems to have visited him there often.

From its position, Greenwich could hardly avoid developing wharves, boat-yards and other maritime businesses. Greenwich ships are mentioned in thir-teenth-century records. By 1400, the town was sufficiently developed to have a church and a market, and it had already acquired its reputation as somewhere that rich London people could reside in the equivalent of villas. The property transactions that took place in the fourteenth century – listed by the antiquarian H. H. Drake in his *Hundred of Blackheath* – contain references to gardens and meadows.

It is thought that the poet Geoffrey Chaucer lived somewhere around Greenwich in the late fourteenth century. The big house next to the river would also acquire a literary reputation, not as enduring as that of *The Canterbury Tales* but certainly significant in the development of intellectual life in England. It was to put Greenwich at the heart of Renaissance culture in England: a position which it occupied for as long as that culture persisted.

## Chaucer

Geoffrey Chaucer may very well have lived at Greenwich, or somewhere near, between 1385 and 1399, since he served almost continuously as a commissioner of the peace for Kent in those years, and in 1390 was appointed to a royal commission (of walls and ditches) along the banks of the Thames between Greenwich and Woolwich. It may be that he owned one of these gardens, to judge from a poem he wrote on a daisy. At the end of May, he came home after a day's roaming in the meadow, and had his servants make him a couch upon the fresh-cut turves of 'a little arbour that I have'. There he fell asleep … and the poem is an account of his dream. From Greenwich he could presumably have watched the pilgrims heading for Canterbury as they made their way across Blackheath. The one or two references he made to Greenwich by name are not very complimentary. Many a shrew lived there, he wrote – a view that may have been personal or topical, rather than a general reflection.

**Geoffrey Chaucer: Greenwich resident? Posthumous portrait, artist unknown.**

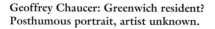

In the late 1420s the manor of Greenwich came into the possession of Humphrey Duke of Gloucester, the youngest brother of the dead King, Henry V. Humphrey was then Protector and Defender of England, as the uncle of Henry VI who was only a child. Earlier in his career, he had won sufficient popularity from the citizens of London to be called the Good Duke. The epithet appears to derive from the valour with which he fought the French, both during Henry V's campaigns there, and later on his own account, when he made a buccaneering raid on the Pas de Calais and Flanders. At Agincourt he had fought with reckless disregard of his own safety, until he collapsed with a wound 'in his hammes'. He would have been left for dead, had not his brother, the King, stood between his outstretched legs, repelling the enemy. London merchants approved of fierceness in battle: anything to the detriment of their commercial rivals in France suited their cause. Returned from the wars, Duke Humphrey seems to have deliberately played for popularity with the crowd. By the time he acquired Greenwich, however, he was not quite so much the Good Duke: in fact he was doing everything he could (not quite successfully) to rule England as a despot.

To secure a power base for himself, Humphrey succeeded in marrying Jacqueline, Countess of Holland, Zealand and Hainault. It was not an entirely straightforward union to achieve since she was already married to the Duke of Brabant. The latter, supported by the mighty Duke of Burgundy, had no intention of relinquishing more of his former spouse's lands than he was compelled to. So Humphrey set off for Hainault with a force of five thousand soldiers in an attempt to wrest those possessions from him, despite the negative consequences that this might have for English reputations abroad. It ended in ignominy. Humphrey returned home, abandoning his wife. However despicable this may have seemed to his Edwardian biographer, Humphrey's contemporaries do not seem to have judged him harshly. Even a figure from the opposing camp, Jehan de Warin, describes him as a 'prince de grant virtu, large, courtois sage et tres vaillant chevallier de corps, hardy de ceur'. Hardly could there have been a better write-up. Humphrey was the personification of chivalry, for which much could be forgiven him.

From the family badge of his mother, Mary Bohun, Humphrey was known as the Swan: an image of arrogance and aggression, to be sure, but also refinement. And for all his bull-headedness and dissipation, he was also, through the associations he formed, a fountain of learning and humanism in a country as yet unwatered by Renaissance thought. He was dedicated to the new learning and corresponded with the Italian scholars who were the leaders of intellectual life in Europe. 'In no other Englishman of the time do we find the same love of the ancient classics which characterised Gloucester,' commented K. H. Vickers in his biography of 1907. At Greenwich he assembled the greatest private library of his age. We can have no idea how much Humphrey read the books himself. His career suggests a man who was impatient, impetuous, clever certainly, but without much gift of forethought. Contemporaries regarded his capacity for sexual indulgence as excessive even in a prince. He was not, in short, a contemplative sort of man. Nevertheless, he absorbed the latest ideas about siege warfare and artillery.

As it happened, Humphrey had a particular connection with Greenwich. He could number Elstrudis among his ancestors, his grandfather had been born in Ghent and his marriage to Jacqueline gave him the title Count of Flanders. And Greenwich was clearly important to him, since he decided to rebuild the house there, despite already having inherited all the royal castles in southern England under the will of Henry V. (At different times Humphrey resided at Pembroke Castle, Penshurst in Kent, the manor of Weald near St Albans, and probably at Leicester and Pontefract; in the manner of the age he was not under-housed.) Greenwich had the merit of being close to the capital: even at the nadir of his fortunes Humphrey had supporters in the City of London. There he owned the opulent

mansion called Baynard's Castle, but it appears to have been destroyed by a fire in the late 1420s. Perhaps that gave Humphrey the impetus to rebuild Greenwich from 1432 to 1437.

Between those dates Humphrey obtained the various licences that were the equivalent of building permits, intended partly to keep over-mighty builders (whose strongholds might have formed centres of opposition to the King) in check. They allowed him to empark two hundred acres of land, surrounding it with a fence high enough to contain a deer herd. A licence to crenellate entitled Humphrey to fortify his house. This could just have meant that he was building a large house of stone: the fortifications to which such licences refer were not necessarily more than decorative. But since Humphrey also built towers and turrets it is likely that this eminent soldier took the defensive aspect of his mansion seriously. These were volatile times, great men were constantly in danger from the mob and personal safety often lay in the possession of armed retainers – any of the top people in England would have kept a band of fifty or so. Humphrey's works include a tower that stood on the site of the present Royal Observatory, which, under the name of Duke Humphrey's Tower, remained a local landmark for centuries. The purpose of this tower must have been to allow a watch to be kept on the Dover Road. Still, the house he created must have been more of a sumptuous residence than a bristling castle, to judge from the name he gave it – the manor of Plesaunce, or Bella Court.

Unfortunately no image has come down to us of this house. The name suggests that it was intended to celebrate beauty and the softer arts of life, so absent from the military and political worlds that he was accustomed to inhabit. The term 'pleasance' was used to describe the detached buildings, surrounded by their own moats, which monarchs had recently started to build in the grounds of their castles: Humphrey's brother Henry V had created one at Kenilworth. It reflected the growing desire for privacy on the part of royal personages. This privacy hardly seems absolute by today's standards, since the King was always surrounded by people; but in his pleasance he was more likely to be surrounded by people of his own choosing, without the press of hangers-on, observers and supplicants who filled his other houses.

Unlike the Plesaunce itself, the creation of the Duke's library is well documented. His introduction to the Italian humanists came through Zano Castiglione, the Bishop of Bayeux, a Frenchman of Italian descent. When Zano was sent to the Council of Basel to represent Henry VI, Humphrey commissioned him to buy as many books as he could. It is likely that Zano initiated a correspondence between Humphrey and Leonardo Bruni, known by the classicising sobriquet of Aretinus (from his home town of Arezzo). In the age before printing, merely to possess a collection of books was a contribution to scholarship. It was not easy to assemble them, given the labours of copying. The difficulties were particularly severe in the case of foreign works. The fashion for Italian literature was so great throughout Europe that

*Opposite:* **Henry VI, from a fifteenth-century manuscript given to Margaret of Anjou by the 1st Earl of Shrewsbury. The King is shown giving Lord Shrewsbury the sword as Constable of France.**

Humphrey Duke
of Gloucester,
brother of
Henry V, whose
mansion beside
the Thames at
Greenwich
prefigured the
later royal palaces
there. Reckless
soldier, notorious
libertine and
flawed statesman,
he was also an
early patron of
Renaissance
learning, whose
library, housed at
Greenwich,
formed the basis
of the Bodleian
in Oxford.

the copyists could not meet the demand. Foreign patrons like Humphrey had to rely on authorities such as Aretinus to supply them with texts, and Renaissance scholars were hardly scrupulous in matters of business. They had a habit of selling their expertise to whichever prince offered them most. All of which makes the scale of Humphrey's bibliophilia more impressive. In book collecting he displayed the persistence that was absent from his public life.

At home Humphrey made himself the centre of literary life, and through his influence England became a little less of a backwater, untroubled by the great intellectual tide flowing through Italy, than it might have been. The focus of his interest was the classics, not contemporary literature. Nevertheless, he befriended John Lydgate, the greatest English poet of his day (not a particularly glorious day, it has to be said). The scale of Humphrey's library can be imagined from the extent of his benefactions to the University of Oxford. It was Humphrey's gifts of books that rescued Oxford from obscurity. This was a time when there were almost no books at the University, and all the teaching of students was done orally. So when Humphrey gave 129 books in 1438 the University's capacity to investigate outside ideas was transformed. There followed a further 150 books over the next few years. 'Gifts of books in such numbers were unique in the history of the University, and continued to be so for some time to come,' comments Vickers. They go some way towards justifying the tag of Good Duke Humphrey, which in other respects seems so strange. John Capgrave, who produced his *Chronicle of England* under the patronage of the Duke, may have overdone it when he called Humphrey 'the most lettered prince in the world'. But his house at Greenwich must have seemed a beacon of modern thought, housing not only a splendid collection of books but, from time to time, the most glittering literary figures of which England could boast. The Italian scholar Titus Livius joined Humphrey's household and wrote the *Vita Henrici Quinti* to commemorate Henry V.

By the standards of Niccolò Machiavelli, writing *The Prince* early in the next century, Humphrey had neither the steadfastness of purpose, nor perhaps the ultimate ruthlessness, necessary to the successful Renaissance prince. His life ended in disaster. As soon as he freed himself from marriage to Jacqueline by papal decree, he married his mistress, Eleanor Cobham, who had been one of Jacqueline's ladies in waiting. She was beautiful, charming and ambitious, and it was said that her hold over Humphrey was obtained through sorcery. Certainly she had an interest in the Black Arts, as did he. It was a weakness that could be exploited by Humphrey's enemies, who resented her meddling in affairs of state and, further, aimed a blow at her husband when they struck at her. She was convicted of sorcery, compelled to perform a series of humiliating public penances through the streets of London, then consigned to prison for life. Humphrey found himself alienated from his weak-minded nephew, the young and mentally unstable Henry VI. The King listened increasingly to those counsels, opposed to Humphrey, who urged him to conclude a truce in the war with France, and cement the *rapprochement* by marrying a Frenchwoman. This he did, taking the fifteen-year-old Margaret of Anjou as his bride. Humphrey's enemies succeeded in poisoning her mind against him. This gave them the confidence to plan an end to him.

In 1447, an unsuspecting Humphrey set off for Bury St Edmunds, with what could be regarded as a relatively compact retinue of eighty horsemen, to attend the Parliament there. On his arrival he was arrested. It is quite likely that an unnatural death had been planned for him. In fact, the shock of the arrest seems to have brought on a stroke, which paralysed him and deprived him of speech. After a few days he died. The fate that could have been in store for him had he not done so was then visited upon his supporters. Five of the most prominent of them, including his natural son Arthur, were tried by his enemy, Lord Suffolk, and sentenced to be hanged, drawn and quartered. The accusation was that they had been plotting with Humphrey against the King, during a seditious meeting at Greenwich. It is a reflection of the unpopularity of these events with the populace that, just as they stood at Tyburn with a rope around their necks, they received a reprieve. According to one account they had already been quickly hanged, laid out on the ground and their bodies scored for quartering. Later Eleanor's accusers, the Bishop of Chichester and the Bishop of Salisbury, were both murdered. The Abbot and Convent of St Albans (Duke Humphrey's favourite place of devotion) paid £433 6s 8d for making the Duke's tomb, which still stands in the Abbey, and also paid two priests a stipend to sing daily masses.

A traitor's end: the condemned man was half hanged, then drawn and quartered (as shown in this sixteenth-century engraving). One of the quarters of Jack Cade, the adventurer who led a desperate insurrection in 1450, was exhibited on Blackheath, where his followers had camped.

As soon as Humphrey was dead, Greenwich and many of his other possessions passed to the young Queen. To make it truly hers, she set about a campaign of decoration. Robert Kettlewell was summoned from the royal palace at Eltham to become 'Clerk of the Quenyswerkys of the maner of Plesaunce'. Into a bay window went fourteen feet of new glass 'floushyd cum margaritis' (flushed or coloured with daisies), the daisy being the Queen's device, a play on her name. Daisies had decorated everything at Nancy when the wedding took place. The King's flower was the hawthorn bud, and that also appeared in the glass. There must have been flowers, too, in the garden, where the Queen had an arbour. The flowers in the glass were made by John Pond; John Pruddle provided more stained glass for the chapel. Rather surprisingly, in view of the animosity between Margaret and the late owner of Greenwich, it included 'one escutcheon of the arms of the Duke of Gloucester, 2s': a curious gesture of piety towards the man whom her faction was popularly supposed to have murdered.

For what appears to have been the first time in England, Margaret organised her palace around two wards, or courts, one for her own apartments and one for the King's: a pattern which was to become standard in great royal residences. Brought up in France, Margaret was familiar with luxury, and there is a suggestion of it in her adornment of Greenwich. Flemish tiles were installed in her chamber, as well as a door studded with dice-headed nails. There was a vestry next to the chapel 'for safe keeping of the jewels', and apparently something described as a bathing vat for her ablutions. Altogether Margaret's house beside the Thames must have made a pretty

Margaret of Anjou. Her marriage to Henry VI in 1445 led to the downfall of Duke Humphrey, who had opposed it. He died, perhaps murdered, two years afterwards; she then occupied his house at Greenwich. Portrait medallion by Pietro di Milano.

sight, with its hawthorn buds and daisies and gaily contrasting pink brick and white stone. But the image of comfort and domesticity which it offered was an illusion. Whatever the appointments of the interior, these were not comfortable times.

Those men who brought about Humphrey Duke of Gloucester's downfall did not have long to enjoy their own eminence. Three years after his death, the Earl of Suffolk, impeached by Parliament, was banished to France, but the ship taking him there was intercepted by the *Nicholas of the Tower*, the crew of which tried and beheaded him. They may well have known Humphrey since the ship had taken soldiers to France for Henry V's wars, and the master, Henry Robinson, was a Greenwich man. The discontents caused Jack Cade to lead an uprising of Kentish men and women, who, like Wat Tyler's rabble, assembled on Blackheath, next to Greenwich, and camped there for over a month. Cade himself may well have been Irish. An adventurer and an impostor, he simply saw the insurrection as his chance for – who knows what? A few days of power, during which he could wear scarlet clothes, behead insubordinates and terrify the solid citizens of London. Many of his followers, though, were local people, quite a number from Greenwich and apparently respectable. A few of them had been personally associated with Humphrey and were out to avenge his death which everyone thought had been murder. More surprisingly, they were accompanied by one Richard Henham, a Greenwich carpenter who had lately supplied beds to the Queen at the Plesaunce, and his wife.

Blackheath, an open space only a few miles from London, was a natural rallying ground for the discontented. Its proximity to Greenwich, so imbued with the spirit of Duke Humphrey, must have redoubled its relevance as the place where forces opposed to the regime which had apparently done away with him should congregate. Jack Cade's rebellion, which culminated in the execution of the Earl of Suffolk's associate, Lord Saye and Sele, was followed by the predictable reprisals: Cade himself was hunted down and butchered, one of his quarters being exhibited on Blackheath. Today he is commemorated by Cade Road. The men living around Blackheath, including those at Greenwich, were forced to ask the King's pardon on their knees, naked except for their shirts. There is some reason to call Cade's rebellion the first armed conflict in the Wars of the Roses. Only two years later, in 1452, another force assembled on Blackheath, composed of supporters of Richard, Duke of York; on this occasion the King backed down before the confrontation came to a head.

Once those wars had begun, it became too unsafe for Margaret of Anjou to linger at Greenwich, in this hostile neighbourhood, so she decamped for places of more solid Lancastrian support, such as the Midlands. Eventually even they were too hot for her, and she withdrew to France. The young Duke of York, his father having died fighting the Lancastrians at the Battle of Wakefield, entered London in 1461 and was crowned Edward IV. After a progress around England, he came

41

to Greenwich to hunt in Duke Humphrey's park. He was superbly built, six foot four tall, and the epitome of chivalry. It is difficult to think that he did not marry for love. Certainly his choice of a wife, in 1464, otherwise seems eccentric, and she was famous for her black-haired beauty. She was Elizabeth Woodville (or Widville), from the manor of Lee, just on the other side of Blackheath from Greenwich. Her mother was Jacquetta of Luxembourg, whose first husband had been Duke Humphrey's elder and more responsible brother, the Duke of Bedford; in her widowhood her eye fell upon Sir Richard Woodville, famed, according to the French chronicler Monstrelet, as 'le plus beau Chevalier' to exist anywhere. Soon after Edward IV's marriage to Elizabeth Woodville, he granted her 'the lordship and manor of Plesaunce, otherwise called Grenewiche, with the Tower of Grenewiche and the parks there'.

To the new King, it must have seemed that the union would help win over the Lancastrians to his rule. But Elizabeth Woodville was no better than Margaret of Anjou at putting other interests above her own. To the established aristocracy, the Woodvilles were nothing. These upstarts pushed themselves forward at every opportunity, particularly when there was a chance of enrichment. Eventually, after the King's sudden death, the Queen's unpopularity was a factor in allowing his brother, the Duke of York, to usurp the throne as Richard III. Greenwich was to preside over the most egregious example of Woodville self-promotion when the marriage between Thomas Grey, Elizabeth's son by her first husband, and Anne, heiress of the Duke of Exeter, took place there. Anne had previously been contracted to a nephew of that Earl of Warwick who has come down in history as Warwick the Kingmaker. Without Warwick's support on the battlefield, Edward IV would not have become King. Both Edward IV and his Queen seem to have suppressed whatever gratitude they may have felt, finding it uncomfortable to have such an over-mighty friend behind their throne. The Greenwich wedding presaged the next outbreak of conflict in the Wars of the Roses. The slighting of Warwick interests continued, and the Kingmaker was forced into exile in France. But he returned with Margaret of Anjou, and this time it was Edward who was driven to take refuge overseas – though he was to return and defeat Warwick six months later. Warwick was killed on the field; so, soon, was Henry VI's son, the Prince of Wales. Henry himself was murdered in the Tower. Thereafter Edward ruled in peace, showing intelligence and capability.

Edward IV was fully possessed of the Renaissance idea of magnificence, whereby it was not enough for a great man simply to be a great man – he had to show himself one through the splendour of his possessions, the prodigality of his gifts and the display of his effulgent self to his people. About the time of his temporary exile in France, his supporter Sir John Fortescue applauded this concept in *The Governance of England*:

*Opposite:* **Edward IV in about 1520. Six foot four and the epitome of chivalry, he believed that a king should display his power through magnificent surroundings and possessions. This set the tone for royal houses such as Greenwich. Note the tiers of jewels on his chest.**

43

Elizabeth Woodville, the beautiful widow of Sir John de Grey. Edward IV made her his queen. She was a local girl to Greenwich, having been raised at the nearby manor of Lee. Edward granted her 'the lordship and manor of Plesaunce, otherwise called Grenewiche'. Her sons were the Princes in the Tower, murdered by Richard III, but her daughter Elizabeth married Henry VII.

Item, it shall nede that the kyng haue such tresour, as he mey make new bildynges whan he woll, ffor his pleasure and magnificence; and as he mey bie hym riche clothes, riche furres … riche stones æ and other juels and ornamentes conuenyent to his estate roiall. And often tymes he woll bie rich hangynges and other apparell ffor his howses … ffor yff a king did not so, nor myght do, he lyved then not like his estate, but rather in miserie, and in more subgeccion than doth a priuate person.

Needless to say, Edward IV glowed with this charisma of riches, while the more simple tastes of Henry VI seemed niggardly. Fortescue lashed him for his 'grete pouertie' and reluctance to keep a 'worshipfull and grete housolde'. According to this yardstick, ostentation was all. It was a principle that prevailed in different forms until the death of Queen Elizabeth 140 years later. During that time Greenwich would blaze like gold.

Paradoxically, though, Edward IV's own special contribution was to establish a house of Observant Friars just next to the palace, on a piece of land 'where the game of ball used to be played'. They were a branch of the Franciscan order and lived according to a strict rule of poverty. Over the next fifty years they won many rich donations from the royal occupants of the palace, as well as from local people. Permission to found the friary was obtained from the Pope in 1481. By then the person and habits of the King made a notable contrast to the austere Observants, for he had come to look as fleshly as his reputation for 'boon-companionship, vanities, debaucheries, extravagance and sensual enjoyments', as a contemporary put it, would lead one to expect. This corpulent man died suddenly, at the age of forty, in 1483. It was now all over for the Woodvilles. Many of Elizabeth's kinsmen were put to death, as were the little Princes in the Tower who were her sons. She herself survived the two years of Richard III's reign, and was assigned a pension by Henry Tudor when he came to the throne as Henry VII in 1485. Henry cemented the reconciliation between the Lancastrians and the Yorkists by marrying her daughter, Elizabeth of York. But he kept Greenwich for himself. Henry VII loved Greenwich.

# IF YOU ARE THE DAUPHIN OF FRANCE, I WISH TO KISS YOU

H ENRY VII EXPRESSED HIS LOVE for the Plesaunce, which he renamed Placentia, by demolishing most of it. But he built it up again into a new palace, bigger and more modern and far more splendid than the old.

It took some time for Henry VII to show that he was a king who would build. The first decade of his reign was spent consolidating his position; to embark on lengthy campaigns of construction cannot have seemed a priority until his own survival on the throne looked more certain. Blackheath was again the scene of insurrection when a great body of Cornishmen occupied it in 1497. It did not take much to defeat them, and carpenters from Placentia who had been building the 'Queen's barn' downed tools to watch the battle. Later, the Protestant martyr Hugh Latimer remembered helping his father buckle on his armour 'when he went unto Blackheath field'. (He mentioned it in a sermon preached before Edward VI.) There was a terrible slaughter, after which the dead were buried in heaps. With Jack Cade's rebellion of 1450, the first blows had been struck in a civil war that lasted decades. Now it was again among the furze-bushes of Blackheath that it finally petered out. (A commemorative plaque to the Cornish marchers was erected in the Park wall just east of the Blackheath Gate in 1997 to mark the 500th anniversary.)

Another obstacle to building was Henry VII's initial shortage of money: fighting had emptied the royal coffers. But from the mid-1490s until his death in 1509 Henry VII spent £29,000 on his principal houses and even more on works of piety, such as the completion of King's College Chapel, Cambridge, and his own memorial chapel at Westminster. Foremost among the palaces were that which he renamed Richmond (formerly Sheen: he had been Duke of Richmond before taking the crown) and Placentia. It was a sign of the affection in which all the Tudors would hold Greenwich, where the future Henry VIII, Queen Mary and Queen Elizabeth were born.

Rich or poor, Henry VII came to the throne determined to celebrate. Magnificence was a weapon in his political armoury. The idea that an English king should express his power through the splendour of his appearance, his houses and his entertainments dated back to Edward IV, who modelled his household on that of his brother-in-law, the Duke of Burgundy. A further incentive in Henry VII's case was the many years of privation he had suffered before coming to the throne.

Henry VIII on board the *Henri Grace de Dieu*, or *Great Harry*. It was built at the dockyard which the King established at Woolwich, near Greenwich. The dockyard at Deptford was even closer. To a king who took immense interest in every development of his ships, and enjoyed acting the part of a captain (as in this picture), the location of these dockyards, handily lying either side of Greenwich, must have contributed to his high regard for this palace.

So stupendous pomp accompanied his coronation, his wedding and such occasions as the creation of the little Prince Harry as Duke of York. He would give feasts for hundreds of people at a time. He loved books and music, but he also loved hunting. For that reason he preferred a country life, surrounded by fine horses, greyhounds and hawks. Greenwich must have satisfied this side of his nature, for it was in a completely rural location; yet it was close enough to London for the King, necessarily suspicious, to know everything that happened in his capital.

Richmond Palace had some of the fairy-tale quality associated with contemporary French architecture; with its little forest of bell-shaped domes, it suggested an enchanted castle – perfect and symmetrical. Greenwich was an altogether different proposition. There was no attempt to make it look like a fortress; this in itself was a novelty after so many years of civil war. It had no moat. Nor was it remotely symmetrical. From the chapel that stood at the eastern end of the site a long irregular façade unfolded westwards along the river, in a succession of projecting bays, buttresses and gables. Most of this range was two storeys tall, but towards the west end stood a squarish tower or donjon of five storeys. The donjon was a medieval survival. As Simon Thurley comments in *The Royal Palaces of Tudor England*, here it fused with the urban character of the Burgundian palaces in Bruges and Ghent. Henry VII would have been familiar with the latter buildings from his years of exile as Duke of Richmond. It was also the Dukes of Burgundy who had elevated brick,

Placentia, the palace built by Henry VII at Greenwich in 1500–4. The donjon (towards the right), which forms the principal entrance, is the only hint of a military tradition. Otherwise Placentia was revolutionary for its informal, domestic character, which influenced many subsequent great houses of Tudor England.

hitherto regarded as a convenient but humble material, to an acceptable level of dignity for a palace. Brick became the Tudor building material *par excellence*, and one of its first uses by a Tudor monarch was at Greenwich. In size, Placentia was not much smaller than Hampton Court.

The King's rooms overlooked the river; other accommodation was arranged round a series of courtyards. Apparently only a fireplace and one wall from the old Plesaunce were incorporated into Henry's new structure: probably the timber of which much of the previous house had been constructed had decayed. But the foundations would seem to have been reused, since archaeologists have discovered that the outline of the previous building was preserved within the new. The master mason Robert Vertue and his men carried out most of the work between 1500 and 1504, at a cost of £900. At the same time the prominent carpenter Thomas Bynks, six times Master of the Carpenters' Company, was being paid for wood-work in the chapel, gallery and two closets: one may have suspicions about the quality since contemporary contributions which he made to Richmond Palace were soon in need of repair, and a gallery he built there fell down. In 1504 Henry VII kept Christmas at Greenwich with the Marquis of Dorset and several other great figures. For the remaining few years of his reign, Greenwich frequently became the setting for the great religious festivals, such as Christmas, with all their associated junketing.

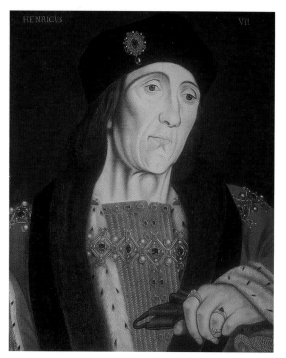

Henry VII, the builder of Placentia. By the time the house was finished, in 1504, the worries of kingship, and the death of his queen and eldest son, had sapped his taste for courtly hospitality. This image, painted after his death, captures the sadness which haunted his last years – and formed such a contrast to the vitality of his teenage successor, Henry VIII.

But Henry's heart was no longer in these celebrations. By the time Greenwich was finished, the gloom and parsimony, for which Henry's character tends to be remembered, had closed in. His earlier high spirits and love of display had evaporated. Two of his sons, including the eldest, Arthur, had died. Then his Queen, Elizabeth of York, died in childbirth in 1503. The King who came to occupy Greenwich for the first time the next year had lost much of his vitality. Although still in his forties, his hair had thinned, those few teeth that he had were black, his skin had turned sallow. It was too late for Placentia to provide the backdrop to spectacular shows of gaiety and revelling. It was left to his glamorous young son, Henry VIII, to fill the palace with people, vigour, courtship, colour, feasting, gorgeous clothes, enticing women and swaggering men. In time Placentia would also witness, and to some extent participate in, the darker late years of Henry VIII's reign; but how distant they must have seemed when Henry inherited his kingdom – and the enormous personal fortune of a million and a half pounds that Henry VII had amassed through prudent kingship – at only seventeen.

\* \* \*

When Henry VIII became King in 1509, he was a young man, extremely handsome, so strong and brave that he often challenged all comers to fight him; he spoke French and Latin, understood Italian, composed music as well as played it on various instruments, sang tunefully and balanced his love of luxury with reading and frequent religious devotions. He was modern, thoughtful and sophisticated, though susceptible to the romance of the past. Magnificence was at the heart of his aesthetic philosophy: he wanted to show himself to be a great prince and the sheer volume of his possessions was a factor in this display. He came to own no fewer than sixty-three houses. It was an exceptional number: Henry VIII was the most prodigious royal acquirer and builder of houses that England has ever known.

Among this great tally of houses, Greenwich, where Henry VIII was born in 1491, occupied a special place. It meant pleasure. His architectural contribution to the palace built by his father consisted of kennels, stables, tennis courts, a cockpit, a tiltyard with distinctive towers for storming in mock combats, and armour workshops – as well, it must be said, as the rebuilding of the chapel. Always impatient, eager to consume every gratification as soon as the thought of it came into his head, he insisted on these works being rushed up with all speed. When a banqueting house was built in 1527, the workmen laboured throughout the night, working by the light of candles.

One of the attractions of Greenwich was its relative accessibility, thanks to its position on the river. Henry travelled there by barge, and his gaily caparisoned oarsmen must have made a fine sight, as they took the King down the river. Shortly after the divorce from Catherine of Aragon, Anne Boleyn was escorted from Greenwich to the Tower, four miles away, by a flotilla of barges of the Crafts of London, 'deckyd', as Archbishop Cranmer wrote in a letter, 'after the most gorgiouse and sumptuous maner'. The journey was accompanied by the blaring of trumpets and other instruments, 'as combly donne as neuer was lyke in any tyme nyghe to our rememberaunce'. Guns fired a salute for the length of the way. It was by river, too, that most of the building materials arrived. Those coming from London would be embarked at the Tower, to avoid the hazard provided by London Bridge. This was the only bridge over the river, and its narrow arches created dangerous rapids: hence an entry in accounts of the 1540s, recording payment to a Greenwich waterman for the carriage of timber and 'shewtyng the bridge' at 4d a load. (It was no better by 1662, according to an anecdote about a Frenchman told to Samuel Pepys by John Falconer, Clerk of the Ropeyard at Woolwich, on 8 August that year. 'When he saw the great fall, he begun to cross himself and say his prayers in the greatest fear in the world; and as soon as he was over, he swore *"Morbleu c'est le plus grand plaisir du monde"* – being the most like a French humour in the world.') Another impediment was the weather: in February 1517 the Venetian ambassador was prevented from going to Greenwich because the river had frozen. In 1536 the King and Queen Jane were forced to ride from London to Greenwich for the same reason.

Houses were something of a hobby to Henry VIII. As he grew older and freed himself from the domination of Cardinal Wolsey, he took considerable personal interest in the improvements of those that he owned. In moving between his admittedly large number of residences, he was following the practice of all English monarchs since William the Conqueror. Henry VIII would descend upon his farther flung properties, as well as the houses of his courtiers, during the summer, as part of a progress around his realm to show himself to his people. In the winter, the court shifted in a random pattern between the different houses around London, of which Greenwich was one. There were various reasons for this, one being to thoroughly clean those that had recently been vacated. The winter movements followed a previously prepared timetable known as the 'giest'. This could be interrupted by the great dread that the King had of plague. The court would decamp as soon as an outbreak occurred in the vicinity of where they were staying, or alter course if any case had

*Opposite:* **Castle Loyal, which provided the scenery for a challenge at Greenwich, at Christmas 1524. A captain and fifteen gentlemen offered to defend the castle, along with the four ladies inside, against all comers, in four forms of combat: the tilt (on horseback with lances), the tourney (on horseback with swords), the barriers (on foot with swords) and a general assault. In the event, the construction went awry and the assault was abandoned in favour of a tournament.**

been found near their intended destination. Plague caused Henry VIII to leave Hampton Court and come to Placentia in the summer of 1530, presumably taking the further precaution of ejecting any inhabitants of the area who looked sickly: Privy Purse expenses show that he paid £18 8s later that year 'to compensate such poor folk as were expelled the town of Greenwiche in the time of the plague'. It may be that plague sometimes reached Greenwich earlier than London, on account of the sailors who passed through it; but conditions were not, on the whole, so favourable there for its spread as in the rotten and crowded streets of the capital. Yet Greenwich was sufficiently close for news of important events to reach the King's ear quickly.

Part of the principle of magnificence was that the pleasures enjoyed by Henry VIII at Greenwich and elsewhere should generally be taken in public. Jousting, maying, dancing, feasting, hunting – these activities, which Henry certainly loved, often had a ceremonial importance that went hand in hand with the personal enjoyment they afforded. Those that did not were invested with an elaborate symbolism, sometimes gratuitous, sometimes overworked, but radiating the values with which Henry wanted his name to be associated. They focused on chivalry. The age of knight errantry, if it ever existed, was at, or beyond, its last gasp. Warfare was becoming an increasingly indiscrimate activity as a result of gunpowder. The last battle in which knights had ridden to the field in full armour had been Flodden in 1513. But it was the golden age of chivalry that provided the visual language for the pageantry of his court. In this he followed the example of the glamorous Burgundian court where Philip the Good had established the Order of the Golden Fleece in 1430.

Courtly love played a big part in it. At Christmas 1511, the great hall at Greenwich saw the erection of a mock castle called *Le Fortresse Dangerus*. Henry and five companions, dressed in russet-coloured silk, stormed it, bringing out the six ladies, similarly clad, who had been inside. They all danced before Queen Catherine, who was enchanted. On May Day in 1515 the Queen led a cavalcade of nobles, ambassadors and ladies, all richly dressed, out of Greenwich to meet the King and a hundred noblemen in a wood, probably on Shooters Hill. There were twenty-five damsels to accompany the Queen, all riding white ponies. The King and his party wore green and carried bows, as though they were foresters or possibly Robin Hood. This scene was watched by an enormous crowd, said to have numbered twenty-five thousand people. Folk must have thought it was worth travelling some distance to watch the pageant. On another occasion, the populace made such a press that they were able to tear the costly robes and golden embellishments off the courtiers' backs, even stripping the King 'into his hosen and doublet'; the guard came quickly to prevent further loss of apparel.

It could be said that chivalric fantasy provided a means of dignifying the wenching and whoring that were a concomitant of Tudor pleasures, certainly those of the King. Henry did not smile upon those who broke the illusion. Duke

Humphrey's Tower, now repaired and named Mireflore, was convenient for amorous purposes. On one occasion when Henry was being rowed to Greenwich, he invited one of his courtiers, Sir Andrew Flamock, to join him in a versing competition, whereby they would each supply a line on the theme of the lady Henry was about to visit at Mireflore:

> Within this towre
> There lieth a flowre
> That hath my hart.

Sir Andrew's contribution was so dirty that Henry dismissed him from his presence.

*Opposite top:*
**Seating plan for the banquet at Greenwich on 7 July 1517. At the top sat (from left to right) Cardinal Wolsey, the Queen, the King, the King's sister Mary and the Imperial ambassador. The food came disguised as animals or castles, and the company sat at table for seven hours.**

A Tudor palace was essentially a theatre. When the King and his court were not there to people the rooms, they would have been empty and almost bare of decoration. The King's rich furniture, gaily coloured tapestries and other signs of opulence preceded him from house to house. There is a similarly theatrical quality about many of the events and practices which happened there. Even the washing of the King's hands before eating, with water brought by noblemen of high degree, was a matter of ritual and display. Many of the entertainments were carefully planned and staged. They made a tremendous impression, at a time when reports of such happenings were sent around Europe by letter. One series of reports has survived in the archives of Venice, thanks to the assiduous correspondence of successive Venetian ambassadors and secretaries. They offer the best description of Tudor Greenwich that can be found.

Naturally the Venetian reports concentrate on great occasions of state, such as the betrothal in 1514 of Henry VIII's sister Mary, then a radiant girl of sixteen, to Louis XII of France, age sixty-two, represented for the occasion by the Duke of Longueville. The ceremony took place in a chamber on the first floor, hung with cloth of gold that was embroidered with the royal arms. The betrothal of the future Queen Mary, Henry's three-year-old daughter, to the Dauphin of France in 1518 was even more sumptuous. Cardinal Wolsey placed a ring set with a large diamond on her finger, and the Lord Admiral of France passed it over the second joint. The little girl is supposed to have lisped: 'Are you the Dauphin of France? If you are, I wish to kiss you.' Two days later a joust was held, followed by a grand supper. The Venetian ambassador noted the precise number of gold vessels: thirty-two vases, the smallest being a foot high, and four drinking glasses that were two

*My Lord Goes by Water to Greenwich.*
**Cardinal Wolsey's barge, approaching the privy steps to Placentia. This illustration from a manuscript *Life of Wolsey* dates from 1578, nearly fifty years after his death.**

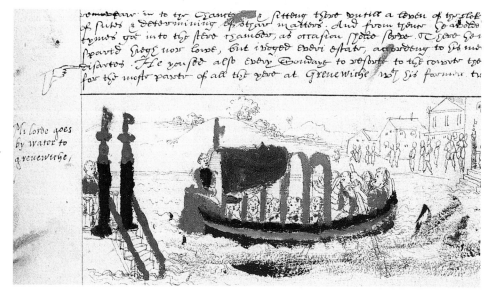

54

foot high. The fact that such reports were made and sent round the world helps explain why the accumulation of material possessions, with little discrimination of taste, was so important to great men such as Henry. Supper was followed by a pageant celebrating the peace and marriage between England and France. It was laden with symbolism: a rock bearing trees that represented the different powers affected by the union; a lady with a dolphin on her lap; knights emerging from the rock to fight a tourney; a Pegasus to bear tidings of the betrothal to the world. Henry was dressed in splendour, wearing a robe that was stiff with gold brocade and lined with ermine. The French admiral happened to admire it, upon which Henry threw it from his shoulders and gave it to him.

Even these celebrations were outdone when the Emperor Charles V came to Greenwich in 1522. The palace was crammed with people, but there was still not enough room. Some of the Emperor's retinue had to be billeted on towns-people. It suggests the scale of Greenwich at this time that there were twenty-seven dwellings of sufficient amenity to accommodate them. The Vicarage took four guests, 'The Syne of the Greyhound' (presumably an inn) put up ten. Several houses had been built alongside the palace, by courtiers wanting something more by way of privacy than palace lodgings could offer. Beyond these couple of dozen substantial houses the town would have consisted of little more than a few shacks. Its only independent life was as a fishing village. Beyond that it serviced the palace which dwarfed it in scale.

Given the theatrical temper of the court, it is not surprising that Henry should have delighted in stage productions, such as pageants and the new Italian fashion of masques. When these

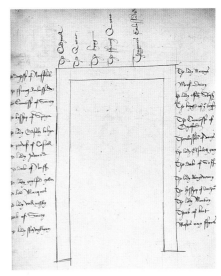

Score card for the tournament of May 1516. The strokes by each name kept the score, as in boxing. Blows to the head, to the upper body and broken lances are recorded, as well as the number of courses run.

took place, tiers of benches would be lined up either side of a hall; in front of each bench was a bar of wood that spectators could lean on as they watched the perfor-mance. These productions would involve courtiers, the gentlemen being masked. At the end of the dance with which they would finish, the men would take off their masks to reveal that – to everyone's incomplete astonishment – one of them had been the King. On one occasion the floor on which this took place is described as having been laid with cloth embroidered with gold lilies. The ceiling was painted with a map of the world, around which the signs of the zodiac were held up by giants. 'Some of the damsels are so beautiful as to be supposed goddesses rather than human beings,' wrote Gasparo Spinelli, the Venetian secretary in London.

Henry VIII jousting. Henry VIII excelled at all the tournament sports. He built his first permanent tiltyard at Greenwich, overlooked by towers which could be stormed as part of a mock combat.

When Henry VIII came to the throne he had great physical powers, and loved to exercise them. His favourite sport as a young man was jousting, or tilting, which combined drama and adrenalin in equal measure. Two knights on heavy horses, their gay caparisons flying, thundered towards each other in full armour, each with the object of breaking the other knight's lance. It was thrilling – and dangerous – for the competitors, colourful for the spectators, the whole thing wrapped up in the chivalric values by which Henry VIII was so entranced. Sometimes Henry would joust every day. Tilting could only take place at the palaces which had the necessary tiltyard and stabling, so the King gave them preference in the early years of his reign. Later, when a lance had splintered inside his helmet and a heavy fall had left him concussed, he became more enamoured of tennis, which could also be played at smaller, relatively more private houses. But for tilting, Greenwich was supreme. Before Henry's time, the structures provided for tournaments – principally a grandstand for the royal party – were all temporary affairs, run up for the occasion. At Greenwich, Henry built a permanent tiltyard, overlooked by a viewing gallery and two tall towers of brick, seen rising high

above the other palace buildings in early representations. It dates from 1514; there was also to be a tiltyard at Hampton Court, based on the one at Greenwich, but it took so long to finish that it was never used in his lifetime.

Two prerequisites for tilting were horses and armour, and Greenwich was well provided with both. Henry was a famous horseman; when he hunted, he would tire out, it was said, as many as eight or ten horses – a scarcely imaginable feat. There were several stables at Greenwich, for hunters, brood mares, work horses and so on. Also, it was at Greenwich that Henry VIII built his armour workshops in the 1510s. Over the previous century the English had stopped making the fine armours that were now such a status symbol across Europe. A suit of armour made an appropriately sumptuous present for one monarch to give another, and Henry VIII found himself in the dreadful position of being unable to offer any of English manufacture. Some of Henry VIII's contemporary sovereigns – Maximilian and John Frederick of Saxony – actually sat at the armourer's workbench, bashing metal with their own tools. Henry did not go as far as this, but he took a close interest in the design. In 1524 he ordered, according to Hall, 'a newe harnesse

made of his owne devyse and fashion, suche as no armorer before that tyme had seen'. Henry was trying this armour in a joust against his brother-in-law, the Duke of Suffolk, when the lance splintered inside his helmet – an accident that could have cost him his sight or even killed him. Initially the metalworkers who made Henry VIII's armours came from Milan, but they did not stay long, their place being taken by Germans. As deftly jointed as a lobster's tail, their armours, hammered out on anvils known as the Great and Little Bear, were diapered and damascened with decorative flourishes, and sometimes inlaid with gold. For all that, they never reached the extremes of fantasy and elaboration seen in some continental work: relatively speaking these were sober suits. Jacob Halder, master workman at Greenwich from 1576 to 1607, left a record of some of the more elaborate Greenwich productions of the reigns of Queen Mary and Queen Elizabeth, in a book of his designs for armour, now in the Victoria and Albert Museum.

*Above:* **George Clifford, 3rd Earl of Cumberland, wearing the fantastic star armour which he had made in the Greenwich workshops. This miniature by Nicholas Hilliard was painted in about 1590.**

*Right:* **Sir Christopher Hatton in his armour, from a book of designs by Jacob Halder, master workman at Greenwich from 1576 to 1607. Most Greenwich armours were more sober than this.**

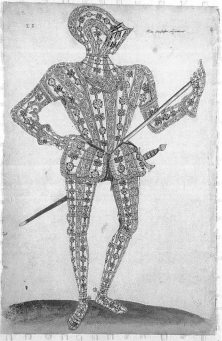

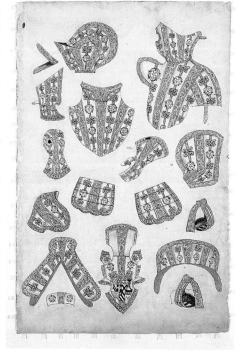

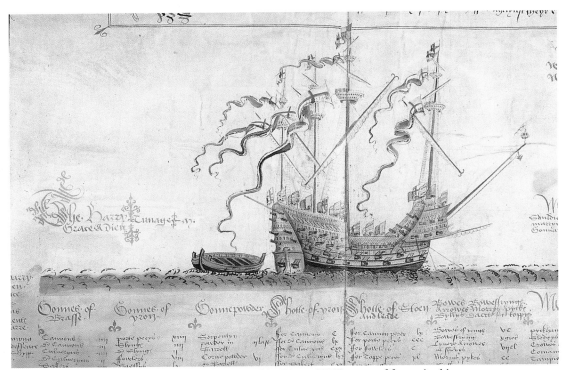

The *Great Harry* in 1546. It was the biggest vessel in Henry VIII's navy of forty-six ships.

## Deptford and Woolwich

When Henry VIII was twenty-one, and had just been enjoying a period of 'Solemptne Justes' at Greenwich, he ordered all his ships and galleys to be prepared, with all their rigging and ordnance. The soldiers who were to man them were mustered on Blackheath, and their captains appointed. This preceded a review of the fleet – the first on record – which took place at Portsmouth. Unfortunately, the French had as much of an eye upon the emergence of English sea power as Henry, and the Battle of Brest Haven soon followed in 1512, during which the chief ship of the English, *The Regent*, was burnt.

This concentrated Henry's mind on England's vulnerability by sea, her lack of great ships and of any but one or two which were permanently equipped for war. To remedy this, he established the dockyard at Deptford, adjacent to Greenwich, in 1513, and the one at Woolwich, a few miles to the east, shortly afterwards. At this period, dockyards were *ad hoc* establishments – little more than a collection of storehouses. It was therefore an innovation when John Hopton, comptroller of ships, made a pond in a meadow next to the storehouse at Deptford, constructing 'a good hable and suffycient hed for the same pond and also certyn hable sleysis through the which the water may have entre and course into the foresaid ponde as well at spryng tydes as at nepetydes'. The dock was to be big enough to take the ships *Great Galley, Mary Rose, Great Bark, Less Bark* and *Peter Pomegranate*. By the end of the reign Deptford had become the most important of Henry's dockyards. The dockyard at Woolwich grew up around the construction of the mighty ship which Henry commissioned after the loss of *The Regent*, the *Henri Grace de Dieu*, or *Great Harry*.

The brilliance of Henry VIII's Greenwich is caught in a verse by the antiquarian Leland, originally written in Latin.

Lo, with what lustre shines this wished for place!
Which, star-like, might the heavenly mansions grace.
What painted roofs! What windows charm the eye!
What turrets, rivals of the starry sky!
What constant springs! What verdant meads besides,
Where Flora's self in majesty resides,
And beauteous all around her does dispense,
With bounteous hand, her flow'ry influence.
Happy the man whose lucky wit could frame,
To suit this place, so elegant a name,
Expressing all its beauties in the same.

Colour, fantasy, sparkling glass and flowers – the charm reaches down to us even now, centuries after the last vestige of the buildings has disappeared.

However, the crisis of the royal divorce from Catherine of Aragon, and the subsequent rupture with the Church of Rome, cast their shadow over Greenwich. The glow faded from the previously rosy reports of the Venetian ambassador. With the instalment of Anne Boleyn he was moved to speak in such 'lewd fashion' of the King and his Council that he had to be recalled, making Venice without an ambassador in England for over fifty years. Before that happened, the Venetians had described what must have been a hair-raising sermon preached before the King on Easter Day 1532 by the Observant friar William Peto. Peto 'gravely reproved such as repudiate their wives, declaring that by no means can they be saved; and, although appearing to speak generally, he threatened the island with excommunication, saying that the ruin of kingdoms always proceeds from the evils of flatterers'. Henry VIII seems not to have missed the point: he rose and stalked out.

Earlier in his reign, Henry VIII had gone out of his way to praise the friars for 'their strict adherence to poverty, their sincerity, charity and devotion'. It was in their church that his marriage to Catherine of Aragon had been celebrated. She remained devoted to them, often worshipping in the friary church, sometimes at night. She appointed one of the friars to be her confessor and expressed a wish to be buried in the friary. After her departure, the existence of these poor and godly monks, just the other side of the palace wall, must have seemed a living reproof to the luxury and goings-on of the court. Worse for Henry, they were not to be silenced. And when Henry's representatives arrived to take an oath from the friars, acknowledging the King to be supreme head of the Church, every one of them refused. They were arrested or dispersed. Of those that were arrested about thirty died, some of starvation. One, after torture, was strangled with the cord of his habit.

In the second half of his reign, Henry VIII was less drawn to Greenwich. There was a time when he had spent nearly every Christmas there, as in the years 1526, 1527, 1530, 1531, 1532 and 1533. After that, the only years that he spent Christmas at Greenwich were 1537 and 1543. As he grew older and fatter, and one wife followed another, some of the brilliance must have gone out of the revels, with their high-spirited chivalry. Following the ruin of Cardinal Wolsey in 1529, Henry VIII had the novelty of Hampton Court to enjoy; and given his restless nature and delight in architectural effects, this new palace, barely finished, must have seemed preferable to the one built by his father, with its uncomfortable memories and recalcitrant friars.

But Greenwich retained the love of Henry VIII's children. His son, the boy king Edward VI, enjoyed himself there, according to entries that he made in his diary in 1551 when he was fourteen: 'March 31. A chaleng made by me that I, with 16 of my chaumbre, shuld runne at base, shote, and rune at ring, with any 17 of my servauntes, gentlemen in the court.' Running at ring was an exercise performed on horses, one of many which encouraged the important accomplishment, both for wartime and everyday, of riding well. Two high posts were erected, with a small ring dangling from a crossbeam at the end of a string. Contestants had to impale the ring on the end of their lance. It was good practice for jousting. The young King and his courtiers were soon having another go at it, Edward noting carefully the black silk coats 'pulled out with white taffeta' worn by his side and the yellow taffeta of the opposition. 'My side lost,' he concluded in dismay.

Edward VI as Prince of Wales, in about 1539, by Hans Holbein the Younger. The boy king enjoyed tournaments at Greenwich. He died there in 1553.

Two years later Greenwich was also the scene of Edward's pathetic death. It happened not in Placentia but in the mansion of Old Court, immediately to the east of Greenwich, which the Lord Protector, the newly created Duke of Northumberland, had got out of the King. Northumberland had the consumptive boy moved from Placentia into his own house, when doctors diagnosed that he had only three days to live. This did not give Northumberland sufficient time to organise his plot to put Lady Jane Grey, granddaughter of Henry VIII's sister Mary, on the throne. (Lady Jane had been married against her will to Northumberland's equally reluctant son, Lord Guildford Dudley; she had been brought up near Greenwich, at Lee.) Edward VI's last days were spun out by means of arsenic, which temporarily stopped the haemorrhages. It must have caused the dying King terrible pain. His hair fell out and his extremities turned gangrenous. By the time he was actually dead, the body was in such a horrifying state that it could not be shown immediately. There was a rumour that the corpse subsequently produced and buried in Westminster Abbey was not that of the King at all, but a similar-looking youth who had been murdered in his place. The distorted remains of the King, according to this version, were disposed of somewhere in Greenwich.

The whole escapade seems as improbable and grotesque as a revenge tragedy by an Elizabethan dramatist. It ended in the predictable disaster: Lady Jane was Queen for ten days, imprisoned, then – following an uprising during which Sir Thomas Wyatt camped his band of rebels on Blackheath – she, her husband and members of their family were executed. Northumberland had already been beheaded on the accession of Mary Tudor. (Despite what seems the total eclipse of the Dudley family, one of Northumberland's sons would soon shine again as Elizabeth's favourite, Robert Dudley, Earl of Leicester.) As a Roman Catholic, Mary reinstated the friars at Greenwich, her mother's champions Peto and Elston among them. But the times had changed, and townspeople pelted them with stones. Nevertheless, it is from Mary's reign that we are allowed our first glimpse of the royal palace of Greenwich, through two tinted drawings made by the Flemish artist Anthony Wyngaerde, who was in the employment of Philip of Spain. These are the first detailed depictions of the place, and show the great rambling length of its river frontage. (Placentia was engraved in the eighteenth century by James Basire, who must have used historical sources since the building itself had long disappeared; but he used his artistic licence to the extent of omitting much of the façade – it would not otherwise have conformed to the proportions of a conventional plate.)

Unlike her father, Queen Elizabeth, despite her long reign, built virtually nothing. The Office of Works, responsible for royal building operations, became little more than a palace maintenance department. Still, it is a sign of her regard for Greenwich that Queen Elizabeth, so careful with her finances, spent more on it annually than on any other palace except Whitehall. It became her principal summer residence 'for the delightfulness of its situation', according to the German visitor Paul Hentzner, who travelled through England when Elizabeth was an old woman, in 1598.

There are occasional accounts of ceremonies and entertainments which took place at Greenwich during Elizabeth's reign: a muster by men-at-arms from the City of London in 1559; a water pageant, in which a mock castle was attacked by pinnaces, on Midsummer's Day 1561; the distribution of Maunday gifts, with the Queen washing the feet (previously prepared by the yeoman of the laundry and the sub-almoner with copious supplies of flower-water) of thirty-nine paupers in 1572. Generally, the pace of revelry had slowed since her father's time. But Greenwich was acquiring a new significance through its association with the great maritime adventures of the age, including the defeat of the Armada. Many names from that greatest of seafaring counties, Devon, recur in Greenwich. It is easy to see why: when Devon sailors were not fighting the Spanish, they were engaged in trade. This would have taken them to the wharves downstream of London, and some of them stayed. Sir Francis Drake's early years were spent plying along the coast in a small trading boat, sometimes crossing over to Zeeland and France, but probably more often sailing up the Thames estuary towards London. Later he joined his relation Sir John Hawkins at Deptford, and eventually it was from here that he left to circumnavigate the globe in the *Pelican*, later renamed the *Golden Hind*. After a banquet at Deptford served on board the *Golden Hind*, the Queen knighted Drake with a gilded sword. Some of the attraction of Greenwich to Queen Elizabeth must have been its proximity to Deptford, only a mile or two away. There would always have been something of interest for her to see in Deptford. It was while she was being rowed between Greenwich and Deptford that a bystander accidentally let off an arquebus, which put a bullet through both the arms of one of her oarsmen. The offender was strung up at the gallows, only to be reprieved when the noose was in place. The London merchant Henry Machyn records a mock naval battle put on for the Queen's entertainment at Deptford in 1560. Four pinnaces attacked a brigantine, with men hurled into the water, pikes and stones being thrown and 'as grett shutyng as cold be'. There were more than four thousand people present, though how many were combatants is not clear.

Not that Queen Elizabeth needed to make the journey to Deptford to keep an eye on maritime developments: ships of all kinds must constantly have been passing beneath the very windows of Placentia. After the Armada, Sir Thomas Cavendish brought the fabulous prize that he had captured from the Spanish Main up the Thames for the Queen to see. When she boarded it, every sailor wore a gold chain.

If the episode of Sir Walter Raleigh and his cloak, thrown down to allow Elizabeth to cross a 'plashy place' without muddying the royal shoes, took place at all, it took place at Greenwich. Raleigh had been in Ireland, where the Spanish had landed and built a fort at Smerwick. The province of Munster had flared up in rebellion. After taking a prominent part in the successful assault on Smerwick, Raleigh was rewarded with the job of bringing the happy news to the Queen. She had been walking in the park, when he stepped out of the gatehouse, tall, dark-bearded and gallant. What came next – or a somewhat cinematic version of it – can be pictured from chapter fifteen of Sir Walter Scott's *Kenilworth*:

> The young cavalier we have so often mentioned had probably never yet approached so near the person of his Sovereign, and he pressed forward as far as the line of warders permitted, in order to avail himself of the present opportunity … Unbonneting at the same time, he fixed his eager gaze on the Queen's approach, with a mixture of respectful curiosity and modest yet ardent admiration, which suited so well with his fine features, that the warders, struck with his rich attire and noble countenance, suffered him to approach the ground over which the Queen was to pass, somewhat closer

In 1558, the Flemish artist Antony van Wyngaerde, who was later taken into the employment of Philip II of Spain, sketched two views of Greenwich, as part of a series showing English scenes. They give the first visual impressions of the palace built by Henry VII.

*Top:* This view shows the long riverfront, taken from the other side of the Thames. The river at this time provided the principal means of travel to and from Greenwich. On the far left of the building is the chapel, towards the right the donjon-like tower that formed the principal entrance. This is the only hint of the military tradition to survive in the architecture of Henry VII's palace. Its domestic character set the tone for the subsequent great houses of Tudor England. But given that the palace at Greenwich was constructed soon after the conclusion of the Wars of the Roses – which to contemporaries may not have seemed a conclusion at all – it shows immense confidence on the part of its builder.

There is a road running along the waterfront, which passes through an archway in the base of this tower. The buildings surrounded three courts: the Conduit or Fountain Court, the Cellar Court and the Tennis Court. Rising above the roofs can be seen the towers overlooking Henry VIII's tiltyard. Adjacent to them are the armour workshops. To the right of this can be seen a garden and orchard, and the cemetery of the friary, whose buildings abut the palace on the right. On the hill at the back stands Duke Humphrey's Tower.

The drawing also shows the extent of the town at this time. There are houses scattered along the river's edge to either side of the palace with several boat houses. Some twenty houses had been judged capable of accommodating those members of Emperor Charles V's retinue who could not be fitted into the palace when he visited in 1522; nevertheless, there is nothing on a scale to rival the palace. The old church of St Alfege, which collapsed in 1710, can be seen on the far right.

*Bottom:* Here Placentia is shown from a spot near the present site of the old Royal Observatory. In the foreground is the Park, where people can be seen practising archery. The Dover road runs between the Park and the palace grounds, walled on either side to keep travellers off the royal turf. On the road stands the ancient gatehouse giving access from the palace garden to the Park. It was supposedly at this point that Sir Walter Raleigh threw down his cloak for Queen Elizabeth to step upon.

To the right of the garden the armoury buildings rear their lofty towers; and to the right again comes the spacious tiltyard with its barriers running north and south to keep the vast mail-clad war-horses from crushing their riders in collision. On the skyline is London, with the spire of St Paul's Cathedral and the silhouette of the Tower of London clearly visible. But most of the country round about was still pasture. At the bend on the left of the river, Deptford is little more than a hamlet.

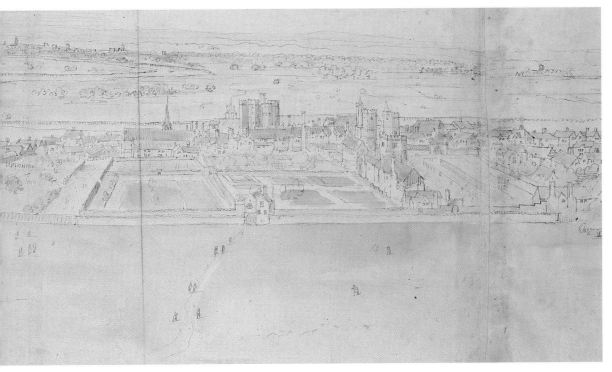

than was permitted to ordinary spectators. Thus the adventurous youth stood full in Elizabeth's eye – an eye never indifferent to the admiration which she deservedly excited among her subjects, or to the fair proportions of external form which chanced to distinguish any of her courtiers. Accordingly, she fixed her keen glance on the youth, as she approached the place where he stood, with a look in which surprise at his boldness seemed to be unmingled with resentment, while a trifling accident happened which attracted her attention towards him yet more strongly. The night had been rainy, and just where the young gentleman stood, a small quantity of mud interrupted the Queen's passage. As she hesitated to pass on, the gallant, throwing his cloak from his shoulders, laid it on the miry spot, so as to ensure her stepping over it dryshod. Elizabeth looked at the young man, who accompanied this act of devoted courtesy with a profound reverence, and a blush that overspread his whole countenance. The Queen was confused, and blushed in her turn, nodded her head, hastily passed on, and embarked in her barge without saying a word.

It is too great a piece of romantic historical imagination for one to quibble with the fact that virtually all of it – if not the whole – is invented.

We can picture Queen Elizabeth at Greenwich, at the end of her reign, through Hentzner's detailed description of his visit. The Queen was then sixty-five, 'very majestic' as Hentzner writes: indeed the living icon that is familiar from the portraits of her. An oblong face, fair but wrinkled; small black eyes; rather a hooked nose; thin lips; and (not evident in the paintings) 'her teeth black (a defect the English seem subject to, from their too great use of sugar)' – those were her features. She was dripping with jewels, with heavy earrings, a long necklace, a small crown on top of her red wig, a collar of gold and jewels about her neck and pearls 'the size of beans' sewn onto her white silk dress. It is hardly surprising that 'her air was stately', given the weight of this garniture; for all the blaze of possessions her manner of speaking remained 'mild and obliging'.

It was a Sunday, and she was on her way to the chapel rebuilt by Henry VIII. To get there she had to pass through a throng of people. Her guard of Gentlemen Pensioners alone numbered fifty. The Presence Chamber swarmed with courtiers, including the Archbishop of Canterbury, the Bishop of London and various members of the Council. They all filed into the chapel in order of precedence. 'First went Gentlemen, Barons, Earls, Knights of the Garter, all richly dressed and bare-headed; next came the Chancellor, bearing the seals in a red silk purse, between two; one of which carried the Royal scepter, the other the sword of state, in a red scabbard, studded with golden fleurs-de-lis, the point upwards.' As she went along, the Queen bestowed a few words, switching easily between English, French and Italian, to the different people who had come to address her. They did so on bended knee; in fact it was etiquette for all to kneel when she turned her face towards them. The Queen was followed by some ladies, 'very handsome and well-shaped'. In the ante chapel the cry went up 'Long live Queen Elizabeth!' To which she answered: 'I thank you, my good people.'

After chapel, dinner. Not being of the inner circle, Hentzner did not see the Queen eat; even so he could witness the extraordinary ritual with which her food was prepared. It reads rather as though it were a dumb show put on for the benefit of the many visitors. It certainly impressed Hentzner, who describes it minutely:

> … a Gentleman entered the room bearing a rod, and along with him another who had a table-cloth, which, after they had both kneeled three times with the utmost veneration, he spread upon the table, and, after kneeling again, they both retired. Then came two others, one with the rod again, the other with a salt-cellar, a plate, and bread; when they had kneeled, as the others had done, and placed what was brought upon the table, they too retired with the same ceremonies performed by the first.
>
> At last, came an unmarried Lady (we were told she was a Countess), and along with her a married one, bearing a tasting knife; the former was dressed in white silk, who, when she had prostrated herself three times in the most graceful manner, approached the table, and rubbed the plates with bread and salt, with as much awe as if the Queen had been present: when they had waited there a little while, the Yeomen of the Guard entered, bare-headed, clothed in scarlet, with a gold rose upon their backs, bringing in at each turn a course of twenty-four dishes, served in plate, most of it gilt; these dishes were received by a gentleman in the same order they were brought, and placed upon the table, while the lady-taster gave to each of the guards a mouthful to eat, of the particular dish he had brought, for fear of any poison. During the time that this guard, which consists of the tallest and stoutest men that can be found in all England, being carefully selected for this service, were bringing dinner, twelve trumpets and two kettle-drums made the hall ring for half an hour together.

The Queen ate in a private chamber, with just a few attendants. Only after she had taken what she wanted were the dishes provided to the ladies of the court.

All those trumpets and kettle-drums indicate the importance that music had for the Elizabethan court. There was a great call for musicians, who performed for dancing, pageants and plays as well as the religious services. Among the Gentlemen of the Chapel, as the musicians attached to the Chapel Royal were known, was the composer Thomas Tallis. Like many of the musicians, he chose Greenwich as his home and in 1585 was buried in the parish church. Engraved on a brass plate before the altar rails was an inscription quaintly describing his life and virtues, in verse which hardly reflects the quality of his music:

Enterred here doth ly a worthy wyght
　　Who for long tyme in musick bore the bell:
His name to shew was Thomas Tallys hyght
　　In honest veruous lyff he dyd excell.
He serv'd long tyme in chappell with grete prayse,
　　Fower sovereygnes reynes a thing not often seen
I mean kyng Henry and prince Edward's dayes,
　　Queene Mary and Elizabeth our queene.
He maryd was though children he had none,
　　And Lyv'd in love full thre and thirty yeres,
With loyal spowse whose name yclipt was Jone
　　Who here entomb'd, him company now bears,
As he did lyve so also did he dy
　　In mylde and yet sort. O! happy man:
To God full oft for mercy did he cry,
　　Wherefore he lyves let death do what he can.

The Greenwich historian Beryl Platts has identified portraits of Elizabeth's Greenwich musicians in a painting known as *Queen Elizabeth Dancing with Robert Dudley, Earl of Leicester* at Penshurst Place in Kent.

Queen Elizabeth dancing La Volta with the Earl of Leicester. The musicians on the left are probably Alfonso Ferrabosco (bass viol), Caesar Galliardello and Richard Farrant (treble viols) and John Lanier (sabeca), all of whom lived at Greenwich.

## Christopher Marlowe

The poet and dramatist Christopher Marlowe was murdered at Deptford in 1593. His death took place in Eleanor Bull's house, presumably a tavern, which lay on the waterfront. According to the inquest, one Ingram Frizer stabbed him in the head as a result of a dispute over the bill; it was accepted that Frizer was acting in self-defence, and he was pardoned. But Frizer's story, supported by the other two in the room at the time, does not bear scrutiny. It is more likely that there was a political motive in his murder – perhaps to protect his patron Thomas Walsingham from association with the atheist views for which Marlowe was about to be tried.

**It is not absolutely certain that this portrait shows Marlowe. If it does, he was both remarkably handsome and self-possessed at the age of twenty-one, the age of the young man in the picture.**

We know so much about Elizabeth's Greenwich players – and here they are: Alfonso Ferrabosco, playing the instrument in which he specialised, the bass viol; behind him the two 'treble viols' (violins), his fellow-countryman, Galliardello, and the English Richard Farrant; with, on the extreme left of the group, the young John Lanier, his sabeca strapped on a harness round his shoulders.

The musicians were not tied to Greenwich but many of them made their home there. Several generations of Laniers, Ferraboscos, Mells and Comeys – all families of musicians – appear in the parish register. There was also a boys' choir attached to the court, and these Children of the Chapel had their home at Greenwich. We can imagine them, perhaps, singing in Shakespeare's production of his own *Midsummer-Night's Dream*, given there in 1594.

Music may have been one of the attractions that persuaded other figures from the court to base themselves at Greenwich. There were already quite a number of them in Henry VIII's time, their names being recorded in the survey of the town made to discover how many extra beds could be found to accommodate

Charles V, Holy
Roman Emperor
and the most
powerful
monarch of his
age. He visited
Greenwich in
1522, and this
portrait dates
from about that
time.

Charles V's entourage, during his visit in 1522. As well as 'Master Cornyshe' (William Cornish, Master of the King's Chapel), the list includes 'My Lord of Kentes howse'. The largest of them was the 'Swanne House', which occupied the site of the present Market and had extensive lands stretching up Crooms Hill. Its name almost certainly derives from the swan that was the badge of the Bohuns. For a time it was occupied by Henry Courtney, 11th Earl of Devonshire, created Marquis of Exeter, who was beheaded in 1539.

Clearly the royal presence at Placentia helped stimulate development of the town, as well as lending an air of fashion to the neighbourhood. The area continued to attract city merchants, such as the linen draper John Lambarde who bought the manor of Westcombe, just east of Placentia. The name of Lambarde requires a genuflection from any writer on Greenwich, since his son William, who was a lawyer, wrote the first history of Kent. It was a long time after his father's death in 1554 before William Lambarde could fully enter into his inheritance at Westcombe, because of a dispute with his younger brother. Rather unexpectedly, he fell to remodelling the house at the very end of his life, in the late 1590s. A month after moving into what he liked to describe as his 'poore cabben', he wrote to a friend describing, with mock humility, his life 'upon barrein Blackheath, wheare my wife and I are (for a few weekes) now begynners of a poore housekeeping'. In the early eighteenth century this house was knocked down and a new one put up by Captain Galfridus Walpole, the brother of the future Prime Minister Robert Walpole and Treasurer of Greenwich Hospital. This house was in turn demolished in the Victorian period, to make way for development.

William Lambarde's antiquarian bent was recognised by Queen Elizabeth who made him Master of the Rolls (the Rolls Chapel being the forerunner of the present Public Record Office) and Keeper of the Records in the Tower of London. One morning in 1601 he visited her at Placentia, to present a copy of his *Account of the Records of the Tower*. It is intriguing to imagine this meeting between two old people, one of them preoccupied by history as represented in old documents, the other a figure of history in her own right. They discussed a picture of Richard II which Baron Lumley (himself an obsessive antiquarian where his own pedigree was concerned) had found nailed to a basement wall in his house and then given to the Queen. It was not long before both the antiquarian and the old Queen were dead; and with the departure of the stilted figures of the Elizabethan court Greenwich entered another era, projecting it into the vanguard of architectural taste.

## Greenwich Charities

The antiquarian William Lambarde founded the almshouses called Queen Elizabeth's College in 1575. It was the first public charity to have been established since the Reformation, as well as the first of a series of charities to be bestowed upon Greenwich. Queen Elizabeth's College had an annual income of £104, which supported poor men and their wives. The original almshouses were rebuilt in an Elizabethan manner in 1819, and are the first sight of Greenwich experienced by visitors arriving by train, since they stand opposite the railway station.

In 1613, Henry Howard, Earl of Northampton, founded Trinity Hospital, otherwise Norfolk College, for the relief and maintenance of twelve poor men of the parish of East Greenwich, as well as eight poor men of the parish of Shotsham in Norfolk. Thirty years after Trinity Hospital was established, John Roan endowed the Grey Coat School, with the Free Grammar School, endowed by Rev. Abraham Colfe, the vicar of Lewisham, following a dozen years later. Sir William Boreman founded the Green Coat School for the education of boys from East Greenwich in 1656, while the girls' equivalent, the Blue Coat School, arrived in 1752. So when the Seamen's Hospital was established in 1694, it took root in soil that had already been well watered by charitable activity. The Hospital in turn spawned the Royal Naval Asylum, instituted for the support and education of sailors' orphans in 1800, as well as an infirmary. There cannot be many locations in Britain where so much charitable endeavour has been concentrated in one place.

# Love and Kindness Increase Daily between Them

I N APRIL 1603, King James VI of Scotland, soon to be crowned also James I of England, began his journey from Edinburgh to his new capital of London. He had travelled to Denmark before, in a rather rash undertaking to bring back his bride, Anne, the Danish King's fifteen-year-old daughter, in person (there had been such stormy seas that the superstitious James thought that witches had been working spells on him). But he had never so much as set foot in the country over which he would reign. So he was as curious to see England, as he journeyed south, as his new subjects were to see him. First he entered Berwick, where 'he was receved with great ioy as kinge', according to Sir Roger Wilbraham, who had served Elizabeth I in various official positions and would receive preferment under James. All his way he was met 'with great solemnity and state', everywhere being greeted by large troops of horsemen, waited on by sheriffs and gentlemen, presented with orations and gifts, and generally entertained with as much show as the neighbourhood could muster. At Newcastle-on-Tyne the King had the gaols emptied of all their prisoners, except those held for really serious crimes such as papistry, and spent great sums of money, which he did not really have, releasing debtors. At York a conduit ran all day with wine. At Newark-upon-Trent he summarily hanged a pickpocket who had been disguised as a courtier – an exercise of the royal will that went against the English tradition.

On 3 May he arrived at Theobalds, in Hertfordshire, the princely residence of the deformed, puny but wily Robert Cecil, who would translate from being Queen Elizabeth's chief minister into his own. He came to like Theobalds so much that he forced Cecil to exchange it for the opportunity to build the new house of Hatfield: not such a bad swop, given the endowment that James felt compelled to give with it. Countless numbers of people streamed from London to see their new King arrive at Theobalds – so many that a private road had to be quickly made to let him through. Even larger crowds assembled along the remainder of the route. About four miles from London James was welcomed by the Lord Mayor and 'such unspeakable number of citizens, as the like number was never seene to issue out upon any cause before'. Finally he reached the Charterhouse in the City of London, where he stayed for four nights, before decamping to the

Detail from *A View of Greenwich Park*, by Adriaen Van Stalbemt and Jan Van Belcamp, 1632. Charles I and Henrietta Maria appear in the foreground with their family and courtiers, including Inigo Jones. In the background the unfinished Queen's House can be seen, covered by a temporary roof of thatch.

Greenwich Park and Placentia in the early seventeenth century. Duke Humphrey's Tower can be seen on the left, Trinity Hospital on the far right. Hunting, a sport of which James I was inordinately fond, is being pursued outside the gatehouse to the park (soon to be replaced by the Queen's House).

Tower to escape the ever-present throng, going out secretly by coach or barge to view London, the Palace of Whitehall and the jewels there. But his incognito did not do him much good; he found himself besieged by a multitude of hopefuls who thought that their best chance of receiving a royal favour was to strike while the iron was hot, endlessly swarming 'about his maiestie at every back gate & privie dore to his great offence'. So after four days at the Tower he announced that anyone who hoped for a knighthood would have to wait until the coronation, and removed to Greenwich.

Greenwich came to assume an important place in James's affections even though it did not possess quite the associations for him that it had for his predecessor. James enjoyed nothing so much as the country life. He spoke of London as 'that filthie toune'. Hunting was his greatest diversion: a poor physical specimen who could not walk very well, he became a different man on a horse, and spent so many hours in the saddle that little else could get done. There were complaints

that he neglected official business, but James did not care. He argued that it was good for his constitution, and it was essential to the well-being of the nation that it had a healthy king. Greenwich was the nearest place to London where he could hunt. It was not the best place: that was to be found on the borders of Cambridge and Hertfordshire, around Theobalds and Royston. He also had a preference for Newmarket where he established one of many racecourses. Still, sport at Greenwich was not to be overlooked. It came into its own, however, in the spring, when the hunting had finished, and the Hertfordshire and Cambridgeshire houses were shut up. Then James established a 'standing' or semi-permanent court at Greenwich, whose country airs he much preferred to Whitehall.

In that first year of his reign, this pattern of occupation lay in the future. James was content, to begin with, just to survey his new possessions. On 22 May, Giovanni Carlo Scaramelli, the Venetian Secretary in England, reported that the six men-of-war and two armed pinnaces which Elizabeth had commissioned before her death were being sailed down to Greenwich for James to inspect. Six days later Scaramelli himself visited Greenwich for his first audience with the new King. The throng of courtiers wanting to establish themselves in the King's favour had scarcely abated.

> I went there and found such a crowd that I never saw the like even at Constantinople in time of peace. There were upwards of ten or twelve thousand persons about. All the efforts of the guards hardly enabled me to reach the first, let alone the inner chamber, owing to the throng of nobility. At length having arrived at the chamber where the King was, I found all the Council about his chair, and an infinity of other Lords almost in an attitude of adoration.

The exact manner of James's greeting was carefully noted, as a means of judging his attitude towards the Venetian state (he took six steps forward, one back, made a gesture of greeting, stood while the ambassador spoke to him and sometimes removed the hat from his head). A hunting fall had put James's arm into a sling. From his dress – a suit of silver grey satin, with a black cloak lined with crimson – he 'would have been taken for the meanest among the courtiers, a modesty he affects, had it not been for a chain of diamonds round his neck and a great diamond in his hat'. The diamond in the hat was supposed to be fabulously valuable.

Altogether, in the English context, James was an oddity who could hardly have seemed more different from Elizabeth I. Contemporaries knew the Queen as being a 'comely' woman, with a strong constitution, who was 'solemn and ceremonious', rigid in her ideas about the hierarchy that constituted social order, parsimonious, utterly majestic in her bearing but prepared to speak to strangers and 'her people' when they came her way. James, by contrast, was not well made: his legs had been bent through rickets, so he liked to lean on the shoulder of one of his courtiers when he walked. His tongue, we are told in a spiteful account, was too big for his mouth, which made him apt to spill his drink and food as he ate. In contrast to the ossified stiffness that had turned his predecessor into a living icon, James had no regard for convention, and his offhand manner and sometimes curious choice of clothes were apt to make him appear slightly ludicrous. Both Queen Elizabeth and King James had their favourites, but the word took on a different connotation at the Jacobean court: James, this funny-looking man, brought up in a world of extreme violence, often in danger of his life, educated under the aegis of the dour Scottish Calvinist George Buchanan, felt an emotional pull towards the sort of dashing young men whose passage through life seemed so much easier than his own. He became besotted with one after another of them. He behaved in a physically affectionate manner towards them in public; no one knows what happened in private but it is assumed that the intimacies were taken further. He heaped them with favours: it reflected a nature that was naturally generous. Whereas Elizabeth had been 'strict in her giving, which age and her sex inclined her unto', James disregarded the precarious state of the royal finances and gave with both hands. He indulged others, and he indulged himself. Corruption was second nature to the sycophants who surrounded the King. Everything was for sale, including peerages and the specially created title of baronet. The court became a byword for licentiousness, duplicity, greed, reckless extravagance, triviality and self-interest. 'Here I am tied about my own business,' wrote Sir Henry Wootton from Greenwich Palace to a friend in 1611, 'which I have told you like a true courtier; for right courtiers indeed have no other business but themselves.'

The differences between the two monarchs must have been particularly apparent at Greenwich, such a manifestation of the Tudor dynasty, as well as Elizabeth's own birthplace for which she retained a special fondness throughout her life. To James it was not wreathed in family history, and the only resonance that it had for him was that which it acquired through his residence there.

Some of the differences between the two monarchs can be explained by James's personal story: for one who was constitutionally a coward – James pioneered a fashion for quilted doublets which he regarded as being poignard-proof – the Scotland amid which he had previously lived must have been frightful. Having become King at the age of thirteen months, he was vulnerable, throughout his youth and later, to kidnap attempts, some of which succeeded. England was less turbulent; it was also richer. The Gunpowder Plot shows that his life was less than completely secure, even so. In the circumstances, it is perhaps not surprising that he enjoyed himself while he could. Like Henry VIII he associated Greenwich with pleasure, but his pleasures were different to his predecessors. He did not care to show himself to the populace. He liked the spectacle provided particularly by masques, a taste that was even more developed in his Queen. But he did not trouble to put on many of those great ceremonial occasions with which the multitude had been delighted by the Tudors. The Stuart court was inward-looking and self-absorbed. This was to contribute to its downfall with the Civil War; but its more personal character created some touching moments which make its protagonists seem recognisably human – all too human sometimes – to the modern age. Greenwich saw as much of this side of the Stuart royal family as anywhere.

It is worth dwelling on the tone of the Jacobean court, set by the King himself; for out of it emerged the first of the Greenwich masterpieces – the Queen's House – that we can see and visit for ourselves. Nothing, apparently, could form a greater contrast with the debauchery, ostentation and venality that typified the court; but then James himself was something more, too. For a monarch he was formidably learned, a King who loved bookish conversation, was an authority on witchcraft (it was probably to flatter him that Shakespeare included witches in his patently James-pleasing *Macbeth*), instigated the Authorised Version of the Bible and himself wrote tracts such as the presciently anti-smoking pamphlet *Counterblaste to*

*Tobacco*. Furthermore, Greenwich came to be associated more and more with his Queen, Anne of Denmark; eventually he gave it to her, though he continued to use it as well; and it is her personality which finally pervaded it.

Anne was an easygoing woman, certainly not erudite like her husband, but (according to some sources) intelligent, wise enough to stay out of the mess that was James's government, without being unaware of it. Above all she was what would now be called a party animal. 'She likes enjoyment and is very fond of dancing and of fetes,' reported Nicolo Molin, the Venetian ambassador, in 1607, when she was twenty-three. England was said to have a hunting King and dancing Queen. She had been pretty as a girl; interminable pregnancies and miscarriages, as well as the disappointments of her marriage, took their toll, and by the time she came to Greenwich she had lost her looks. Her ladies knew her, rather engagingly, as Rina, a contraction of Regina. She seems to have had a kind nature. Not surprisingly, given the King's preoccupation with hunting as well as his weakness for male favourites, the King and Queen were not always in each other's company. Nevertheless, as their last child, Sophia, was born in 1607, they evidently continued to have sexual relations beyond what might be considered the call of duty (they had already secured the succession by producing three boys). Anne was long-suffering, but James was not entirely callous towards her feelings. He insisted that she was shown the respect appropriate to her station. When James first entered his new kingdom, it had been without Anne, who was pregnant with a baby that miscarried. No sooner had he arrived at Berwick than he wrote to the Privy Council ordering them to make ready 'such Jewells and other furnyture which did appertaine to the late Queene [Elizabeth], as you shall thincke to be met for her estate; and also coachs, horses, litters, and whatsoever els you may thinck meet'. He knew his Queen. She was a heedless and incurable spendthrift, and it fell to James to bail her out. He did so with good grace.

The judgement on their relationship given by the James apologist Bishop Goodman may seem quaint by today's standards, but nevertheless shows some wisdom in assessing the sort of happiness that the partners of a royal marriage could achieve. 'The King of himself was a very chaste man,' he wrote in his *Court of King James* (meaning, presumably, that he did not pursue other women)

and there was little in the Queen to make him uxorious; yet they did love as well as man and wife could do, not conversing together. She had many suits from the King; the King did prefer many upon her recommendations; when she died and left some things unfinished which she had past, the King made all good; whatsoever she gave the King made it good; and it was no small matter that she should give all her linen to Mrs. Anna, so mean a gentlewoman. Nor were they small sums of money which she had from the King, that she should be continually in building, both at Denmark House and in Greenwich.

*Opposite:* **James I's long-suffering queen, Anne of Denmark, painted by Paul van Somer. In the background of this painting is Oatlands Palace. James, though distracted by his epicene favourites, gave her both Greenwich and the money to begin the Queen's House there. This painting dates from 1617, about the time the Queen's House was begun.**

## *Thomas Howard, Earl of Arundel*

Thomas Howard, Earl of Arundel, inherited one of the great courtier houses built near Placentia, with an acre of garden. It was built by the Earl of Northampton, founder of Trinity Hospital, who died in 1614, leaving his splendid new house – 'my mistress,' as he tenderly referred to it – to his great-nephew Lord Arundel. It was in this Greenwich house that his art collection was housed. Arundel was described by John Evelyn as 'the father of Vertu in England, the great Maecenas of all politer arts and the boundless amasser of antiques'. He seems to have started collecting in 1615 soon after inheriting the Greenwich house. In 1617 disaster struck. George, Lord Carew, wrote to Sir Thomas Roe, ambassador at Constantinople: 'The Erle of Northampton's new-built house at Greenwich (by the negligence of servants) is burnt all but the gallerye to the ground, wherein the Erle of Arundell, whose house it was, lost a great part of his householde stuffe, which was of great value.' According to another account, the loss of the contents, while including 'some rich moveables', was not as great as it had first seemed. The loss to Greenwich, however, was all the worse, since Arundel did not rebuild the house and moved his collection to Arundel House in the Strand.

Later a tavern called the Blue Boar was constructed on the site. It was incorporated into the grounds of the Seamen's Hospital, and the tavern demolished, in 1716.

In all respects, the Jacobean history of Greenwich reflects the feelings of affection that seemed to exist within this baffling royal marriage. There had been a curious incident at Theobalds in July 1613, when the court had been hunting. The Queen took aim at a deer, but instead shot Jewel, the King's favourite hound. There could hardly have been a worse offence in James's canon of values than so unfortunate an interference with his hunting (he was implacable in his severity against poachers). No one can have been very surprised that, as Master John Chamberlain wrote to his friend Sir Dudley Carleton, 'he stormed exceedingly awhile'. But the anger abated, and he assured her not to be upset by it, 'for he should love her never the worse'. The next day he sent her a diamond of immense worth (£2,000) as a legacy from the deceased Jewel. 'Love and kindness increase daily between them,' continued Chamberlain; 'and it is thought they never were on better terms.' James was someone who did not wish unduly to distress those close to him, so long as he could do what he wanted. So he responded generously to what seems to have been a more emollient attitude towards his favourites on Anne's part. On 25 November 1613, Chamberlain could report: 'the Queen by her late pacification hath gained Greenwich into jointure.' In other words the King gave Anne the palace to which she had become particularly attached. His generosity was all the more remarkable in view of the possessions that she had already received at the time of his entry into Britain: Denmark House (later Somerset House) in London and Oatlands in Surrey.

Greenwich had acquired something of a reputation for healthiness. It had been one of the places to which Henry VIII had repaired to escape the plague, and so it remained for the new dynasty. But it also seems generally to have been associated with the benefits of a change of air. Certainly this would seem to have been the opinion of Robert Burton, author of *The Anatomy of Melancholy*, who regarded 'variety of actions, objects, air' and 'places' as being 'excellent good' in treating melancholy. He quotes Barclay the Scot's commendation of 'Greenwich tower for one of the best prospects in Europe, to see London on the one side, the Thames, ships and pleasant meadows on the other'.

Admittedly, in early December 1610 the Queen found she did not like the air at Greenwich that winter, and with some reason: a week later her friend Lady Drummond had died, it was feared of plague, and a few days later one of her companions was also taken off. Plague, however, could strike anywhere. Five years later, when the Queen was ill, her doctors and the King urged her to take the baths at Greenwich, where she accordingly went. She seems never actually to have entered the baths, because, as the Venetian ambassador reported, 'some of the physicians thought that she ought to be half covered, while the others said it should be up to her neck, so that in consequence of this difference in opinion she had abstained'. It was to Greenwich that she went to have those of her children that were born in England.

She was there, waiting to give birth, in the early spring of 1605, when James set off to visit her. Clearly the prospect put him in a good humour, to judge from the jaunty tone of the letter he wrote, apparently to Viscount Cranborne and the Earls of Suffolk and Northampton, before leaving.

A cartel of challenge to a trinity of knaves.
If I find not at my coming to Greenwich that the big Chamberlain have ordered well all my lodging, that the little saucy Constable have made the house sweet and built a coke pit, and that the fast-walking Keeper of the Park have the park in good order and the does all with fawn although he have never been a good breeder himself, then shall I at my return, finding those things out of order, make the fat Chamberlain to puff, the little cankered beagle to whine, and the tall black and co[a]l-faced Keeper to glower. As Sir Roger Aston said, if my wife shall not produce a fair young lion at this time, the Constable shall bear the blame; if I have not good fortune at the beginning of my hunting the Keeper shall have the shame, and never be thought a good huntsman after; and if I get not good rest all night, the big Chamberlain's fat back shall bear the burthen of all. And so

farewell as ye deserve. And as for the bearer, I have made choice of this worshipful Knight of the Bath to carry this cartel, who swears he will venture all the hairs of his beard in my quarrel.

The 'fat Chamberlain' seems to have been Lord Suffolk, the 'little beagle' Lord Cranborne and the 'coal-faced Keeper' Lord Northampton, according to G. P. V. Akrigg in the *Letters of King James VI and I* (1984). The letter reveals a lot about James: his droll humour, his passion for hunting and his hopes for another son. The last was disappointed; the baby was a girl who died in infancy. But Greenwich had again become the birthplace of a royal child – the first in England for seventy years.

James was often at Greenwich during the spring and summer months. In 1606 he had the stone-vaulted undercroft (beneath the present Queen Anne Court) inserted below the Tudor banqueting hall as underpinning and to stop flooding. It is the only piece of the Palace which survives, apart from a 1515 reservoir building of Henry VIII's time which is now part of the Chantry, 34 Park Vista. On at least a couple of St George's Days, James held the Garter ceremonies at Greenwich, with all the knights assembling, as now happens each year at Windsor. The pleasures of cock-fighting,

**Masque design of a hunting scene, perhaps one of Inigo Jones's Arcadian settings for *Pan's Anniversary, or the Shepherds' Holiday*, written by Ben Jonson for the King's birthday in 1620 and performed at Greenwich.**

mentioned in the letter above, were supplemented by those of bull-baiting and bear-baiting, to which the Queen was equally attached. The same could be said of gambling (gambling was part of the appeal of the cock-fighting and other blood sports). Among the salaries disbursed at Greenwich, according to a 'true collection of the fees and offices of his Majesty' drawn up in 1618, were those to the Keeper of the Park, the Keeper of the Wardrobe and the Keeper of the Lodge, Meadow and Garden. The Keeper of the Wardrobe had a particular importance, given (contrary to the impression made upon Giovanni Carlo Scaramelli) James's excessive vanity for clothes. Perhaps it was for this reason that he set up a silk factory near Greenwich at Lewisham. 'He is so charmed with the industry that he has brought over a number of workmen from France,' wrote the Venetian ambassador in 1608. 'They promise excellent results, and he has set up all the plant and expects in a short time to manufacture here as much as is at present imported.'

Inigo Jones, painted by William Hogarth after Van Dyke. Painter, masque designer, antiquarian, connoisseur and architect, Jones blazed a meteoric path through the courts of James I and Charles I. This image suggests his vigour, refinement and spirit – as well as the personal charisma of a man who won a place in the affection of royalty.

A detail of the garden at Greenwich emerges from an account of a contretemps between the future Charles I, aged sixteen, and the King's favourite George Villiers, who would become Duke of Buckingham. He would become Charles's favourite too, but as a boy Charles had hated him. Charles, Villiers and James I were standing together by a statue of Bacchus at Greenwich; it happened to be one of those novelty fountains which the overdressed aristocrats of seventeenth-century Europe found hilarious. By surreptitiously turning a pin, water could be made to spurt out suddenly and soak unsuspecting bystanders. Villiers was standing in just the right place, and the temptation for the royal youngster proved too much: 'the water spouted in Sir George Villiers his face, whereat he was very much offended,' wrote Sir Edward Sherburn to Sir Dudley Carleton: 'the king observing his discontentment was so exceedingly moved against the Prince for doing it, as besides the hard words he gaue him, which was that he had a malicious and dogged disposicion, gaue his Highnes 2 boxes in the eare.'

On 21 June 1617, John Chamberlain wrote to Sir Dudley Carleton: 'The Queen is building somewhat at Greenwich wch must be finished this sommer, yt is saide to be some curious devise of Inigo Jones, and will cost above 4000li.' The painter, masque designer, antiquarian, connoisseur and now architect and Surveyor of the King's Works Inigo Jones had been blazing his meteoric way through the half-light of the Jacobean court for a dozen or so years. He must have dazzled and astounded contemporaries; as one might expect, this did not always make them love him, and the accounts that have come down of him – notably the lampoons made by Ben Jonson after the pair had fallen out – suggest that he was mightily full of himself. 'Huomo vanissimo e molto vantatore,' concluded an Italian, having watched him pronounce on some of Charles I's newly arrived Italian paintings. An impression of vanity is not entirely excluded from Van Dyck's memorable portrait drawing of him, though this suggests many other qualities too, such as intelligence, refinement and spirit. He is shown with his eyes straining to discern some distant vision. Contemporaries seem to have thought of him as arrogant, and it would hardly be surprising if he was: to achieve anything new in architecture requires self-confidence. A double dose must have been needed given the chaotic finances of the Stuart court. Perhaps the most surprising thing is that so little was written about Jones. He was prominent at the highest levels of the court, friendly with kings and queens. Van Dyck's record is enough to show that he must, in all senses, have cut a striking figure. His name alone – Inigo is very unusual – might have made him stand out. Yet tough as he was, he was invisible to the diarists and letter-writers on whom historians depend for court gossip. Maybe he adapted himself so well to his environment that they did not notice him.

Jones was the son of a London clothworker. How it was that he transcended his modest background to become such a figure of taste is a mystery. In his twenties he travelled in Italy for several years. He was not rich and we do not know how he supported himself. Perhaps he hitched himself to the train of a nobleman. While there, he would seem to have focused his eyes on the world of the antique, as seen in ruins and interpreted through the Renaissance – and not just its architectural aspect either. In 1606 a friend wrote a Latin inscription on the fly-leaf of a book he was giving Jones, expressing the hope that through Jones 'sculpture, modelling, architecture, painting, acting and all that is praiseworthy in the elegant arts of the ancients, may one day find their way across the Alps into our England'. Already he seems to have become the *homo universalis*, as regards his interests, that he would later be proclaimed by his achievements. By some means he entered the service of King Christian IV of Denmark, not yet twenty and brother of the English Queen. It was an unlikely milieu for this man of refinement to be happy in: the booziness of Christian IV's entourage scandalised English observers when he visited London in 1606 – though it has to be said, on that occasion, that Danish misbehaviour was equalled by James I and his court. Before long Jones was back in his native land, having transferred from the service of the brother to that of the sister. His first work for Anne of Denmark was to stage a court masque.

The masque was not an entirely new phenomenon: we have seen that Henry VIII acted in masques at Greenwich. But in the Jacobean and Caroline courts it reached a zenith of sophistication, technical complexity and symbolic meaning. It was a form of entertainment that particularly delighted the Queen. There was something of the pantomime about it, with an emphasis on outlandish costumes and seemingly magical transformations of scene. The best masques, though, must also have been very beautiful. Certainly they were lavishly expensive: for the price of some productions it would have been possible to build a country house. And they could be erudite too. A number were written by Ben Jonson, in classicising vein. Words, however, took second place to dance. The object of the masque was to demonstrate the virtues of the monarch, in an entertainment in which the court itself participated through dancing. At one point the masquers would dance and take partners from the court, dissolving the barrier between the ideal, as represented on stage, and the real, as embodied in the audience. With its arcane symbolism, it reflects the growing insularity of the court. For these revels were mounted for the royal family's and their courtiers' own delectation, without any thought of impressing the people beyond. To take a prominent part in the staging of masques was certain to attract the attention of the King and Queen, and Jones seems to have been friendly with, in particular, Charles I. By then he was established. At the beginning of his career, masque design gave him a way of demonstrating the ideas he had developed through contact with Italy, without committing his patrons to the cost of building a palace.

An early design for the Queen's House, by Inigo Jones. It shows the caprice of a building that straddled the Dover road, the two principal wings being connected by an archway.

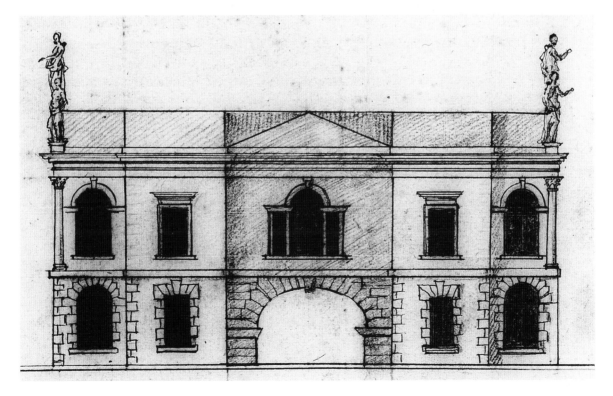

85

In one way, none of this need detain us very long, since only one masque was ever presented at Greenwich during James I's reign. Called *Pan's Anniversary, or the Shepherds' Holiday*, it was performed on the occasion of James I's birthday in 1620. The pastoral theme was, perhaps, appropriate to the out-of-town setting. The audience would have been quick to appreciate the parallel between James himself and the great god Pan, in whose honour the masquers dance, the identification being underlined by the lines spoken by an Arcadian figure:

> Of Pan we sing, the best of hunters, Pan,
> That drives the hart to seek unused ways,
> And in the chase more than Sylvanus can.

Not that hunting was the only kingly occupation, as another Arcadian suggests:

> Of Pan we sing, the best of shepherds, Pan,
> That keeps our flocks and us, and both leads forth
> To better pastures than great Pales can.

The Christian King must strive to emulate Christ's own example as the Good Shepherd. The author of the work was Ben Jonson, who gave the Shepherd some charming verses evoking the flowers of the countryside. It was not, however, one of the more elaborate masques, Jones's set design showing only a hilly landscape framed by fluffy trees.

In another way, the spirit of the masque penetrates the extraordinary building known, after Anne of Denmark, as the Queen's House. Today it is difficult to appreciate the impression that this little villa, with its sparse decoration and rectangular profile, must have had on contemporaries. Our eyes have become habituated to the hundreds of similar structures that came after it – generally, such was its originality, long after it. But seventeenth-century England had literally seen nothing like it. It was begun in 1616, and by then Jones had made a second trip to Italy, in the train of the young Earl of Arundel who was to become one of the greatest collectors and patrons in English history. Jones was by no means exclusively interested in architecture: a sketchbook suggests that he was perhaps more concerned to study the Italian Mannerist painters whose work he admired. Nevertheless, he bought architectural textbooks, notably the *Quattro Libri* of Palladio, and set out to visit the buildings illustrated in them; he also met Palladio's disciple Vincenzo Scamozzi. It would have been enough to turn him away from the provincial style of English architecture, with its encrustations of ornament. He did not respond to the richness of Mannerism or the baroque, the 'aboundance ... brought in by Michill Angell', preferring the severity of the ancient ruins and 'the sollid, proporsionable ... and unaffected' style of Andrea Palladio. But there is nothing even among the serene country villas of Palladio that equates to the austerity of the Queen's House. The only explanation is that it emerged from Jones's study of the theory of architecture, in the works of Leon Battista Alberti and others. Jones did not borrow a fashion from Italy, he used the principles he discovered there to invent his own. So the Queen's House is not only completely unlike anything that had previously been constructed in England, but has no real parallel anywhere else in Europe either.

From 1613 Jones had been Surveyor to the King's Works (he had previously, for two years, served as Surveyor to Henry, Prince of Wales, who died in 1612). It was a remarkable appointment since Jones had yet to prove himself as capable of constructing anything very substantial. Admittedly the post was largely a matter of administering the repair of palaces and the preparations necessary to put them in readiness for the King and Queen. But it shows the favour he had come to enjoy at court, and the confidence that was placed in him. Confidence was again needed to give Jones the commission of the Queen's House. All that he had actually built by this time was a church monument in Shropshire and some outbuildings at James's Newmarket Palace. (The latter provided what must have been essentials to the court of this monarch: stable, brewhouse and kennels. Drawings for them show that they were proposed in the fanciful style of his masque designs, but they were probably not executed like that; they no longer exist.) So in every respect the Queen's House was a novelty. Clearly this was how it struck contemporaries, to judge from John Chamberlain's reference to the Queen's House as being 'some curious devise'. One feature that fully justifies this description is the plan. Built on the site of the old gatehouse mentioned in Gille Delaporte's report to the Abbot of Ghent, more than three hundred years before, it took the form of an H, the downstrokes of which stood either side of the London to Dover road, with the crossbar forming a bridge at first-floor level. Quite why the Queen wanted the road to pass through the middle of her house is unclear. It cannot have been very convenient, particularly given the privacy which the royal family valued. The idea that it provided a means of passing from the palace precincts into the park beyond without the indignity of walking across the public road does not seem justification enough (they could have constructed a tunnel). There is a little, perhaps, of Raleigh's cloak about it: the building provided a permanent means of keeping the Queen's feet dry.

The reason why the Queen wanted this charming box to be built there at all is no more certain. It was at the bottom of the gardens, some way from the palace, yet seclusion could not really have been the motive, given its position relative to the road. At least some of the 'curious' quality of the house derived from its being a caprice. The whimsy would have been very much to the taste of someone as enraptured with court masques as Anne. The other architectural works at Greenwich of which we hear at this period seem to spring almost directly from the world of the masque. Duke Humphrey's Tower was yet again transformed, this time into what the Venetian ambassador Pietro Contarini called 'the fabled tower of Oriana'. Near the palace itself, deliberately within earshot, was built a new aviary, through whose tall windows, covered with copper nets, birdsong poured forth. Very much in the spirit of *Pan's Anniversary*. One explanation might lie in the nature of some forms of hunting in the seventeenth century. Hunting could involve participants, such as James, in long, invigorating and almost addictive hours in the saddle; but there were also more formalised versions that did not entail much galloping over the countryside, at least on the part of the principal spectators, since the game – hare or deer – was coursed by dogs along a designated track, conveniently placed in full sight of a building that served as a viewing plat-form. It is likely that the Queen's House was intended to serve as a grandstand, both for hunting and military parades. As built, the side facing the Park has a log-gia which would have done very well for this purpose. It is also possible that the Queen's House was conceived, from the start, as a place to receive important visi-tors whose first impression of Britain would have been Greenwich. There is more evidence from the reign of Charles I that suggests this intention.

The Queen's House has come to be regarded as the *fons et origo* of all Classical architecture in Britain. One aspect of this is the harmony of the proportions, achieved through numerical relationships. This had been a prominent element in the architectural theory of Palladio. Contemporaries were much struck by Jones's preoc-cupation with numbers: Ben Jonson ridiculed him for it. To anyone steeped in the culture of Renaissance Italy, it would have seemed self-evident that spaces based on pure geometry pleased the eye and engendered a feeling of equilibrium. Jones had imbibed this idea during his travels, and he applied it by designing an exactly cubic hall for the Queen's House. One wonders whether this was how all Jones's patrons saw it. Perhaps the Jacobean court, presided over by a King who was an acknowl-edged expert on witches, as well as being intensely superstitious, responded differ-ently to the magic of numbers. Did they picture Inigo Jones's number theory as leading them forward, towards an age of harmony and humanism, or as harking back to the medieval world of sorcery to which some of them were still attached? Certainly the Queen's House was a wonder and a mystery – and so it remains. The mystery is due in part to Anne's death in 1619, before the house had been finished.

* * *

In about 1632, Adriaen Van Stalbemt and Jan Van Belcamp painted an elegant view of Greenwich. It shows a hunting scene. In the foreground, sublimely detached from the activities of the chase, Charles I, wearing a black broad-brimmed hat and with a cloak thrown over one shoulder, escorts his Queen, the dark-eyed summation of elegance Henrietta Maria, to the top of a slight rise in the Park. She holds the hand of her daughter. It is an affecting image, painted at a time when the King and Queen, after a disastrous start to their marriage, had come, quite publicly and against convention, to love each other very much. They are not alone. They are not surrounded by the great press of people who might have mobbed one of the Tudor monarchs, but a select band of courtiers. To the left of the royal group stand a couple talking pleasantly between themselves. The younger of the two, with his hand on his hip and a smile ruffling the moustaches of his pointed beard, is Endymion Porter, a gallant who was as colourful as his name, having been one of the two trusted friends to accompany Charles, then Prince of Wales, and the dazzling Marquis of Buckingham on their madcap, incognito dash to Madrid to woo (unsuccessfully) the Infanta Maria, sister to the King of Spain, in 1623; subsequently it was Porter who made the first of Charles's overtures to the painter Sir Anthony Van Dyck, which would end in the latter's residing in England. The other, more soberly if still fashionably clad, wearing a close-fitting cap, is none other than Inigo Jones. In the middle distance behind them can be seen the Queen's House, with the Park wall extending to either side of it, but complete only up to the first floor and thatched over at that level – the state in which it was left on Anne's death and for the next ten years.

Much had happened in the thirteen years since Anne of Denmark's death. The desperate state of the royal finances had been revealed by the delay that took place before the pomps of her funeral could be staged – her body lay unburied for ten weeks. Inigo Jones designed the immense catafalque, in the manner of Bramante's *Tempietto*, erected in Westminster Abbey for James's own obsequies in 1625. With his death the court sounded a different note, which resonated, as much as anywhere, at Greenwich.

The court of James I had been 'a nursery of lust and intemperance … and every greate house in the country became a sty of uncleanesse'. So wrote the Puritan critic Mrs Hutchinson. But even she had to admit that the Caroline court was a different place. 'The face of the court was much chang'd in the change of the king; for King Charles was temperate, chast and serious. … The nobility and courtiers, who did not quite abandon their debosheries, had yet that reverence to the king to retire into corners to practise them.' Who can say what corners were provided by Greenwich? What comes down to us from Charles's reign, in the completion of the Queen's House, is witness only to the culture and elegance of the court.

There is a painting in the National Maritime Museum at Greenwich which shows the palace from the north side of the river. It suggests that, in the newly elegant age, Greenwich had become a place of fashionable resort, where sophisticated

*Top:* Detail of Inigo Jones, wearing a close-fitting cap, with Endymion Porter, from the painting reproduced on page 72.

*Below:* The unfinished Queen's House from the same painting. It bears little resemblance to the building we know today.

Greenwich Palace in the reign of Charles I, with a man of war at anchor in the Thames. The twin towers of Henry VIII's armoury stand in the centre. The square castle-like structure on the rise to the left is a mystery: it has never been identified.

couples might stroll side by side along the bank of the Thames, albeit under the gaze, in this case, of a peasant woman and her child. The foreground of the picture shows a rowing boat bearing more elegantly dressed people. Skiffs dart across the water: the activity on the river must have been constant. But the most imposing sight is that of a fine man of war at anchor, its St George's flag beating proudly in the breeze. The artist is unidentified, but clearly Flemish. With, apparently, one exception – the entirely unexplained inclusion of another great house on the left of the painting – the picture is topographically accurate. If it is accurate in the style of life represented, we can conclude that the charms of Greenwich had been discovered by a wider spectrum of people than just the court. On such a day as that depicted, it must have been a joy to make an outing along the river there. It was painted about 1630, just as work on the Queen's House had recommenced.

The change at court had not happened suddenly at James's death. For some years before that date the old King, tired and senile, had virtually surrendered the governance of the country to the Prince of Wales and the now Duke of Buckingham. The favourite whom Charles had once hated he now adored. And as much as the young Prince, soon to be King, loved this captivating, greedy, impossibly sumptuous man, his young bride, understandably, hated him.

Charles first saw Henrietta Maria when he passed through Paris, with Buckingham, on his way to woo the Spanish Infanta. Incredibly, he managed to gain entrance to the Louvre unrecognised. There he and Buckingham found themselves watching the ladies of the court as they rehearsed a masque, in which Henrietta Maria, aged thirteen and dancing prettily, played the character of Iris. She was the youngest daughter of King Henri IV of France, assassinated while Henrietta Maria was still in her cradle, and the amply proportioned Marie de Medicis. ('Floors, as well as courtiers, trembled at the approach of this emphatic and portentous royal widow,' writes Carola Oman in her biography of Henrietta Maria.) Once it had become clear that no acceptable terms could be reached for Charles's marriage to the Infanta, a 'wooing Ambassador' was despatched to Paris in the personable shape of Lord Kensington, who reported back that Henrietta Maria was 'the loveliest creature in France and the sweetest thing in nature'. We must take this description as an arrow fired by a cupid to royalty. In some obvious respects this fourteen-year-old girl fell short of perfection. She had heavily hooded eyes, a long nose and rather protruding teeth: only later did she blossom into the creature of elegance recorded by Van Dyck. She was also very short – even by comparison with the also diminutive Charles.

If these were defects, they were sufficiently overlooked for the couple to marry (Charles being represented by proxy) in 1624. What could not be overlooked afterwards was the size of her retinue. It comprised a gaggle of courtiers, a bishop, twenty-nine priests, various aristocratic nannies and over four hundred attendants,

## Greenwich, USA

In 1640 a group of English settlers from the New Haven colony purchased some land for 'twentie-five coates' on what was then known as Elizabeth's Creek, in Connecticut, from the American Indians. The Englishman who came up with the name of Greenwich would seem to have been Richard Ferris. Born in Leicestershire, he was the son or nephew of an Elizabethan courtier who bore the same name. It has been supposed this Ferris spent time in the palace at Greenwich, and some of its fabulous reputation perhaps lingered in the mind of the Connecticut Ferris. While the names of the original settlers of Greenwich are known, none seems to have come from Greenwich in London. Perhaps the name of Greenwich was, to people of English origin, synonymous with sophistication and splendour.

Greenwich, Connecticut, in turn gave birth to a number of other Greenwiches across the United States. There is also a Greenwich at Hunters Hill, New South Wales, Australia, complete with a Woolwich Docks.

to whom (refusing to learn English) she spoke French. They encouraged her in her dislike of English customs, the English court and her English husband. Charles himself did not behave impeccably. She was a lively young girl; later her vivacity would supply the verve that the over-formalised court would otherwise have lacked. (Her love of the theatre, though, would scandalise Puritans.) At twenty-five, Charles was beset with cares; polite but chilly; habitually soulful; not able to enter into the frivolities that delighted his wife. But the general opinion was that, of the two, she behaved worse. It is a harsh if inescapable judgement. She was only acting exactly as the thing she was: a child.

Two events happened to redirect the course of the marriage. In 1626 the King, normally so courteous, felt himself to be driven beyond endurance, and expelled Henrietta Maria's compatriots. Their departure showed them for what they were, since they plundered all of their young mistress's possessions that they could lay hands on. Charles's masterfulness at last made Henrietta Maria respect him. She may have reflected that, without her own court, it was in her own interests to submit to his will, since Cardinal Richelieu had no wish to see her back in France. Then in 1628 the Duke of Buckingham was stabbed to death, just as her own father had been. Devastated by the loss, Charles turned to her. She did what she could to console him. From that moment grew the love that united them in a dangerous and finally tragic destiny. One of its first expressions seems to have been a resumption of work on the Queen's House at Greenwich. Charles gave Greenwich, so long associated with English queens, to Henrietta Maria the year after Buckingham was murdered. That same year Henrietta Maria was at Greenwich, in preparation for the birth of her first child.

Since Queen Anne's death, Charles had been in possession of Greenwich. He used it in the summer of 1619: we know that from a surviving letter dated from Greenwich in June that year. It had been intended that the palace would have been one of the first places she saw on arriving at Dover: the plan had been to travel more or less straight there, by way of Canterbury. This had not proved to be possible because of plague. Perhaps it might have made a more favourable impression on the young Queen and her entourage than the one they formed, coloured by what they regarded as the meanness of their reception (there was no money for splendid ceremonies). During the disastrous war with Spain in 1626, Charles had watched with gratification as a large and heavily laden 'berton', a type of merchantman, owned by Hamburgers trading with England's enemy, was brought up the river, following its capture by an English ship. It must have been one of the few episodes of that misconceived campaign to give him any pleasure. Charles and Henrietta Maria followed precedent by making a stay at Greenwich a regular feature of the early summer months.

It was some years into their marriage before Henrietta Maria became pregnant for the first time, and she had become anxious at the delay. When that happy state came upon her, she retired, in accordance with royal tradition, to Greenwich. Everything seemed to be well as she entered the sixth month of her pregnancy. She was walking in the Park: indeed that exercise, particularly since it was apt to be taken up-hill, was one of many causes to which her premature labour, ten weeks early, was ascribed. It happened so suddenly that the *sage-femme* from France, whom her mother had organised to attend, never arrived. Instead, the 'poor town midwife of Greenwich' was rushed into the royal chamber, and promptly swooned from the drama of it all. She was replaced by a surgeon, and just as well, since it was a very difficult delivery. Charles constantly appeared at the bedside, emphasising that the mother's life had to be saved at all costs. And Henrietta Maria did survive. The premature baby, a boy who was hastily christened Charles-James, died the same day. A barge took his little body up-river to Westminster, where he was buried in the Abbey the same night. A superstitious soul, Henrietta Maria never returned to Greenwich to give birth to a child, and she was to have many.

Perhaps it was to help Henrietta Maria overcome the gloomy associations which Greenwich now had in her mind that the project of the Queen's House was revived. The unhappy birth had happened in May 1629. Within a few months, according to the Paymaster of the Works's accounts, the Queen's House had become the subject of 'sondry necessary workes and Reparacons', including the construction of a new roof (of thatch, since it was temporary). It was in a happy mood that Henrietta Maria followed the progress of the building – she visited the site often – for in 1630 she gave birth to the future Charles II, at St James's Palace.

Adriaen Van Stalbemt and Jan Van Belcamp's painting does not show the Queen's House in the state we know it. They depict it as a single-storey structure (presumably this can be explained by its unfinished state), with a row of eight round-headed windows arranged either side of a big central arch. Over the arch is a triangular pediment. If this is the building that existed in 1632, Jones completely reworked it. It would not be surprising if he did. In 1617, this had been one of this earliest attempts in architecture; in the intervening years he had been busy with one great commission after another – lodgings for the Marquis of Buckingham at Whitehall Palace; rebuilding the Banqueting House at Whitehall Palace after a fire; erecting St Paul's Church, Covent Garden, and laying out the piazza in front of it. He might well have revised his ideas – or come up with new ones – while the Queen's House stood neglected. It is part of the enigma of this crucially important building, to assume pride of place in the pantheon of neo-Palladianism after its publication in Colen Campbell's *Vitruvius Britannicus* in 1715, that no elevational drawings survive to show its evolution. The catalogue of the Royal Academy's 1990 exhibition of Inigo Jones's complete architectural drawings, includes a drawing (now lost) of an elevation of the north front of about 1640, by an unknown Italian draughtsman. It is the only elevation to come down from before the Restoration. It shows the Queen's House as it can still be seen: a seven-bay façade of square-headed windows, those on the ground floor set into rusticated masonry, the central

**The Queen's House in 1781. Originally, the loggia probably served as a grandstand for both hunting and military parades. In 1661–2 John Webb made the building into a square by building two further bridges over the Dover road. By the time of this engraving, the road had been moved.**

window of the first floor having a balcony, a round head and a tablet above. Along the skyline runs a parapet, giving a chastely rectangular profile. Two chimneys rise above it, as they do today; the drawing also shows two turrets. These would have been little banqueting rooms, following the Elizabethan practice. In the sixteenth century there had been a vogue among country-house builders for providing rooftop eyries to which guests could repair for the last course of a meal. Roofs were important: it was common practice to walk up and down on the leads. So it must have been at the Queen's House. The lost drawing shows that this side of the building, facing the river, may have been decorated with mural paintings of trophies, sacrifices and triumphs. This suggests that the House was intended as a place to receive guests arriving by water, perhaps with theatre or poetry. Because of its position east of London, Greenwich was often the first stopping place for arriving ambassadors and other great people. There they rested until ready to make their grand entrance into the capital. In 1636 the newly arrived Spanish ambassador stayed at Greenwich incognito for more than a week, unable to appear publicly until preparations for his first official appearance, which he wished to make 'in the most pompous and magnificent manner', according to Anzolo Correr, the Venetian ambassador, had been completed. The Caroline court may well have wanted somewhere to receive such resplendent personages, incognito or not. It retained this function into the eighteenth century, long after the palace itself had disappeared and the ground between the Queen's House and the river was the site of the Seamen's Hospital. The architect Nicholas Hawksmoor, writing his *Remarks of the Founding and Carrying on the Buildings of the Royal Hospital at Greenwich* in 1727, remembers that Queen Mary wanted to add four pavilions to the Queen's House to make that 'little Palace compleat' into 'a Royal Villa for her own Retirement, or from whence Embassadors, or publick Ministers might make their Entry into London'. The Queen died in 1694 and the pavilions were never built. But the Queen's House continued to serve as a reception depot for very grand arrivals to England. On a foggy evening in September 1714, a rowing barge arrived and King George I, yet to be crowned, stepped on to English soil for the first time at Greenwich. He was taken by torchlight to the Queen's House. (Such was the excitement at the Hospital that the sculleryman was later forgiven for the loss of 40s worth of pewter pots which vanished in the commotion.) George III's bride, Princess Charlotte, would have landed at Greenwich, had not fickle September weather forced her ship to put in at Harwich. The future Queen Caroline, who was to have a close, not to say intimate, association with the area when she lived in Blackheath following her separation from the Prince of Wales, disembarked at Greenwich in 1795.

Charming, pretty, scheming, devout, frivolous, a great breeder of children and concerned mother, Henrietta Maria had, alas, no feeling for English politics. Any

intervention she made in her husband's affairs was disastrous. Charles can only
have been increasingly preoccupied with the gathering storm. Yet, temperamentally averse from business of state, even he was able to detach himself from the
ominous unfolding of events to a surprising degree. Together they were able to
exercise their shared love of art in finishing the Queen's House. On 18 May 1635,
Correr reported to the Doge and senate: 'On Wednesday his Majesty went to

One of Inigo Jones's studies for chimneypieces in the Queen's House, c.1637. It is based on a French precedent, perhaps in tribute to Queen Henrietta Maria.

Greenwich with the queen. It is thought that they will both stay there at least six weeks, the king to enjoy the pleasures of the chase, and the queen to see the completion of a special erection of hers, which is already far advanced.' Two years later they once again went 'to see some buildings of the Queen at Greenwich'. By this time, 1637, most of the carving of the interior had been finished, though the year still witnessed a dispute between Inigo Jones ('Mr Surveyor') and the Commissioners of the Navy over the impressment of Thomas James and Richard

Durkin. They were carvers. The Navy wanted them to adorn the *Sovereign of the Seas*, being built at Woolwich.

Chimneypieces were designed, made and installed in the late 1630s. Painters were at work too. The Tuscan artist Orazio Gentileschi, patronised by the Duke of Buckingham and installed in his Whitehall house, had lingered there after the latter's assassination, awaiting payment from the King, much to the annoyance of

## *Charlton House*

Charlton House, at Charlton, next to Greenwich, was built by Sir Adam Newton in about 1607–12. Newton was the tutor to two Princes of Wales: Prince Henry, who died in 1612, then his brother, the future Charles I. His emoluments went beyond the salary of £200 he received each year. There were gifts, the income for his privilege to let some tenements in the Tower, the Secretaryship of the Principality of Wales, and the Deanery of Durham, all of which made him a rich man. He was created Baronet in 1620. His house was revolutionary in architectural terms, because of the position of the hall, running from front to back.

**Engraving of 1776 by William Watts after Paul Sandby. Sandby was Chief Drawing Master 1768–90 at the Royal Military Academy in nearby Woolwich.**

Buckingham's widow. Now he was at work on panels for the ceiling of the Great Hall and the cove of the ceiling of the Queen's bedroom. The theme of the Hall paintings was Peace surrounded by the Muses and the Arts, neatly combining the feminine beauty and cultural sophistication that characterised Henrietta Maria. The accounts mention carved picture frames, dispersed during the Commonwealth. There were also a large number of sculptures, according to the *Inventory* made by the Parliamentary Commissioners in 1649-50. They included Bernini's famous bust of Charles I, made from the triple portrait, showing each profile and the full face, painted by Van Dyck. (It was a countenance 'doomed', pronounced Bernini when he saw it. 'Never have I beheld features more unfortunate.' Van Dyke also undertook a triple portrait of Henrietta Maria, and stayed at Greenwich to paint it.) The fine arts of sculpture and painting combined with the applied arts of furniture and decoration in the enrichment of this building. An item in the accounts read: 'To … Zachary Tailer Carver for carving Tenn Pedestalls of Timber for

## *Trinity Hospital*

Henry Howard, Earl of Northampton, founded Trinity Hospital, otherwise Norfolk College, in 1613, the year before his death. With an income of £600 a year, it provided relief and maintenance for twelve poor men of the parish of East Greenwich, as well as eight poor men from Norfolk, where the founder was born. The building stands beside the river, east of the Seamen's Hospital, occupying the site of Lumley House: a building owned by the Dukes of Northumberland and of Norfolk in the sixteenth century, until they were each disgraced. Originally the building comprised a chapel, a council room, four rooms for the use of the warden, a room each for the poor men, a common hall, kitchen, wash house, brew house, and two rooms each for the butler, cook and female assistant. The Earl's monument, moved from Dover Castle, rests in the chapel.

Northampton had been brought up at Greenwich, became Keeper of the Game in Greenwich Park and amassed enormous possessions at Greenwich, some of which he was forced to surrender when James I gave Greenwich to his Queen. In contrast to most of the noblemen of his age, he was a formidable scholar, who was fluent in many languages and deeply learned in history, theology and philosophy. But his character receives a stern assessment by the Victorian editor of Hasted's *Hundred of Blackheath*. 'With the talents, tastes, and accomplishments of his father (Surrey); amiable and refined in his manners; apparently pious; extensively charitable; he was, nevertheless, a monster of wickedness and hypocrisy; leagued in the murder of Overbury, the letters in proof of which displayed such a mixture of ferocity and obscenity that the Chief Justice could not read them entire in court; endowing almshouses, and writing on devotional subjects, he, nevertheless, appears to have had no religious principle.'

marble Statuaes to stand on with Bulls heads festons, fruites leaves & flowers att lxs the peece.' Contemporaries regarded the Queen's House, as well they might, as an exquisite production which was the best of its kind. To quote one of them, Henrietta Maria 'hath so finished and furnished, that it far surpasseth all other of that kind in England'. By the end of the century, it had become an icon, not just of taste but of the Stuart monarchy. Hence its preservation. It would have been all too natural to sweep it away as part of the grand baroque development of the Seamen's Hospital; the Queen's House was out of style and out of scale. Instead Queen Mary, herself a Stuart, insisted that it was kept as the focus of the composition.

The Queen's House was not Henrietta Maria's only contribution to Greenwich. She also created a garden at the palace which had fountains, statues, a grotto and timber seats. In his monograph on the Queen's House for the *Survey of London*, George Chettle, the Inspector of Ancient Monuments who supervised the 1930s

This engraving from 1796 of the Duke of Norfolk's Almshouses, or Trinity Hospital, shows their original elegant setting; they are now overshadowed by the Greenwich Power Station built in 1902–10.

restoration of the building, illustrates a drawing for an Italianate fountain, with water pouring from the mask of man into a shell; it is set in an arch supported by herms to either side. Henrietta Maria loved plants, and had asked her mother to send her flowers and fruit-trees from France. It is pleasing to imagine her in this setting, relishing the charms of life, rejoicing (as she did) in her happiness, to be joined by her beloved husband – for Greenwich was a place where he could retire to reflect on the disasters that were besetting him.

But gardens vanish, and so do kings and queens. We can now only speculate what Henrietta Maria's garden looked like. As for the Queen's House, there were only three years for the royal family to enjoy it. It was finished in 1639. On 10 February 1642 Henrietta Maria and Charles spent a night at Greenwich for the last time. Henrietta Maria was on the way to Dover, from where she would embark with her daughter Princess Mary to Holland. The princess was engaged to William Prince of Orange. It was a sign of the low ebb of Stuart fortunes that she had made so poor a match, and was being taken out of the country when she was only ten. It was an excuse for Henrietta Maria to try to raise money for her husband on the Continent. From Greenwich, Charles went north with the Prince of Wales. In a couple of months the Civil War had begun. Henrietta Maria returned, but not to Greenwich – London was not friendly to the Royalist cause – and not to a life of gardens, art and masques. She landed in Yorkshire, and was now, as she called herself, 'Generalissima', riding at the head of the troops she had brought over. But not all the exertions of this diminutive, high-spirited, dark-eyed woman, capable of great courage in dreadful circumstances, could save her world from its fate. Just a fortnight after the birth of her last child, a daughter, in the summer of 1644, Henrietta Maria embarked from Falmouth, in Cornwall, to France. She was convinced she was dying. 'Adieu, my dear heart,' she wrote to her husband. Her ship was pursued and attacked; with its rigging damaged, it limped to the shore of Brittany, where the local people at first thought the royal party were pirates. The Queen of England, persuading them otherwise, managed to scramble ashore over the rocks, and sheltered in a thatched hut. For the next five years she could only watch, Generalissima no more, as the last act of her husband's tragedy was played out. In 1649 his composed figure stepped out of a window of Inigo Jones's Banqueting House in Whitehall on to the scaffold where the two executioners, grotesquely dressed in tight woollen clothes and false beards, awaited him.

Poor Inigo Jones had sometimes been at the King's side during the War: his architectural knowledge made him an expert on fortification. In 1645 he was among the many Royalists who sought to hold out in Basing House, in Hampshire, against a siege. He was consulted on its defence, but the garden walls could not withstand the pounding of artillery and the Roundheads poured in.

They killed indiscriminately. Jones, hated for his contribution to the masques in the 'Queen's Dancing Barne', was stripped naked, and the old man had to make an unceremonious escape, wrapped in a blanket. The beheading of Charles I broke his heart, and in 1652 he died (as the architect John Webb, who married a close relation of Jones's, wrote in 'The Vindication of Stonehenge Restored') 'through grief, as is well known, for the fatal calamity of his dread master'.

LONDON                Grænwich             Theems flu.

POTENTISSIMO AC SERENISSIMO CAROLO II. DEI GRATIA MAGNÆ. BRITANNIÆ. FRANCIÆ ET
HIBERNIÆ. REGI, FIDEI DEFENSORI. etc:
*Magnificis. Nobilibus. Amplissimisque Dominis D.D.Cornelio a Vloofwyck. Andreæ de Graef. Cornelio de Vlamingh van Outshoorn. Iohanni Huydecoper.*
*Civitatis Amstelodamensis Consulibus Meritissimis. Dignissimis humillimi obsequii. ergo D.D.C.Q.*      *Hugo Allart.*

# I HAVE NEVER LIVED SO MERRILY AS I HAVE DONE THIS PLAGUE-TIME

QUEEN HENRIETTA MARIA returned to England six months after the triumphant restoration of her son, Charles II, in 1660. She could not establish herself immediately at Greenwich, since it was in no state to receive her. Instead, she lodged at Whitehall Palace, where Samuel Pepys was among the 'persons of good Fashion and good Appearance' who were officially allowed to watch the royal family dine. But her stay there was brief. Soon she was off back to France, taking her daughter, Henrietta Anne, to be married to the Duke of Orleans, brother of Louis XIV. By the time she returned, in the summer of 1662, Greenwich had been made ready for her, and she went straight there. And on a warm July afternoon the whole court set off to visit her, Charles II being accompanied by the pretty Portuguese girl, Catherine of Braganza, whom he had married the year before.

The intervening years of exile – eighteen of them since her last night at the Queen's House – had told on Henrietta Maria's features. She had always been small; now she looked pinched, 'a very little plain old woman' according to Pepys, and she dressed always in black. To the Frenchwoman that she was, however, the colour was not unbecoming. With consummate chic she was accompanied by twenty-four menservants, in cassocks of black velvet embroidered with golden suns. She was not generally a popular figure. She was regarded as one of the causes of the Civil War and the miseries that came after it. It was perhaps in recognition of this that, in her first years back in England, she withdrew from the public gaze to Greenwich. Later she would make the building that became known as Somerset House, then called Denmark House, after Anne of Denmark, her principal home, the music from the concerts she gave there drifting out over the Thames to beguile the ears of the watermen who plied their vessels on the river.

The Greenwich to which Henrietta Maria returned was a changed place from the one she had left in 1642. London as a whole sided with Parliament during the Civil War. There were probably more Royalists in Greenwich than round the capital, if only as a result of the employment which the court gave to locally settled people, such as musicians. But they seem to have kept their heads down. The hundreds of Royalist soldiers who had been defeated by Fairfax on Blackheath found

Equestrian portrait of Charles II, with Greenwich in the background. Charles II hoped to turn Greenwich into a palace to rival Versailles.

*Opposite:* **Crowley House, begun by the City merchant and zealous royalist, Sir Andrew Cogan, and completed by the regicide MP Gregory Clement – thrown out of Parliament, according to one account, for misbehavior with a serving maid at Greenwich. Under Charles II, it was owned by George Bowerman, who obtained an order to ballast the King's Ships, which he did from nearby Ballast Quay (it survives today). Bowerman sold it to the great Newcastle ironfounder, Sir Ambrose Crowley. The grounds were littered with anchors in the eighteenth century.**

that they were hooted and pelted by the Greenwich watermen when they fled into the town. When, in the last days of the Civil War, the Earl of Norwich camped a band of Royalists in the Park in the hope to raise recruits, he had little joy of it; everyone who wanted and was able to fight for the cause had already joined up.

The proceedings of the manor court of 1645, at the height of the Civil War, suggest that, for most people, life continued much as it always had. Bakers, butchers and brickmakers were fined, as they always had been, for selling underweight goods; citizens neglected to remove muck heaps from beside stables; failed to keep their drains clean; fed their pigs on the highway 'to the grate annoyance of passers by'; persisted in keeping their boats where they should not, and then abusing 'the jurie with verie vile and uncivill language'; and would not take down structures that they had illegally erected beside the dock. These were everyday misdemeanours. Already, though, there is a hint that royal possessions were being treated with a freedom that residents would never have permitted themselves before. Richard Hewes, the seller of underweight bricks, was persistently fined for such offences as 'suffering his hoggs to goe into the King's house' and the 'erecting of cottages on the King's waste'. The waste was the land immediately outside the Park wall. Hewes was also fined for neglecting his office as Surveyor of Highways. The old order was breaking down, and people like Hewes were too busy profiting from the opportunities presented to attend much to responsibilities accorded them under the passing regime.

The advent of the Commonwealth signalled an end for all the *douceur de vivre* associated with the Caroline court. The glorious art collections were dispersed among government buildings, lent to ambassadors, delivered to Oliver Cromwell for his own apartments, embezzled in the confusion or straightforwardly sold. Some paintings went to the court musicians and other functionaries at Greenwich whom Charles had been unable to pay. In 1652 the diarist John Evelyn visited 'Old Jerome Laniere' who had acquired, among other pictures, an intaglio portrait of Queen Elizabeth: he had been one of her servants and said it was an excellent likeness. A couple of loyal souls seem to have bought what they could, to keep safely until the monarchy was restored.

The state apartments in the palace were turned into stables. That degradation must have been a conscious insult to the memory of the men and women who had peopled them until hostilities commenced. Later they housed prisoners from the First Dutch War, 1652–4, which broke out as a consequence of Cromwell's Navigation Act of 1651. For a time the Queen's House was made over 'by the rebels to Bulstrode Whitlock, one of their unhappy counsellors', as John Evelyn recorded in his diary. Bulstrode moved out. Then came the idea that it should be occupied by Oliver Cromwell himself. That did not come to anything, but it may have had the effect of restraining the depredations. Land from around the Park – the waste between the Park wall and the road – was sold to speculators who wanted to build on it. The priory buildings, the kitchen and the privy gardens were acquired by Uriah Babington and Thomas Griffin; Babington had been the King's barber for ten years and was owed nearly £4,000. The Fish Offices were sold, appropriately enough, to Richard Salmon. All these sales were cancelled after the return of Charles II, which meant that the new owners, if they kept their property, had to pay twice.

Throughout the first half of the seventeenth century, courtiers had been building themselves good houses in up-to-date styles around the Park. These also suffered a diminution. Their fate was not so bad as Placentia, since they were bought by new owners, but the shades of the Cavalier court were just as effectively banished. The land attached to Swanne House, standing on the site of what is now Greenwich Market, was divided up into ten building plots. East of the palace, the ardent Royalist Sir Andrew Cogan had built the house that, in the next century, became known as Crowley House, after its then owners (its site is now occupied by the generating station). It had not even been finished at the outbreak of the Civil

Wricklemarsh House, immediately south of Blackheath, as rebuilt in about 1725 for Sir Gregory Page. The estate had originally been owned by the inventor Colonel Thomas Blount. Pepys was impressed by his new coach springs, but not by his vineyard. In Sir Gregory Page's day, Wricklemarsh was famous for the 'princely magnificence' of the house, park and servants.

War, but is reputed to have cost a fortune; Gregory Clement, the Parliamentarian, bought it for £832, supposedly less than a fifth of what Sir Andrew had spent in erecting it. Unabashed by his role as a regicide, Clement shrewdly acquired a pair of stoves from the palace kitchens to help complete it; they were emblazoned with the royal arms. At the Restoration, stoves or no stoves, he was beheaded. Wricklemarsh House, on the other side of Blackheath, had always been home to a Parliamentarian, and so it remained. Its owner, Colonel Thomas Blount, had been one of the two men in Kent whom Charles I refused to pardon in 1642. He relished the military life, to the extent of organising a mock battle between Parliamentarians and Royalists on Blackheath. When John Evelyn was robbed at a place called Procession Oak outside Bromley in 1652, Blount used his magistrate's powers to send out a hue and cry in pursuit of the two cut-throats (though it was as a result of Evelyn's having notices of the theft distributed around London shops by an officer of the Goldsmiths' Company that his property was recovered).

'A very stately seat for situation and brave plantations,' is how Pepys found the Hall, marvelling at 'a Vineyard, the first that ever I did see'. It was typical of Blount. Like so many of Pepys's acquaintance, he had an inquisitive, inventive mind. But the wine was 'good for little', according to Evelyn. Hardly surprising: the description of the soil given by Sir Thomas Hanmer in his *Garden Book*, which 'naturally grows nothing but ling and furze', does not sound very promising. 'The Colonell sayth hee uses no dung nor compost to this barren earth of his vineyard, which is very strange.'

Gone were the fabulous masques and elegant fashions. The tone of life during the Commonwealth can be judged from the kill-joy rules that Greenwich residents, like everyone else, laboured under and sometimes infringed. They incurred fines for the keeping of ninepins, swearing and going to an ale-house at a time when the culprit should have been at church.

As for Placentia, the palace was a wreck. In his *Survey of London* volume on the Queen's House George Chettle remarks that it 'had suffered perhaps greater spoliation than any other of the major palaces'. Placentia was in any case old, and quite apart from the wilful damage inflicted upon it, nothing had been done to maintain it for twenty years. When the King came to inspect the palace at Greenwich in 1661, the gates had to be broken open to enter the park.

In name, Greenwich still belonged to Henrietta Maria, but that did not prevent Charles II from having ideas for it. As an exile, he had been exposed to the bronzing effect of the Sun King: he had seen how things could be done. He had a natural inclination to architecture, too. What he did not have is much money. But the plans he laid for Greenwich were on the grandest of scales. Just as it had suffered most during the Commonwealth, so now it was the subject of Charles II's most ambitious building project. Within a year of his return he had formed the idea of sweeping away the mouldering buildings by the river and replacing them with a new palace. Like so many previous occupants of Placentia, Charles II was entranced by this magnificent site. He had a great affinity for ships, and would have enjoyed the sights of the river.

In October 1661 John Evelyn discussed the site of the new palace with Sir John Denham, the Surveyor of Works. Evelyn's idea was to set it back from the river frontage, making in front of it 'a large Square Cutt' which would 'let in the Thames like a Baye'. A handsome conception, but even in Charles's imagination it must have seemed too expensive to be built. But he was fixed in his intention of 'quite demolishing the old' palace, as the King himself told Evelyn in January the next year. A model for the replacement palace seems to have been in existence. It may or may not have been by Inigo Jones's hagiographer and relation by marriage, John Webb (of Butleigh, Somerset). But it was certainly Webb who designed the one range that was actually built in 1664.

In the meantime Charles had to make ready the Queen's House for his mother's arrival. The Tudor palace was too far gone to save, and most of it came down in the course of 1662. For a time, an apartment was retained for the Earl of St Albans, Henrietta Maria's devoted major domo (said to be her lover or even husband) who was granted the custody of the palace. But these lodgings did not survive long, and in a few years everything except the chapel, now used as a storehouse, had been swept away. For the Queen's House this had the advantage of opening up its view of the river, previously blocked by the old buildings.

*The Royal Visit to the Fleet in the Thames estuary, June 5, 1672*, by Willem van de Velde the Younger. Charles II is on board the *Royal Prince*, at anchor on the right, having summoned a council of war after the Battle of Solebay. The yachts that brought the King and some noblemen down the river are shown on the left. This is probably one of the works painted in the Queen's House where the van de Veldes, Dutch masters of marine painting, were given studio space by Charles II to depict, ironically, English triumphs in the Second Dutch Wars.

It was felt that the Queen's House could be made comfortable – if only its two halves either side of the road could be united. Inigo Jones had conceived the building as a caprice, the backdrop for reception ceremonies, a little palace of art and a grandstand from which to view diversions. He did not think of it as a dwelling house. To convert it into one, the hollows of the H-plan were filled in, at first-floor level, by building new rooms at either end, supported on bridges. This work provided two suites of staterooms on the first floor, all at the same level. Two suites? Clearly Charles did not expect his mother to stay in residence for ever; perhaps he had not expected her to return there at all. His interest in Greenwich began shortly after his marriage, and part of the object in rearranging the Queen's House was to provide matching apartments that formed a King's Side (on the east) and Queen's Side (on the west). The architect responsible was probably Webb, whose additions were so sympathetic to the original as to be virtually identical in style. Fortunately the proposal to erect corner pavilions, which would have destroyed the purity of the façades, never get beyond the digging of foundations in 1663.

Catherine of Braganza, Charles II's queen. It was at Greenwich that she first met her mother-in-law, Queen Henrietta Maria, in 1662. This portrait shows the Portuguese hairstyle and clothes that seemed so outlandish to English eyes.

An account of that day, in July 1662, when Charles II introduced Catherine of Braganza to his mother for the first time, exists in the Portuguese state archive. It must have been an anxious moment for Charles, whose comfort would be materially affected by the relations established between these two women. No doubt he was relieved to discover that his mother welcomed Catherine with every sign of consideration, meeting her on the steps of the building. Catherine needed all her natural good looks to overcome the peculiarly unflattering fashions of hairstyle and dress that she brought with her from Portugal; on their arrival in England, she and her ladies manoeuvred themselves around in farthingales, not seen in England for half a century, and wore their hair in great bunches, like carrots, on either side of their heads. She liked, perhaps loved, the debonair individual whom she had married, and he reciprocated that liking; but he was not to be estranged from his mistress Barbara Villiers, who threw tantrums at the prospect of the King's deserting her. From the moment that

she met Henrietta Maria, however, Catherine had a friend. In a country of Protestants, they had their religion in common. And the younger woman, lacking any knowledge of the world into which she had been thrown, must have been glad to find, in her mother-in-law, someone whose experience of it ran so deep. The royal party moved from the steps of the palace into the presence chamber. Henrietta Maria made Catherine sit in an armchair, while she took another. Charles II occupied a footstool, and the Duke of York, the future James II, remained standing. They refused the refreshments that were offered them: perhaps they doubted the abilities of Greenwich to provide any. But they nevertheless stayed for four hours.

From the windows of the Queen's House, the royal party would certainly have cast their eyes towards Duke Humphrey's Tower, for the hill below it had been transformed into a series of terraces, like an immense staircase. These Giant's Steps, on an axis with the Queen's House, had been completed by April 1662. In that month the diarist Samuel Pepys recorded a visit that he made to Greenwich with, in effect, his boss in the Navy secretariat, Sir William Penn. They arrived by water, 'and there, while something is dressing for our dinner, Sir William and I walked into the Parke, where the King hath planted trees and made steps in the hill up to the Castle, which is very magnificent'. It is no wonder that these garden works

View from the roof of the Royal Observatory, looking across the Giant's Steps, created for Charles II. Beyond the Giant's Steps on the left can be seen Westcombe Manor, previously the home of the antiquary William Lambarde.

113

should have impressed him: they were a novelty for Britain. They were so important to Charles that he had embarked on them before reconstructing the Queen's House. In France he and his mother had seen the works of André Le Nôtre, who had laid out Versailles for Louis XIV. That great man was consulted, and even prepared plans. Who carried them out is not known; inevitably the work executed was done to a reduced scale. A splendid cascade was proposed for the slope occupied by the Giant's Steps. Charles probably had this in mind when he wrote to his sister Henrietta, married to the Duke of Orleans: 'Pray lett Le Nostre goe on with the modell and only tell him this addition that I can bring water to the top of the hill, so that he might add much to the beauty of the descente by a cascade of water.' That was in 1664; the cascade was never built.

The trees to which Pepys refers may have been the first ever to have been planted in this country for visual effect. In the French manner, they were marshalled into avenues, striding out over the landscape as straight as a surveyor could make them. These avenues suited the French style of hunting, not that this was what Charles had in mind; he had not inherited his grandfather James I's passion for the chase. They required a large number of young trees: six thousand elms were planted in 1664. The elms have gone, of course, but a considerable number of the gnarled Spanish chestnuts of this era survive. So do the ruins of his avenues, impressive in their way, though they would have been far more so if the site had been level. Then, for example, Blackheath Avenue would have ended in a splendid vista of the Queen's House and later the Royal Naval College (as Charles II intended it, his palace) beyond it. Instead it ended, so to speak, in mid-air, a statue of Major-General James Wolfe of Quebec being raised in 1930 (a gift from the Canadian people) as its terminal feature. There is a theory that Le Nôtre was never told that the site was not level.

All this was to have provided the setting for the new palace. It was designed by John Webb, originally, as three ranges, enclosing a big open courtyard giving on to the river; the southern block would have been crowned by a dome. Then came a scheme to make the centrepiece the Queen's House, enlarged and domed. In the event only one range – the Charles II Wing of the Seamen's Hospital – was constructed. It is in a heavier style than the great Inigo would have favoured. The length of the block is emphasised by the masonry; in deliberate contrast to this, columns in the centre and pilasters at the end rise up through the full height of building to the cornice. There is a centrepiece with a pediment; but again, the ends are emphasised by attic storeys in which the vertical thrust of the pilasters is continued. These tensions justify the claim that this is a Baroque building – the first in England.

The progress of the construction can be followed in the accounts. In January 1664 the foundations were staked out. The next month various entries show boxes and portfolios being made for keeping architectural drawings. In May Webb

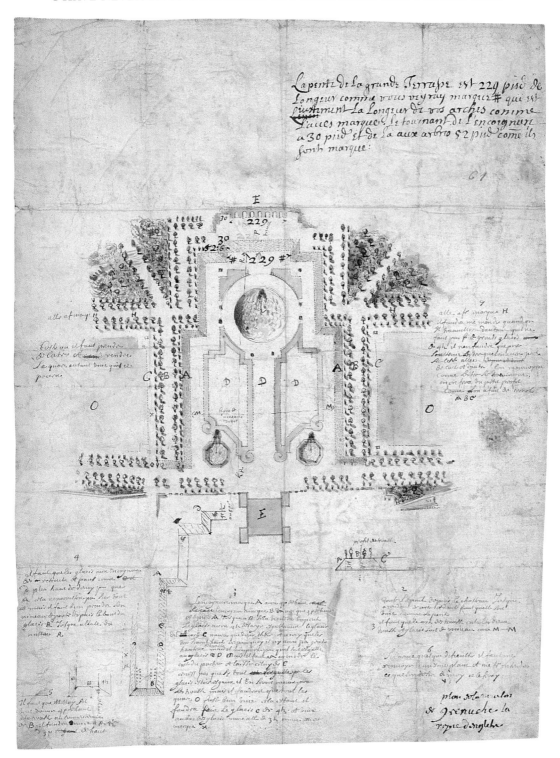

received £6 for journeys to Lyndhurst and Portland to arrange the supply of stone. In June, Richard Gammon, the Clerk of the Works, was paid 8s for 'bringing a Trunck with drawing out of Sumersetsheire', while a labourer, Thomas Fisher, received a compensation of £2 for having been 'dangerously hurt in the worke'. In January 1665 Gammon was again off to Somerset, collecting prints and drawings that Webb was sending the King. Already, on 4 March 1664, Pepys noted: 'at Greenwich did observe the foundacion laying of a very great house for the King, which will cost a great deal of money.' By November 1665 works at Greenwich Palace had cost £75,288 6s 4d. One block of Webb's palace had been constructed: it was to be the only one. When Parliament had invited Charles to take the throne, they had sent him a chest containing £50,000 for his personal needs; the sight of so many golden coins, after years of frustration and poverty in exile, made him laugh out loud. But the cornucopia of the royal finances was by no means infinite, and by the end of the 1660s Charles was forced to concede that he would never realise his vision of a new waterside palace. Perhaps it was as well for him: the country might not have appreciated such an emphatic display of absolutism.

Webb died in 1672. The previous year he described himself, in a new version of his *Historical Essay on the Origins of the Chinese Language*, as 'very fairly at leasure, until his Majesty shall bee gratiously pleased to proceed towards the perfecting of his new Royall Palace at Greenwich; the designing and ordering whereof comanded formerly my cheifest time'. (The *Historical Essay* shows how far Webb shared the inquisitiveness of his times; it was a brave venture, since he never visited China nor learnt to read Chinese.) Admirers of English architecture must be grateful that not more was completed, leaving the field relatively clear for the altogether greater geniuses of Wren and Hawksmoor, architects of the Royal Naval Hospital. Still, as Pepys recorded in July 1665, the King was 'mightily pleased with his new buildings'. Later Wren's son, also Christopher, was generous enough to call it 'a graceful *Pavilion*'. And the new range was soon put to good use – not as a resplendent setting for monarchy, but as temporary offices for naval administration during the Great Plague of 1665.

\* \* \*

Thus it was in Greenwich that, from August 1665 till January 1666, Samuel Pepys had his office. He knew Greenwich already. Official business was always drawing him to the yards at Woolwich and Deptford, where he inspected rope, timber and canvas, poked into stores, investigated fire risks and organised contracts, leases and surveys. They must have made an extraordinary contrast with the other worlds he inhabited – court, City of London and Royal Society – where his contemporaries were struggling, in the difficult circumstances of the time, towards sophistication and learning. Here was a pandemonium of activity, with the clamour of hammers on wood or anvil, the killed-pig squeal of saws, the constant shouts of men, the mingled smells of sweat, pitch, raw wood and baked cordage. Skilled men led teams of smiths, carpenters, sail-makers, rope-makers, gun-founders, powder-makers and the like. Then there were the victuallers who supplied bread, beer and other stores. About the purlieus of the dockyard moved a demi-world of parasites and thieves. It was not only work that drew Pepys to the heaving tumult of the docks. At Deptford lived the mistress whom he invariably refers to as 'Bagwell's wife', William Bagwell being a ship's carpenter for whom he obtained 'preferment': Pepys never scrupled to use his powers of patronage to his own sexual advantage.

To Pepys it was only a short walk from Deptford and Woolwich to Greenwich, or vice-versa. Sometimes he had a specific reason for going, when a warship was moored there, or more often one of the King's yachts. But it seems that he also simply enjoyed the walk. In the Spring of 1663 he found it 'very pleasant along the green corne and peas'. Once (on 22 April 1664) he rose at four a.m., left his home in Seething Lane, went to Greenwich by river and, in the cool and mist of the early morning, 'walked with great pleasure to Woolwich, in my way staying several times to listen to the nightingales'. It was not always free from adventure. At night, he would be sure to have some stout fellow go with him carrying a blazing link or a lantern. Walking to Greenwich after having inspected the *Royal James*, in May 1663, 'I was set upon by a great dog, who got hold of my garters and might have done me hurt; but Lord, to see in what a maze I was, that having a sword about me, I never thought of it or had the heart to make use of it, but might for want of that courage have been worried.'

Samuel Pepys, by Sir Godfrey Kneller. Pepys knew Greenwich well, from its proximity to Deptford dockyard which he visited often for his work at the Navy Board. He lived in Greenwich while the Navy Board was evacuated there during the Great Plague.

Pepys and his contemporaries, like the Cavaliers of an earlier generation, viewed Greenwich as a place of resort. It was somewhere to go for an outing. 'Away back home,' he writes in May 1665; 'and not being fit for business, I took my wife and Mercer down by water to Greenwich at 8 at night, it being very fine and cool, and moonshine afterward – mighty pleasant passage it was. There eat a cake or two, and so home by 10 or 11 at night, and then to bed.' He spent a happy summer afternoon in 1662, visiting Greenwich to see the King's yacht, the palace and the Park. Afterwards he went to one of the taverns that had a reputation for music.

PROSPECTUS

*Prospect Towards London.*
**Engraving by Francis Place of about 1700 showing the Royal Observatory with Greenwich Park from the south-east. The parish church of St Alfege can be seen in the centre of the view. The houses of Crooms Hill appear on the left.**

Music was always delightful to Pepys, and Greenwich supplied it in various forms. There was a 'Musique-house', where, on 21 August 1663, 'we had paltry musique till the Maister Organist came … and he did give me a fine voluntary or two'. When staying in Greenwich during the Plague, he attended St Alfege's church, attempting to place himself nearest to those members of the congregation with a reputation for good voices. (When, on 3 December, he was prevented, through being invited into Colonel Cleggatt's pew, he had the compensation of being 'in sight by chance, and very near, my fat brown beauty of our parish, the rich merchant's lady, a very noble woman'.) He was too early to enjoy the new organ fitted into St Alfege's in 1672–3, the organ builder being Ralph Dallans, apparently a Greenwich man, to judge from the fact that when he died, while building it, he was buried in the church (the organ was finished by his partner). Even Pepys's barber at Greenwich played the violin, and was much in demand for dancing. His wife's taste for dancing had troubled Pepys when it first showed itself; still, he was inclined to indulge her in this taste for 'mirth' – hang the expense. There was other mirth to be had at the Greenwich taverns, such as the Ship and the Bear.

It is a sign of Greenwich's gentility that Pepys had friends round about. Foremost among them, and typical of the salty character of the area, was Captain

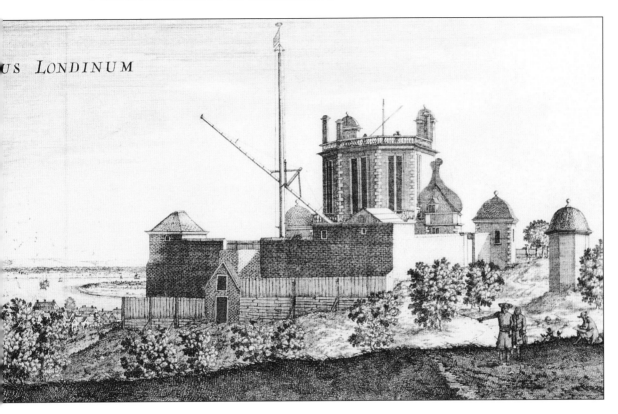

Cocke, a hemp merchant who served as Commissioner for the Sick and Wounded and Prisoners of War in 1664–7. Since hemp was a naval necessity, and Pepys responsible for procuring it, they inevitably saw much of each other; he was also good company, though boisterous. His house stood next to the mansion built by Sir Andrew Cogan, on the east side of Greenwich: Pepys describes it as 'a most pleasant seat, and neat'. Pretty Mrs Cocke had what to Pepys seemed a most unfortunate disposition, since she freely berated her husband for his errant ways. Though they seemed to live frugally, the garden yielded an abundance of apricots, mulberries and other fruit. Then there was the lawyer Mark Cottle, Registrar of the Prerogative Court, 'with a very pretty house, and a fine Turret at top, with windeing stairs, and the finest prospect I know about all Greenwich, save the top of the hill – and yet in some respects better than that'. It was called the Belvedere.

At Wricklemarsh House, the Colonel Blount whose hue and cry had been despatched after Evelyn's robbers, was a member of the Royal Society: that august body of scientists and scientifically inclined gentlemen – the 'college of virtuosoes' – of which Pepys himself would become President. There was much wondering at the ingenuity (and about the practicability) of Blount's 'Way-Wiser', a kind of odometer, and a new type of coach springs, which a committee of the Royal

Society tried on Blackheath. 'It is very fine and likely to take,' wrote Pepys, perhaps optimistically. Innovations of this type were important, at a time when the number of hackney coaches – there were thought to be as many as twenty-five thousand in London – was increasing to such an extent that the watermen began to fear for their livelihood. The Royal Society returned to Colonel Blount the next year, considering a new type of 'chariot' in which 'the coachman sits astride upon a pole over the horse, but does not touch the horse, which is a pretty odde thing; but it seems it is more easy for the horse, and, as they say, for the man also'.

In August 1665 Pepys enjoyed a 'good merry dinner' at the house of George Boreman, Keeper of the Wardrobe and Privy Lodgings at Greenwich. He was no doubt the son of Sir William Boreman, also present on the occasion, a remarkable figure who had paid £650 of his own money to keep the Queen and her household in food during the siege of Exeter, and later to transport them to London. As a result of his services, he was made Clerk Controller of the Household and given the responsibility – presumably, like all contracting work, lucrative – of planting Charles II's trees in Greenwich Park. The office of gamekeeper at Greenwich, worth 12d a day, was granted to him in 1663. At the dinner, they partook of a 'good venison pasty'. Where the venison could have come from is something of a mystery. Certainly it was not local: there were no deer left in the parks at either Greenwich or Eltham.

A walk to Sayes Court, at Deptford, brought Pepys to that other diarist, John Evelyn, the greatest connoisseur of his age, whose parade of learning Pepys found alternately fascinating and tiresome. Pepys leaves a vivid impression of the evening he spent there in November 1665. 'Evelyn, among other things, showed me most excellent painting in little – in distempter, Indian Incke – water colours – graveing; and above all, the whole secret of Mezzo Tinto and the manner of it, which is very pretty, and good things done with it.' (The art of mezzotint printing had recently been introduced to England by Prince Rupert, once the 'Mad Cavalier' at the head of Charles I's horse, who described it to the Royal Society in 1662.) The talk then turned to gardening, and Evelyn read some of his own poetical effusions – before Captain Cocke came in 'as drunk as a dog'.

Less than a fortnight after establishing himself at Greenwich during the Plague year, Pepys invited Lord Rutherford to his lodgings. 'We supped together and sat up late, he being a mighty wanton man with a daughter-in-law of my landlady's, a pretty conceited woman, big with child; and he would be handling her breasts, which she coyly refused.' It was not until December that Pepys had a go at fondling her himself (she was hoping her husband could be made a lieutenant), but in the interim he had been applying himself to making ready the King's ships for the Second Dutch War of 1665–7, as well as to other distractions. Prime among the latter was Mrs Penington. Pepys had a taste for modest and seemingly virtuous women, and felt it 'very strange' that this daughter of a knighted alderman did not, after a short acquaintance, repel the

## John Evelyn

John Evelyn, the greatest connoisseur of his age, moved to his wife's property of Sayes Court, Deptford, in 1652. There he created an elaborate garden out of what had previously been 'a rude orchard, and all the rest one entire field of 100 acres, without any hedge, except the hither holly-hedge joining to the bank of the mount walk.' He lovingly planted walks, groves, enclosures and plantations, his pains being rewarded, after the Restoration, by visits from both the Queen Mother, Henrietta Maria, and King Charles II. The latter took a particular interest in a fantastic beehive he had been given by a don from Wadham College, Oxford.

Like all gardeners Evelyn was at the mercy of the winter weather. In January 1684, when it was so cold that the Thames froze over, and a fair, including printing presses, was set up near London Bridge, he 'went to Sayes Court to see how the frost had dealt with my garden, where I found many of the greens and rare plants utterly destroyed. The oranges and myrtles very sick, the rosemary and laurels dead to all appearance, but the cypress likely to endure it.' These comments come from the famous diary that was discovered in an old clothes basket at his brother's house at Wotton in 1817.

Among Evelyn's many projects was Greenwich Hospital, of which he became the first Treasurer, aged seventy-five. It was largely his perseverance which ensured that the money to built it was found.

**John Evelyn, painted by Sir Godfrey Kneller.**

hand he put inside her chemise to feel her breasts. She was, however, exceedingly taken with the contemporary fashion for déshabillé, as portrayed in the paintings of Lely. She must have been proud of her charms. Another time, a barrel of oysters inspired further ardours, though, as with other of Pepys's adventures, he seems to have had to content himself with groping. His hopes must have been high when, having been 'mighty merry and free' with her during supper from the King's Head tavern, he persuaded her to change into her nightgown, à la Lely. He said he would walk up and down while she was changing, his steps taking him along the walled road that crossed the Park. By the time he returned she had gone to bed, much to his chagrin. (But the night was not over: when he got home he found Mrs Daniels waiting for him to discuss her husband's commission.)

For all such adventures, these were grim times. Pepys, humane as well as all too human, pitied 'the horrible Crowd and lamentable moaning of the poor seamen that lie starving in the streets for lack of money – which doth trouble and perplex me to the heart'. The wretched condition of people on the Kent Road also moved him. Further, for all the consolations provided by a Mrs Pennington or a Mrs

## Peter the Great

In February 1698, Deptford was graced, if that is the word, by the presence of the Emperor of Russia, Peter the Great. He came to England to study shipbuilding, and after some time visiting the sights of London, withdrew to John Evelyn's house of Sayes Court. This had already been let to Admiral Benbow, master of the fleet at the Battle of La Hogue, who felt constrained to move out for the royal guest. For four and a half decades, Evelyn had studied to make the house and its garden a reflection of his antiquarian learning and discriminating taste.

These qualities seem to have been lost on Peter. His researches into shipbuilding were accompanied by dissipation and vandalism. He and his entourage ('right nasty,' according to Evelyn's bailiff) slept anywhere, at any hour. In May, after Peter had left, Evelyn had Sir Christopher Wren and the King's gardener, George London, value the damage. They found that doors had been taken down and burnt, three hundred window panes had been smashed, the Dutch tiles in the fireplaces needed replacing, floors were 'dammag'd by Grease and Inck', and what must have been every piece of fabric in

the house – curtains, counterpanes, bedhangings, tapestries – had been torn and soiled. The paintings were riddled with bullet-holes. Outside, all the lawns had been pitted with holes 'by their leaping and shewing tricks upon it'. A particular entertainment had been for the Russians to push each other through the hedges in wheelbarrows; the pride of the neighbourhood was a great holly hedge – not comfortable, one would have thought, to wheelbarrow through – which they broke down. 'To Deptford to see how miserably the Czar has left my house, after 3 months making it his court,' noted Evelyn gloomily on 9 June. It was judged that the depredations amounted to the large sum of £350. The Lords of the Treasury reimbursed Evelyn and Bembow without demur. William III was so pleased that England had received Peter as a guest that he commissioned Sir Godfrey Kneller to paint his portrait. Peter's return present was a big uncut diamond, wrapped, characteristically, in a piece of dirty paper.

**Peter the Great, painted for William III by Sir Godfrey Kneller. This giant of a man, six foot and seven inches tall, recalled his time studying shipbuilding at Deptford with affection, saying that he would have had 'a much happier life as an admiral in England than a Tsar in Russia'.**

Daniels, the removal to Greenwich was a cost that Pepys would have rather not borne. His wife and household were still living at Woolwich, while a maid kept the London house going. Pepys was not the only person seeking to escape the Plague, and his landlady got a good price for her lodgings. But it had to be done. When

Pepys went to the City, he was relieved and surprised when he found shopkeepers, including pretty ones, still on their feet. Like everyone else, he could only watch powerlessly as the Bill of Mortality rose to over a thousand a week. One day when he walked from Woolwich to Greenwich in August 1665, he saw

> a coffin with a dead body therein, dead of the plague, lying in an open close belonging to Coome farme, which was carried out last night and the parish hath not appointed anybody to bury it – but only set a watch there day and night, that nobody should go thither or come thence, which is a most cruel thing – this disease making us more cruel to one another then we are [to] dogs.

It was not until the end of the year that the plague had 'abated almost to nothing', and he could look forward to a return to Seething Lane. This happy event took place on 22 January 1666.

Still, he had to conclude, on 21 December 1665, 'I have never lived so merrily . . . as I have done this plague-time'. In 1669 he gave Greenwich the accolade of being 'a very pretty place'.

* * *

While Pepys enjoyed his time in Greenwich, thanks to the congenial company he found there, the majority of inhabitants of the late-seventeenth-century town did not have such a comfortable time. The houses were miserable, and so was the food. Greenwich was 'like a Spanish Town', being 'under such a scarcity of Fresh Meat', according to J. How's *A Frolick to Horn-Fair* of 1700 (Horn Fair was the ancient fair at Charlton held on St Luke's day, St Luke's emblem being an ox): 'a Gentleman not long ago, brought his Mistress down with a Design to lye all Night in the Town, but was forc'd to go back to *London*, at seven a Clock at Night, against Tide, because never a Publick House in the Town could procure him a Supper.'

In 1710, after the collapse of the parish church of St Alfege's, the people of Greenwich petitioned the Crown for help in rebuilding it. They claimed that the town had long been deserted by its richer inhabitants, and the largest houses were empty. Nine-tenths of the population were supposed to be seafarers. Tradesmen were in trouble after having given long credit. Three thousand widows and children had become a burden on the parish after the Great Storm of 1703 had sunk many vessels; and yet more widows and orphans had been made when three of the ships led by Admiral Sir Cloudesley Shovell, returning from Gibraltar after skirmishing with the French, struck rocks off the Scilly Isles. These figures must have been exaggerated; still, they suggest the poverty that had settled on the town, in contrast to the fine buildings erected in the royal park under the Stuarts. But at least the town got its new church.

Sir Jonas Moore, the mathematician, would talk to Samuel Pepys about subjects such as Moore's duodecimal system of mathematics and the concept of time in the Old Testament. He was responsible for the defences of Tangier, as well as being the prime mover behind founding the Royal Observatory. This portrait was engraved for his *A New System of Mathematicks*, 1681.

One of the books in Pepys's library is said to have been Sir Jonas Moore's survey of the entire length of the Thames. Moore was another of the ingenious figures in Pepys's acquaintance. Very tall, very fat, with grey eyes and the fat man's delicate skin, he cannot have been easily overlooked. Trained as a mathematician, he was also expert in draining the Fens, cartography and fortification. John Aubrey, in his *Brief Lives*, concluded that he 'was one of the most accomplisht Gentlemen of his time; a good Mathematician, and a good Fellowe'. In short, he was the sort of man whom Pepys might be expected to like. It was an era when science was, in some respects, only one stage removed from quackery: even an apparent rationalist like Sir Isaac Newton could also waste much effort in the study of alchemy, in the hope of discovering the philosopher's stone. And Moore had his moments of credulity, too. On one occasion, he told the assembled fellows of the Royal Society, no less, how an Irish boy had been made to fly through the air by the Jesuits, crossing a river in Lancashire, then falling to the ground and breaking both legs when the people below had shouted at him. A mite of gullibility (unless another miracle) may also be inferred from Aubrey's laconic comment: 'Sciatica: he cured it by boyling his Buttock.'

*Effigies* Ionæ (Moore *Matheseos Professoris Ætat: suæ* 45 *An: Dm̄:1660*

Moore never lived at Greenwich, but he was to make a powerful contribution to its history. For he was not only a mathematician, a surveyor and an authority on fortification; he was also an astronomer. It is no wonder that, given his bent, he should have taken study of the heavens into his repertoire. This was an area in which even amateurs could still make a contribution to knowledge, and it also had a highly valuable application. The anxiety that Pepys experienced over trade with Tangier (he was secretary to the Commmission that ran this newly acquired colony) is evidence of the rudimentary state of navigation at sea. Sometimes even the most experienced seamen steered by a combination of intuition and guesswork. Ships that were far from their supposed position on the charts could be wrecked, or fall into enemy hands. As trade by sea expanded and the number of colonies grew, the security of English shipping became a rising concern. Eventually, in 1714, Parliament itself took action by proposing the enormous prize of £20,000 to the person who established a means of calculating longitude at sea. Forty or so years earlier, Charles II had made his own contribution by establishing the Royal Observatory at Greenwich. The prime mover in this work had been Sir Jonas Moore.

It was the sort of project which would have appealed to one aspect of the King's nature. He shared with so many men of his age a fascination with both the arts and the sciences, the difference between which had scarcely been drawn. Thus he had a fondness for curiosities, and collected them from foreign courts. Deeply concerned, as were Pepys and Moore, about the state of his own body, he had a knowledge of certain medicines. Pepys records that he would observe dissections. Less expectedly, he had some grasp of mathematics. The succession of royal yachts that he moored at Greenwich were evidence enough of his love of ships and shipbuilding. Like his cousin Prince Rupert, he had a lifelong passion for chemistry, bringing a professional from France to create a laboratory at St James's Palace. The King had his own

Greenwich as depicted in Sir Jonas Moore's *Mapp or Description of the River Thames*, 1662. Surveying was another of the sciences in which Moore excelled.

View from One Tree Hill in Greenwich Park, with the Royal Observatory on the left (note the stream of people visiting it) and the Queen's House on the right. The town of Greenwich huddles in the shadow of the steeple of the old church. The river is busy with shipping. Painting by Jan Griffier the Elder (1651–1718).

Louise de Keroualle, the French mistress whom Charles II created Duchess of Portsmouth, in 1682. Her badgering of the king, on behalf of a compatriot, indirectly led to the foundation of the Royal Observatory in 1675.

'elaboratory' filled with 'chymical glasses' at Whitehall, where he conducted experiments. Even so, constitutionally averse from anything that would cause him trouble, he might not have got round to founding the Royal Observatory had his interest in science not been reinforced by another predilection – the great weakness to which all the many others in his personality were subsumed – his animal appetite for women.

In 1674, the first woman in his affections was Louise de Keroualle, the voluptuous Breton beauty whom he created Duchess of Portsmouth. She had first made an impression accompanying Charles's sister, Henrietta, Duchess of Orleans, on a visit to the English court. She was later sent back by Louis XIV, to promote what would later have been called an entente cordiale between England and France. It was her mission to meddle in politics, and meddle she did – not only in politics, but any matter where a countryman's interests were affected. To that end she took up the cause of a 'bold and indigent' Frenchman who called himself Le Sieur de St Pierre. He claimed to have found an easy means of discovering longitude by astronomy alone. Had this been possible, it would have been of immense benefit to mariners, since the only method by which longitude could be established involved knowing the ship's local time (easily done by observation) and comparing it to that at a 'prime meridian', which was quite impossible given that there was then no clock which could keep time accurately at sea. Charles II, badgered by his mistress, put the matter of St Pierre's claims to a Royal Commission, its seven members all drawn from the newly established Royal Society. Four of them met on 12 February 1675, taking 'Mr. Flamsteed of Darby' as their assistant. Flamsteed, a young man of twenty-eight, had been staying with his patron, Sir Jonas Moore. As Moore was also a fellow of the Royal Society, it was probably through his influence that he obtained the position. St Pierre's theories were dismissed. Even had they been true, they would have been useless without a complete chart of the movement of the heavens, which did not exist.

A clue to the Duchess of Portsmouth's tactics with the King, highly effective on a man who did not like to be fussed, can be perceived behind a communication sent to one of the Commissioners, Dr John Pell:

His Majesty is so daily imperturbed by Mons. St Pierre the French
Longitude Man, that he commands me to signify to you, that absolutely to
have a final answer, that is that you forthwith give him such data as he
pleads are necessary to the work in hand, and that we may either have the
General Science he pleads to, or at least a quiet from his further impetuosity
etc. You must please to set yourself to this forthwith, and not intermit a day
till it be finished, and an account returned to his Majesty.

St Pierre had every reason to be frantic to obtain the data that he maintained
would prove the truth of his thesis. Already the King had been persuaded by
Moore to appoint Flamsteed as his 'astronomical observator'. The warrant directs
that he should devote his energies 'to the rectifying the tables of the Motions of
the Heavens and the places of the fixed Stars so as to find out the so-much-desired
Longitude of Places'. This was, to say the least, a big job; under the circumstances,
the salary of £100 a year was hardly excessive.

An oil painting by Thomas Gibson shows Flamsteed to have been rather fine-
looking. He had regular features, a straight nose, eyes that seem to survey the spec-
tator coolly – disconcertingly coolly perhaps – and above all a mouth that suggests
determination. It is a face of some delicacy, but nothing in the painting points to
the terrible ill-health that had dogged this man's life. From the age of fourteen, he
suffered from a kind of rheumatism, supposedly the result of a cold caught while
bathing. Until then he had been educated at the free school in Derby, where his
father, who was a maltster, lived (his mother, the daughter of a Derby ironmonger,
had died when he was three). Now he could not walk to school. At fifteen he had
to leave it. But the illness which cut him off from the normal youthful activities
allowed him to concentrate single-mindedly, when he was well enough to concentrate at all, on his passion for astronomy. And it must have taken some concentra-
tion. The book that first stirred his love of the heavens was Sacrobosco's *De
Sphaera*, which had been lent to him. Then he devoured Fale's *Art of Dialling*,
Stirrup's *Complete Diallist*, Gunter's *Sector* and *Canon*, and Oughtred's *Canones
Sinuum*. The first two works are part of the extensive literature that existed on the
subject of making, setting and reading sundials. It was strong fare for a schoolboy.
He constructed his own quadrant and made observations of the sun. In later years
Flamsteed liked to recall that he pursued his studies 'under the discouragement of
friends, the want of health, and all other instructors except his better genius'.
Absolute certainty that he was right, combined with a feeling that the rest of the
world was against him, were, alas, all too typical of Flamsteed. *The Dictionary of
National Biography* quotes 'an old writer' as describing Flamsteed as a 'humourist
and of warm passions'. Ill-health may have enabled Flamsteed to develop in his
chosen subject, but it also seems to have left him crabbed and over-sensitive to

*Opposite:* **John Flamsteed, painted by Thomas Gibson in 1712. This portrait, with its strong features, does not suggest the ill health which dogged the first Astronomer Royal. However, the pugnacious lip hints at the chronic bad temper and argumentativeness which caused him to fall out with other scientists, including Isaac Newton.**

imagined slights. Perhaps the peculiar regime of the astronomer – observing at night, sleeping by day – exacerbated the difficult side of his character.

He was twenty-three when he made the journey to London and was there introduced to Sir Jonas Moore. Moore gave him a measuring instrument which Flamsteed calls 'Mr. Townley's curious mensurator', and obtained lenses for a telescope to fit it. With the mensurator he started making systematic observations, using a quadrant to work out the time (clocks were still a rarity in England). By this time he had entered Jesus College, Cambridge, which enabled him to become ordained as a clergyman shortly after the Royal Observatory was established. In contrast to Pepys and others who took their tone from their King, Flamsteed was pious, unimpeachable in his moral behaviour and rigidly abstemious in his habits. Whether he would have had any interest in the duties of a clergyman is doubtful; but the income provided by a living would have been useful. He had his eye on one near Derby which was in the gift of a friend, but it was not available. So under Moore's tutelage he began to make his way in London instead. At Moore's suggestion, while staying in Moore's apartment in the Tower for some weeks in 1674, he made a table of the tides for use by the King. In an age when the river was the main thoroughfare of communication, such a table would have been highly convenient. Flamsteed also gave the King and the Duke of York each a barometer and a thermometer made from his models, as well as rules for forecasting the weather by them. So Flamsteed's name was already known in the royal circle when the appointment of a Royal Observer came up. But he was in any case exactly the right man for the job. This was principally to observe the fixed stars and the moon's course among them. Flamsteed's motto might have been: observe, observe and observe. (Moore's role was acknowledged by his being given, according to the Latin inscription on a stone cartouche near the front door of the Old Royal Observatory, the title of Keeper.)

But before that could begin, the Royal Observatory needed a home. Sir Jonas Moore favoured a site in Hyde Park; Flamsteed preferred Chelsea College, established by James I but then in ruins, which had been presented to the Royal Society in 1667. The idea of Greenwich came from Sir Christopher Wren. Wren's involvement should occasion no surprise. Though he is principally remembered as the architect of St Paul's Cathedral and some fifty-two City churches, as well as the bones of the Seamen's Hospital at Greenwich, he began his career as a scientist. His father and uncle had both been prominent churchmen who fell foul of the Puritans. So during the Civil War Wren's family had taken refuge with William Holder, rector of Bletchingdon near Oxford. Holder was a scholar and, according to Aubrey, set about further educating the young Christopher, 'of whom he was as tender as if he had been his own child, whom he instructed first in geometrie and arithmetique'. The boy had already been to Westminster School; at the end of the

Civil War he went up to Oxford. His interests there included anatomy, and he moved in the circle of scientific scholars who would found the Royal Society. Of all the subjects that stimulated Wren's intellect, astronomy took pride of place. It was to be his principal occupation until the cascade of architectural work that, as Surveyor of the King's Works, fell upon him after the Great Fire of London in 1666 absorbed most of his energies. Like Flamsteed, he was much fascinated by 'dialling' (the science of sundials) as a boy, and translated the relevant passages of Oughtred's *Clavis Mathematica* at the age of fifteen or sixteen – not into English (it was already in English) but into Latin. His experience of producing models and diagrams predisposed his mind to architectural ways of thinking.

Quite why he proposed Greenwich Park as the best place to build an observatory is unclear; he may well have thought that the skies above Greenwich would be clearer than those over London itself. There was already so much smoke from brewers, dyers, soap-boilers and lime-burners, as well as domestic hearths, hanging over London that in 1661 John Evelyn published proposals to remedy matters called *Fumifugium, or the Inconvenience of the Air and Smoke of London dissipated.* He may have thought the problem would get worse over time, and he would have been right. When Evelyn's work was republished in 1772, the editor, Samuel Pegge, lamented that 'since his time we have a GREAT INCREASE of Glass-Houses, Founderies and Sugar bakers to add to the black catalogue'. Foggy weather was the bane of English astronomers as it was: they did not need to contend with a smoke haze as well. Wren himself was to be the architect of the new building. There is no record of his visiting the site during its construction, however. In the context of his other commissions, it was small beer.

It would seem that Duke Humphrey's Tower had been demolished or was at least in ruins by the time it was decided to build the Royal Observatory where it had stood. During the Civil War, the Tower acquired yet another new name: Greenwich Castle. It was still standing when Jonas Moore drew that survey of the Thames, of which Pepys owned a copy, in 1662. But the royal warrant authorising construction talks of 'the highest ground at or near the Place where the Castle stood', so presumably it was no longer there. The foundations remained, however, and for the sake of economy it was decided to re-use them. 'Provided that the whole sum to be expended and paid shall not exceed £500,' states the warrant emphatically: economy was the keynote of the whole Observatory project. The money to fund the building work came from the sale of decayed gunpowder, which was then reconditioned and, oddly, sold back to the ordnance.

On 27 July 1675 that far-ranging and inventive scientist Robert Hooke (like Wren, also an architect) records in his diary: 'To Greenwich. Set out Observatory. Saw Flamsteed's level. Dined at Nightingales in the Park …' The foundation stone was laid on 10 August at 3.14 p.m., with Flamsteed casting a mock horoscope for the birth of the new building. By Christmas it had been roofed. In May 1676 Flamsteed reported everything except the Sextant and Quadrant Houses – separate structures that stood in the little garden – had been completed. He was then occupying an apartment in the Queen's House, where the loggia served as a platform for his astronomical instruments. It may have been at this time that the two Van de Veldes, father and son, the great Dutch painters of seascapes, were using studio space there, working on their scenes of English triumphs against their own country in the Dutch Wars that had been so much preoccupying Pepys. (They lived in East Lane, now Eastney Street.) On 29 May 1675, Flamsteed left this accommodation and installed himself in the Observatory, prior to a partial eclipse of the sun. It is an indication of Charles II's curiosity about science that he expressed a desire to see it, though in the end he did not come. He would have been pleased to know that the building very nearly kept to the prescribed budget, the final cost coming in at £520 9s 1d.

'We built indeed an Observatory at Greenwich not unlike what your Tower will prove,' wrote Wren to Bishop Fell some years later (referring to the proposed new Tom Tower at Oxford); 'it was for the Observator's habitation and a little for pomp.' For pomp, Wren made the most of the need to create an observation room with very tall windows; he did so in the form of a tower, appearing flat from the front but octagonal within, which gave the Observatory a faintly castle-like appearance – perhaps recalling the building that had preceded it. There are little turrets at the top, for servants' bedrooms, and to either side of the façade facing the palace, Wren applied the curly scrolls called volutes. About half a dozen years later, he gave a little further dignity to this elevation by adding garden pavilions at the corners of the courtyard in front of it. The principal material was red brick – once more enjoying the vogue it had known under the Tudors. But it was a sign of the extreme economy with which the 'pomp' had to be affected that the dressings which appear to be stone are nothing more than painted wood. The bricks had been left over from the building of Tilbury fort.

This was a building to make its effect from a distance: more or less an eye-catcher in the royal Park. This is evident from the position of the front door, tucked away at the side of the main façade: not an entrance to make a grand impression on anyone actually visiting the building. It gave onto a hall on the ground floor, around which were the bedroom, drawing room and dining room of what, in effect, was Flamsteed's one-bedroom flat. Stairs lead up to the justly named Great Room, one of the few Wren interiors to survive in its original condition. The dignity and calm of Wren's architecture seem very conducive to studying the silent mysteries of the night sky. The universe which Flamsteed was observing – soon to be interpreted by Newton – seemed as ordered and mathematically inspired as the canons of classicism. Francis Place made a book of engravings of the Observatory for Jonas Moore, in which plate IX is titled *Prospectus intra Camera Stellatam* ('View within the Star Chamber'). A glance at it shows why the great height was needed. The only means

The Royal Observatory viewed from Crooms Hill in about 1680. The mast on the right allows a very long telescope to be elevated. In the distance can be seen the Queen's House, with (on the far left) the King's House designed by John Webb.

The Octagon Room in the Royal Observatory, engraved by Francis Place. The instruments include the pair of year-going clocks built by Thomas Tompion in 1676. However, since the Observatory was built on the foundations of the demolished castle, it was not aligned on the meridian. Consequently most observations of the heavens were made from a specially constructed shed in the garden.

by which the secrets of the heavens could be unlocked was the telescope. The longer the telescope, the more detail that could be seen. Place shows the ladder and stand necessary to support Flamsteed's eight-and-a-half-foot telescope, which had to be tilted at any angle he wished. To know the precise time at which observations were made was critically important. Consequently, two clocks by Thomas Tompion were fitted into the wall (they seem always to have been a pair, though Place shows three); they were regulated by thirteen-foot pendulums that, unusually, were hung above, rather than below, the clock faces. This reflects the ingenuity of the great Tompion. (The inventor of the first portable watches, Tompion was a genius entirely suited to this mechanistic age, in which the clock seemed to be a metaphor for the universe itself.) The dials of the clocks bear the inscription: *Motus Annus [Year Movement]. Sr Jonas Moore Caused this Movement with great Care to be Made Ao 1676 by Tho. Thompion.* To check that the clocks were themselves absolutely accurate, there was also a three-foot sextant, which Place shows being used by a monk.

One might almost have thought that Flamsteed was spoiled for the variety of spaces and devices available to him for observation. One of the garden pavilions formed a *Domus Obscurata*, or darkened house, for receiving sunspots and solar

PROSPECTUS INTRA CAMERAM STELLATAM

eclipses. There were outbuildings for large sextants, a great quadrant fixed to a wall aligned on the meridian, a sixty-foot telescope suspended from a mast, and a telescope sunk in a well. These were really the working side of the establishment. As Wren would write to Bishop Fell: 'It is the instruments in the Court after the manner I have described which are used, the roome keeps the Clocks and the Instruments that are layed by.' But none of it made Flamsteed a happy man. His private accommodation was cramped – all the more galling in view of the splendid, if little used, octagon above him.

He was provided with an idiot of an official assistant, as a result of which he had to employ another at his own expense; and he was expected to teach two pupils from Christ's Hospital as part of the bargain. He could only make ends meet by taking private pupils as well. From the beginning he was 'much troubled' (as he wrote to Towneley as early as 3 July 1675) 'with Mr Hooke', who 'will needs force his ill contrived devices on us'. These were instruments which Hooke (an authority on microscopes more than telescopes) persuaded Flamsteed to accept, but which had to be replaced later. The worst of it was that he made no allowance for the very expensive equipment without which any observatory would not be worth the name. Not that this was quite all of it. Flamsteed, locked up with his charts and his telescopes, isolated by illness as well as temperament, was a pioneer in the assembly of data; but it was not for him to make sense of it. That fell to his friend, as he originally was, Isaac Newton. Flamsteed said that Newton worked with the ore he had dug. 'If he dug the ore,' Sir Isaac said when he heard it, 'I made the gold ring.'

Newton and his contemporaries saw Flamsteed's observations as vitally important material upon which their own theories about the universe could be developed. To begin with, Flamsteed shared his data willingly with fellow scientists. But Newton's exhortations to publish at least the material that related to the major stars had the opposite effect to that intended. Flamsteed had a grander scheme; he wanted to wait until he was ready; he became secretive. He also became suspicious to the extent almost of paranoia. But he was, after all, the Astronomer Royal, and something was owed to the monarchs who paid his salary. In the first years of the eighteenth century, he announced that he would publish a catalogue of his findings. This was largely to allay the charge that he would not communicate information. The catalogue was only half finished. Newton, against Flamsteed's wishes, commended its publication to Prince George of Denmark, husband of the future Queen Anne, who appointed a committee of the Royal Society to assess its merits. They reported favourably, and what was to prove the agonizing process of publishing the *Historia Coelestis* was started. It appeared in 1712, under the editorship of Edmond Halley, of comet fame (whom Flamsteed called a 'lazy and malicious thief'). Flamsteed protested that the work had been

John Flamsteed, sketched in an observation book by his assistant Abraham Sharp in 1684. Generally, humour was not in great supply at Flamsteed's Observatory.

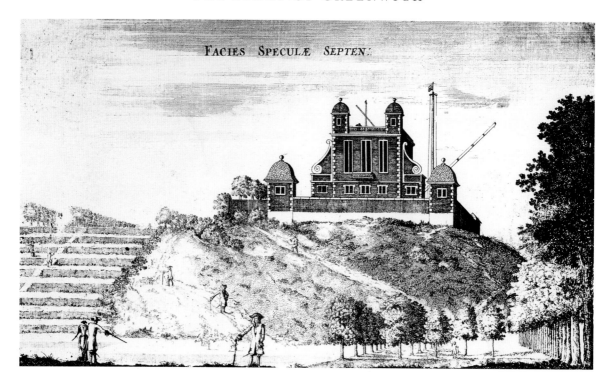

FACIES SPECULÆ SEPTEN:

**View of the Royal Observatory from the bottom of the Giant's Steps. The two summerhouses to either side of the central building appear to have been an afterthought by architect Sir Christopher Wren.**

printed from early drafts, without corrections. By then he had quarrelled with just about everyone who mattered in science. He had driven Newton to call him 'many hard names – *puppy* was the most innocent of them'. The appearance of what he regarded as the pirated edition of his work spurred him to a fury of activity in the last seven years of his life – but the time was too short, and his three-volume version of the *Historia Coelestis*, literally his life's work, did not appear until 1725, six years after his death. He was succeeded as Astronomer Royal by his hated enemy, Halley.

In the history of science, the Royal Observatory was of incalculable benefit to the development of astronomy. For Greenwich, it is worth noting that it quickly became one of the wonders of England, and helped attract admiring interest in the location through the number of educated tourists drawn thither. It was not only the Royal Observatory which attracted them, of course: the Seamen's Hospital, to be described in the next chapter, was also regarded as one of the sights of Europe. But the almost universal, sometimes extreme, enthusiasm expressed for the view from Castle Hill confirms Wren's genius in having promoted this site. The prospect of the earth, as much as that of the heavens, obtained from it inspired raptures. The French lawyer Pierre-Jean Grossley's *A Tour to London; or, New Observations on England, and its Inhabitants*, whose translation by Thomas Nugent was published in 1772, is only a little more hyperbolic than others:

The observatory is as deserving of admiration on account of its situation, as it is respectable for its use; it exhibits the finest, the most exquisite, and the grandest landscape in England. In a space of five or six leagues on every side, the centre of which is occupied by London, it takes in the most agreeable part of the course of the Thames, surrounded by fields, which are covered with villages, palaces, and country houses; a prospect comparable to that of Lombardy at the descent of the Alps, or the Apennines; or rather to that of the country about Rome, seen from the eminences of Tibur and Tusculum, during the most flourishing times of the empire.

To the age of the Picturesque there could be no higher accolade. It was typical of Greenwich that it could combine scientific inquiry with elegance and the highest aesthetic values. Uniting apparently contradictory forces was to become rather a Greenwich speciality, as seen when the most wretched of conditions were relieved by the charitable purpose of the Seamen's Hospital, housed in buildings of ineffable splendour.

## Greenwich Glass

While the Royal Observatory was being built, other industrious souls were busy at the making of Greenwich glass. John Evelyn thought highly of it. In June 1673, after a visit to Blackheath to see the army then bivouacked there, he went 'to the Italian glass-house at Greenwich, where glass was blown of finer mettal than that of Murano at Venice'. Lord Egremont took his daughter Helena and a party of children to the factory in 1738, to watch glass being wrought into fantastic animal and human shapes. However, these novelties seem to have impressed him rather less than the hocus-pocus of the glass-blower: 'The woman pretended she had the art of curing wounds and staunching blood by sympathetical powder, and gave an instance of it, of a cook maid in the town who had been cured so by her.'

# LAST LIGHT ON THE WAVE OF TIME

*Oh, heavy are the sorrows that beset*
*Old age! and hard it is – hard to forget*
*The sunshine of our youth, our manhood's pride!*
*But here, O aged men! ye may abide*
*Secure, and see the last light on the wave*
*Of Time, which wafts you silent to your grave;*
*Like the calme evening ray, that smiles serene*
*Upon the tranquile Thames, and cheers the sinking scene.*

William Lisle Bowles, 1762-1850

I N 1672 THE SEEMINGLY interminable quarrel between the English and the Dutch was persisting, and the Duke of York, the future James II, was the Lord High Admiral in command of the English fleet. Like his brother Charles II, he had always enjoyed being around ships. But neither of them had any great aptitude for naval strategy. James proved a brave rather than brilliant Lord High Admiral. When the morning of 7 June dawned, a fleet of English and French ships was lying in Southwold Bay, off the coast of East Anglia. This force was surprised by an Admiral, Michiel de Ruyter, who, like other Dutch commanders, really did know his business. The battle that followed inflicted terrible casualties on both sides. The Dutch got the better of it. The English position was so bad that the Duke of York had to abandon two successive flagships, the *Prince* and the *St Michael*. By the end of the day there were thousands of English dead. Among the bodies floating in the water was that of Pepys's patron Lord Sandwich, recognised only because of the Garter insignia that he had been wearing. Afterwards, the scenes in Margate, after the allied squadrons had put into shore, were appalling. The Duke of York may have been a deficient King and an indifferent commander, but he was not inhumane. The dreadful sights that confronted him made an indelible impression. He resolved to do something for the sailors who ventured so much on England's behalf.

That James II deserves credit for the idea of a Seamen's Hospital is indicated by a letter which the now elderly Samuel Pepys wrote to John Evelyn in

*John Rosedale, mariner, Exhibitor of the Hall of Greenwich Hospital.* Thomas Rowlandson shows one of the pensioners who acted as guides to the tourists viewing the Hospital – part of a tradition of visiting Greenwich that continues today.

*Opposite:* **Queen Mary II. The foundation of the Seamen's Hospital, proposed by her father James II, became a cherished project for her, particularly after the battle of La Hogue. Though she died of smallpox in 1694, before her vision could be fulfilled, it was implemented, as an act of remembrance, by her husband, William III.**

November 1694, referring to the deposed King as 'my unhappy Master'. He had done nothing to further it during the three years he occupied the throne. But the events that followed his leaving it in 1688, when he fled to France, revived the project in the mind of his tender-hearted daughter, Queen Mary II. England, now ruled by Mary and her Dutch husband William III, was at war again, this time forming an alliance with its former foe, Holland, against the forces of its former ally, France. The latter had been lent by Louis XIV in support of James II's attempts to regain the throne. The French ships were routed by a combined Anglo-Dutch fleet off Cape Barfleur, near Cherbourg, and the transports that had been prepared for the invasion of England were burnt in the bay of La Hogue. It was a triumph for the new order. There could now be no prospect of James's return. But the human cost was, as usual, appalling. King William III, with whom Mary shared the throne, was away fighting in the Low Countries. It was therefore left to Mary to do what she could to relieve the suffering of the wounded of the fleet now returned to Portsmouth. In the early hours of 21 May 1692, a messenger came galloping up to London with the news of the victory. While London celebrated, the practically-minded Queen assembled fifty surgeons from the hospitals there and despatched them to Portsmouth, along with £30,000 in bounty to be distributed among the crews. She also had her Secretary of State, Lord Nottingham, bestir the Treasury 'to hasten … the grant of Greenwich as a hospital for Seamen, which is now depending before you'.

In the end, the Hospital would be Queen Mary's memorial. She could probably not have achieved it during her life. William III was a soldier, without James II's personal involvement in naval life. The project would almost certainly have struck him as impossibly grandiose, at a time when he desperately needed money to pursue his resistance to the expansionist ambitions of Louis XIV. But the Queen's sudden death from smallpox in December 1694 opened his heart towards what had been 'the darling object of her life'. She had been popular with the English people; he, on the other hand, was not much loved. Maybe he hoped that a little of her aura would rub off on him. In any case, he could spare the palace at Greenwich better than other monarchs: being asthmatic, he could not live anywhere so watery. The charter to found a Hospital 'for the reliefe and support of Seamen serving on board the Shipps and Vessells belonging to the Navy Royall' was issued in the names of both William and Mary, and backdated to 25 October, before the Queen's death. Throughout its history the palace of Greenwich had been associated with Queens of England, often being given to them as a token of their husband's affection. Now the King's warmth towards Mary – rather greater than that of some previous monarchs towards their Queens – would be permanently embodied in the institution that was to rise on the site of the previous building.

To give the site showed generosity. And William also subscribed £2,000 towards building the Hospital 'as a further instance of Our Princely Zeal for advancing the Designe'. It was all too typical of the grandees who promised money for the project that this was slow to materialise. Hard evidence of the 'Princely Zeal' only arrived after building work had begun, in the summer of 1697. And then it did not take the form of cash, but of 'Malt Tickets', or credit vouchers against the tax on malt which the workmen would not accept at more than three-quarters of their face value. In these early years, the finances of the Hospital had to be cobbled together out of sometimes very little. Their parlous condition is at odds with the confident scale of the undertaking, planned around four handsome courts that could accommodate over two thousand veterans. The hero of the story is the man who sustained this vision through times when there was no money to realise it. In other words, the Treasurer, John Evelyn.

We encountered Evelyn in the last chapter, as Pepys's erudite friend, creating his garden, pursuing his scientific interests and writing his books at Sayes Court. Now he was an old man – seventy-four when he was appointed Treasurer of the Hospital in February 1694. That year he would let Sayes Court to Admiral Benbow, master of the fleet at La Hogue, who vacated the house to admit Peter the Great, staying at Deptford, remarkably enough, to study shipbuilding. Evelyn, despite his age, still had the energy necessary to pursue the project. It was one to which he had been committed for many years. As long ago as 1664, Charles II had appointed him to be one of three Commissioners for the Sick and Wounded and Prisoners of War, his area of responsibility being Sussex and Kent. Like Pepys, labouring in his office at the Navy Board, Evelyn took his duties seriously, and was active about them. He reserved half St Thomas's Hospital for the wounded who came from the fleet, and took over Chelsea College (to be considered as a possible site for the Royal Observatory) for Dutch prisoners. Apparently their only complaint, when Evelyn visited them, was that the bread was 'too fine'. He kept at it throughout the Plague. Later, he was presented to the King at Hampton Court, who

> in a most gracious manner gave me his hand to kiss, with many thanks for
> my care and faithfulness in his service in a time of such great danger, when
> every body fled their employments; he told me he was much obliged to me,
> and said he was several times concerned for me, and the peril I underwent,
> and did receive my service most acceptably (though in truth I did but do
> my duty, and O that I had performed it as I ought!)

The next month, February 1666, he went to Whitehall to put the idea of a permanent hospital for the sick and wounded before Charles II. The latter received Evelyn in his bedchamber, and warmly approved his proposal. Twelve days later he was again promoting the scheme:

To the Commissioners of the Navy who, having seen the project of the Infirmary, encouraged the work, and were very earnest it should be set about immediately; but I saw no money, though a very moderate expense would have saved thousands to his Majesty, and been much more commodious for the cure and quartering of our sick and wounded, than the dispersing them into private houses, where many more chirurgeons and attendants were necessary, and the people tempted to debauchery.

'I saw no money': that would become a recurring condition throughout Evelyn's long association with the Hospital. If there was little money at the beginning of 1666, there was even less at the end of it, for by then the Great Fire of London had made its overwhelming claim on whatever royal funds might be available for building. So nothing happened for fifteen years.

But the idea did not die, and in 1681 it was resurrected, albeit in a different form, by Evelyn's acquaintance, the philanthropist Sir Stephen Fox. Fox was Paymaster of the Forces; the office had, of course, made him extremely rich. He proposed that Chelsea College should be purchased from the Royal Society and converted into a hospital for four hundred soldiers. From the start, it was intended that this should not only cure the wounded but look after those who were too old or disabled to find further employment. As Evelyn recorded, they were 'to be as in a college or monastery'. At a time of such Anglo-French rivalry, the fact that Louis XIV had already built Les Invalides in Paris must have encouraged Charles II in his support of the project. Fox first sought Evelyn's help as a council member of the Royal Society, but, given Evelyn's enthusiasm for this sort of enterprise, it was not long before the two men were discussing how the institution would function. 'So, in his study we arranged the governor, chaplain, steward, house-keeper, chirurgeon, cook, butler, gardener, porter, and other officers, with their several salaries and entertainments,' he wrote on 27 January 1682. 'I would needs have a library, and mentioned several books, since some soldiers might possibly be studious, when they were at leisure to recollect.' Chelsea Hospital took ten years to build, just a fifth of the time it took to finish the much larger project at Greenwich. Its opening in 1692 reinvigorated the idea of creating a similar institution for sailors.

Many of the subscribers who had said they would give money to the Hospital never did so. The Grand Committee of sixty who were supposed to oversee the project were so grand that they hardly ever met. The burden of raising the money fell upon the aged shoulders of the Treasurer. His probity, which, to judge from the diaries, might have been mildly irritating to his contemporaries, was remarkable in an age when Treasurerships were generally regarded as a bonanza for those who possessed them. It was common practice – indeed expected – that a Treasurer would use the money in his keeping to further his own ventures, and that was perfectly in order so long as the capital was produced for its intended use when required (in the case of Chelsea Hospital, the Treasurer, Lord Ranelagh, did not produce it; and only narrowly escaped trial for embezzlement). In marked contrast to this, Evelyn never drew the salary to which he was entitled. Further, he himself gave £1,000 to the project – half as much as the King himself. The foundation stone was laid on 30 June 1696, with John Flamsteed, the Astronomer Royal, on hand, to observe the 'punctual time by instruments'. The extent of Evelyn's difficulties can be judged by the shortfall in the accounts at the end of the first year: receipts £800, expenditure £5,000.

Evelyn (and his successors as Treasurer) raked together money from wherever they could, their reach sometimes extending in unlikely directions. There was already a charitable fund for seamen called the Chatham Chest, built up from the sixpence a month that had been deducted from their wages each month since 1590. From 1696 another sixpence was taken for the Hospital (the Chatham Chest finally became amalgamated with the Hospital in 1814). Fines on French merchants who had been caught smuggling, about £10,500, were made over in 1697. Early in the next century, Captain William Kidd was brought to the scaffold for having killed a man (he struck him, according to the meticulously detailed indictment, 'with a certain wooden bucket bound with iron hoops of the value of eightpence') while on a ship called the *Adventure Galley*. It was a token charge; Kidd was a notorious pirate. His property was confiscated and given to the Hospital, contributing about £6,500. In 1700 Lord Romney, then Ranger of the Park, ceded the Hospital his right to establish a market in Greenwich: not an overwhelmingly attractive proposition, since it was over thirty years before the Directors of the Hospital did anything about it. A lottery was also staged, exceptionally, at a time when they were otherwise banned. In 1707 the Hospital was granted all the naval prize money from captured enemy vessels which went unclaimed; this was to provide a good income in the course of the next century, with its almost incessant fighting at sea. Rather more dependable was the solid £6,000 a year which Parliament provided from the revenues of the coal tax.

It says something about the gentlemen of substance who lived around Greenwich during the eighteenth century that one of their number, Robert Osboldston, left a bequest of £20,000 to the Hospital in 1714. Like many Greenwich figures, Osboldston derived his fortune from the sea, and he was an enterprising man, having built the North and South Foreland lighthouses. The Hospital also received the income of the dues collected from ships passing these lighthouses, worth £1,400 a year. From 1729 until the Hospital was finally completed in 1751, Parliament granted £10,000 a year towards construction. In the next century, it gave the Hospital a share of the Royal Navy's income from the practice of carrying gold and jewels for merchants.

Charm, diplomacy and persistence were required to amass the funds to carry on the building work. In the early 1730s, the then Governor of the Hospital, Admiral Sir John Jennings, personally paid for the great John Rysbrack to carve a statue of George II out of a large block of marble captured from a French ship. It was hauled on to its plinth in the very centre of the Hospital on 1 March 1735. Two months later the King would have seen it when he embarked for Hanover, earmarking a new German mistress for himself and a German bride for Frederick, Prince of Wales. There it was again when he came back. Not everyone liked it. Lord Egremont made the journey from Charlton House and found the statue 'not like him. His left hand is ill made and too large for his arm.' Whatever its merits as sculpture, it was undoubtedly a fine piece of flattery. And it worked. Before long the King made over the estates of an attractive young Catholic nobleman, Lord Derwentwater, who had joined the Jacobite uprising of 1715. These estates in the Lake District had been forfeited by Lord Derwentwater when he was beheaded as a traitor, though since they were entailed it took the Crown nearly twenty years to get its hands on them. They were of enormous value to the Hospital, producing an income that rose as their mineral wealth, particularly in coal and lead, was exploited: £7,000 initially, £25,000 in 1787 and £39,000 in 1859.

On 12 August 1703, Evelyn noted another momentous event: 'The new Commission for Greenwich Hospital was sealed and opened, at which my son-in-law, Draper, was present, to whom I resigned my office of Treasurer. From August 1696, there had been expended in building £89,364. 14s. 8d.' It was a typically modest entry; without the old man's fund-raising the Hospital would probably never have come into being, though it would still be two years before it received its first pensioners. When Evelyn died in 1706, it was found that the Hospital owed him money. The first forty-two pensioners had moved into the nearly completed King Charles Court, under Captain John Clements, in June 1705.

William Draper did not entirely justify his father-in-law's trust. Shortly after the accession of George I he was replaced as Treasurer by Captain Galfridus Walpole, brother of that rising star, the Paymaster of the Forces Robert Walpole. It was an early example of the sort of political job that would become a notorious feature of Walpole's glory days as Prime Minister. Alas, it was discovered that Draper had, apparently with permission, put some of the Hospital's money to work for him by investing it with a goldsmith called Mr Coggs. Coggs had gone bankrupt. There was a hole of £3,000 in the accounts when Draper handed over to Walpole, and he was prosecuted. He died, but the prosecution continued against his estate. His executors promised to pay from investments that had been made with the South Sea Company. But the South Sea Bubble burst, and the Hospital never saw its money again. It is a tale of financial misadventure rather than excessive venality – by the standards of the time, at least. The contrast invests John Evelyn's name with an almost saintly glow.

\* \* \*

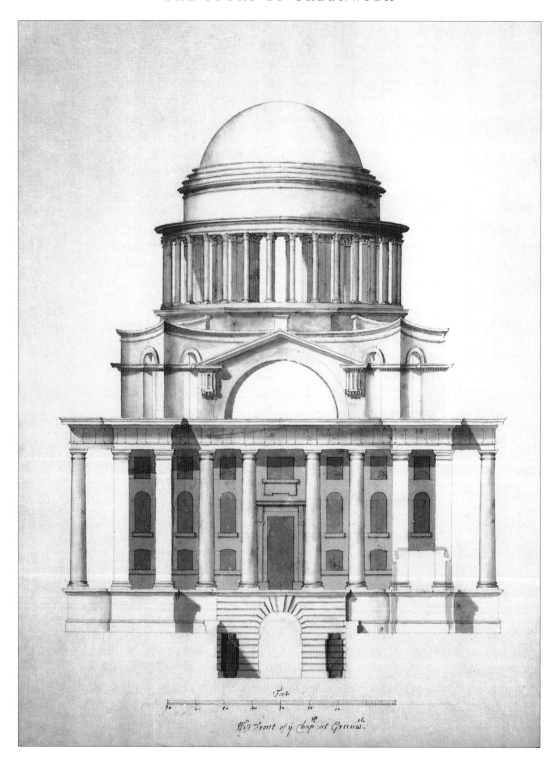

Feet

West Front of y Chap. at Greenw.

By the time Wren inspected the site of the Seamen's Hospital, with Samuel Pepys, in the autumn of 1694, he had become the grand old man of English architecture. He must have been a formidable presence. A gentleman by birth, twice widowed, he had reached the top of two highly reputable callings, science and architecture. He had been President of the Royal Society. He had been Surveyor to the King's Works for as much as twenty-five years. Not only had he taken the leading role in refashioning London after the Great Fire, designing its new cathedral and dozens of churches, but he had come to know all the most important figures of his time, including a succession of monarchs. Pepys, writing to Evelyn, gives Wren the credit for elevating the notion of a hospital for the wounded sailors coming from recent wars into a great and permanent national memorial: 'an *Invalides* with

us for the sea, suitable in some degree to that of Paris for the land.' Something of the rather overwhelming dignity of the man is conveyed through the prose of his son, also Christopher Wren, who describes Wren's involvement at Greenwich in his filial memoir *Parentalia*:

*Above:* **Sir Christopher Wren, painted by Kneller in 1711, was principal architect of the Seamen's Hospital. By 1694, when he first inspected the site, he had been Surveyor of the King's Works for a quarter of a century.**

> he Chearfully engag'd in the Work, gratis, and contriv'd the new Fabrick, extensive, durable, and magnificent, conformable to the graceful Pavilion, which had been erected there by King Charles the Second, and originally intended for his own Palace; contributing his Time, Labour, and Skill, and prosecuting the Works for several Years, with all the Expedition the Circumstances of Affairs would allow; without any Salary, Emolument or Reward (which good Example, tis to be hoped, has been since follow'd;) preferring in this, as in every other Passage of his Life, the public Service to any private Advantage of his own, by the Acquest of Wealth, of which he had always a great Contempt.

Christopher Wren junior must have known that his successor, Vanbrugh, did not scruple to take a handsome salary for his involvement, even though he made very little contribution to the design. But then Wren belonged to a different generation, a different age.

The day-to-day running of the project was delegated to Wren's lifetime Clerk of Works, Nicholas Hawksmoor. When Hawksmoor had the task, many years

*Opposite:* **Sketch by Hawksmoor for a central chapel that would have formed the centrepiece of the hospital, but was never built. As an act of piety to Queen Mary's Stuart forebears, the Queen's House was preserved as the culmination of the main axis.**

later, of justifying the long and costly construction to Parliament, he emphasised Queen Mary's desire for 'Magnificence'. The ear attuned to the particular music of Greenwich may hear in this an echo of Henry VIII's priorities in his development of Placentia. It was to maximise on 'Magnificence' that various other sites that had been proposed for the Hospital – Winchester Castle and elsewhere – were rejected, since they were 'both out of the way, and not frequently seen', while Greenwich was 'in the View of all the World ... [a] noble Situation in the Sight of (the Grand Emporium) London'. But that was in 1727, and Hawksmoor was sensitive to criticisms that the Hospital, which had swelled somewhat in architectural conception, was too ostentatious.

No doubt Queen Mary valued the site, as her predecessors had done, for its prominence on the river, one of the first things that arriving foreigners would see. With that in mind, she did not surrender the Queen's House, which continued in use as a royal staging post on the way to London long into the eighteenth century – despite the oddity of having a royal residence in the midst of a Hospital, albeit a very imposing one. But an equal consideration was thrift. In the last chapter we saw how the one range of Charles II's palace to have been built served as offices for Pepys and his colleagues in the Navy Board during the Plague. In more recent years it had been pressed into service as a gunpowder store, and the upper windows blocked up. According to Hawksmoor, 'workmen' (presumably builders and surveyors) came from London to assess whether the King Charles Block was worth keeping.

> They, as it is indifferent to all Workmen whether they get Money by
> destroying or erecting Fabricks, gave their Opinion that it was nothing but
> a Heap of Stones, and that it might lawfully and reasonably be destroyed,
> and turn'd into Ornaments for slight Buildings, such as the private Hotels,
> or the Houses commonly built by the London Workmen, often burning,
> and frequently tumbling down.

This advice was put to the Queen. But she insisted that it should be retained, as well as the Queen's House which did not form part of the Hospital grant. She became quite agitated about it. Or as Hawksmoor rather charmingly recounts: 'her Majesty received the Proposal of pulling down that Wing, with as much Indignation as her excellent good Temper would suffer her, order'd it should remain, and the other Side of the Royal Court made answerable to it, in a proper Time ... There was no Argument for its being taken down could prevail.' On 24 May 1695, Evelyn records: 'We made report of the state of Greenwich House, and how the standing part might be made serviceable at present for £6000.'

Furthermore, the Queen was equally emphatic that the view, or 'visto', to the river which the Queen's House had enjoyed since the demolition of the Tudor palace should also be retained. How can this be explained? Queen Mary, after all, was a Stuart. She had the Stuarts' attachment to family history. It is unlikely that she regarded the Queen's House with the reverence that it would later be accorded by architects and historians, on grounds of style. Her wish to preserve it must have been based on its status as a Stuart icon – that and economy. Modern-day conservationists should make Queen Mary their patron saint.

The retention of the King Charles Block and the vista from the Queen's House determined Sir Christopher's Wren's plan. He had hoped, initially, to replace the Queen's House with an elaborate centrepiece, in the form of the chapel with a dome almost on the scale of St Paul's, around which the courts in front of it, to either side, would be constructed. This desire remained current into the era of his successor at Greenwich, John Vanbrugh. It was never effected. As a result, the focal point of the grandest parade of baroque architecture in Britain is a small, chastely rectangular house, designed as a garden caprice, an afterthought almost to the long-vanished medieval palace. There is, as the author of the Wren Society volume on Greenwich observes, 'something peculiarly English' about this outcome. Canaletto thought the Queen's House so deficient in presence that he gave it a pediment, which it never possessed, when he painted his famous view of Greenwich Hospital. In the nineteenth century James Dallaway, in his *Observations on English Architecture*, wrote that Greenwich Hospital 'consists of two palaces, exactly repeated, and appearing as wings without a body'. Architecturally it may be deficient; as a gesture of piety towards the early seventeenth-century monarchs who created the Queen's House it resounds with emotion.

**Greenwich Hospital from the north bank of the Thames by Jacques Rigaud, 1736. This engraving appears to have been used by Canaletto in preparing his famous view of 1755. However, Rigaud does not make Canaletto's unexpected error of adding a pediment to the Queen's House.**

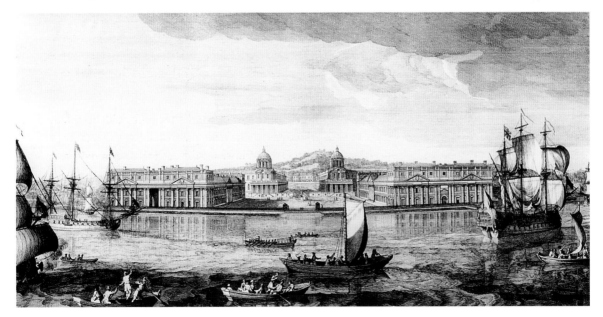

Canaletto's view of Greenwich, 1755. Nothing captures the dignity and splendour of the project so well as this painting. One would hardly guess that the buildings had taken fifty-five years to finish, amid constant anxieties about money.

Wren built up to, and sometimes over, the boundaries of the eight-acre site. (The Hospital was always short of room to expand.) The building went on fitfully, encountering many of the difficulties to which building sites have always been subject along the way. To begin with, work on refitting the King Charles Block, in the north-east corner, raced ahead; and in the summer of 1696 the foundations of a parallel range were being dug. In February 1697, a quantity of lead was stolen, as a result of which a mastiff dog was purchased for £1 2s, with a 4s 6d collar. The Committee for the Fabrick paid a visit of inspection. They were the only sub-committee of the three constituted for the prosecution of work at Greenwich to get anything done; perhaps as a consequence, they felt they could treat themselves royally. The accounts record the bill of fare: four ribs of beef, a leg of mutton, six chickens, ten half-flasks of wine. As Clerk to the Surveyor General, Wren, Nicholas Hawksmoor was paid £20 for making architectural drawings. Early the next year, Wren was asked to submit a drawing and estimate for a hall to be added to the scheme. In the summer, the existing Clerk of Works died and Hawksmoor was appointed in his place. He was expected to live on site, his reward being 4s a day in addition to the £50 a year he received as Clerk to the Surveyor-General. John James, who would design the steeple of St Alfege's Church in Greenwich in 1730, and boasted that there was 'no person pretending to Architecture among us, Sir Chr. Wren excepted, [who] has had the advantage of a better Education in the Latin, Italian and French tongues', was appointed to the seemingly unglamorous position of watchman. Soon the foundations of the Great Hall and cupola, south of the King Charles Block, were getting along, and the terrace wall had been begun.

There were difficulties over the supply of stone: so much of it being needed for St Paul's Cathedral, then also rising. The royal quarry at Portland was at full stretch. Hawksmoor was despatched to Kent, Yorkshire and elsewhere to supplement the Portland stone. Bricks were supplied by that all-round shady individual, Daniel Defoe, best known as the author of *Robinson Crusoe*. By the end of 1699 Wren's design had been engraved, the interior of the King Charles Block was being fitted out and the terrace, or part of it, had been constructed. Then, in 1702, King William died, and Queen Anne appointed a new Commission to direct operations. (It was at this point that John Evelyn handed over the Treasurership to his son-in-law, William Draper.) The Commission included the Prince of Denmark, the Archbishop of Canterbury and other luminaries – soon to be joined by the playwright, man of fashion and now Comptroller of the Office of Works (the post

Daniel Defoe. In the course of a somewhat chequered career, the author of *Robinson Crusoe* at one point owned part of a brick factory at Tilbury. As such he supplied bricks to Greenwich Hospital, the accounts of which first mention his name in 1701. Payments continued until 1703, when he had to give up brick-making due to imprisonment at Newgate.

immediately beneath that of Surveyor of Works), John Vanbrugh. Not that Vanbrugh had very much, if anything, to do with the design of the Hospital at this stage: later he succeeded Wren as Surveyor at Greenwich, for which he claimed the salary that Wren had nobly foregone; but by then the design was more or less fixed. Instead, Hawksmoor's name appears with increased prominence in the accounts. Poor John James was promoted from watchman to assistant to the Clerk of Works. But the labour went on slowly for want of funds. In 1707 Wren wrote to the secretary at the Hospital – who happened to be William Vanbrugh, cousin of the architect – excusing himself from attending a meeting of the Commissioners, on the grounds that it clashed with another Commissioners' meeting about St Paul's. He comments: 'The best business wherein the Commission of the Fabrick of Greenwich can employ their time is to consult of money.'

No doubt they did so, but it did not dim their optimism. That year they commissioned an eager James Thornhill, then thirty-two years old, to paint the ceiling of the Great Hall. He left it to the Board to pay him as they believed appropriate: an arrangement which inevitably led to wrangling once Thornhill's great allegorical scheme – the first on this scale by a British painter – was completed. At this time the name of 'Mr Tejous' appears in the books: presumably this was Jean Tijou, the great Huguenot ironworker. So plans were being laid for embellishment. But little actual building was going on in these years and it was even proposed to abolish the office of Surveyor 'since there has been an order to cease the progress of building'. Posterity must be grateful that they would not compromise Queen Mary's idea of 'Magnificence', however provoking the circumstances. In 1711 it was decided that the apparently serviceable pavilion which had already been constructed beside the King Charles II wing should be taken down and rebuilt in stone.

When Vanbrugh became Surveyor in Wren's place most matters of detail had already been referred to Hawksmoor, who now had a house in Greenwich. Vanbrugh's contribution lay elsewhere. His touch can perhaps be detected in the petition, signed by him and other directors, which was presented to Parliament in 1723:

> As to the building it is a great concern to us to observe that a work so pious in design and so much tending to the reputation of the Kingdom should be now standing to the view of the world as a kind of National reproach from the imperfect figure it makes. It is seven and twenty years since the building was first begun, and notwithstanding the taking in part of King Charles' Palace which lay ready built to hand the structure is not yet two-thirds advanced, the charge whereof has already stood in about £227,000, and by estimation it will require about £150,000 more to finish it; but the work has been for some time past at a total stand for want of money.

The case could hardly have been put better.

## Thornhill's Ceiling in the Painted Hall

James Thornhill, the son of an impoverished Dorset gentleman, set out to prove himself a home-grown alternative to the fashionable French and Italian painters who were decorating the salons and staircases of the aristocracy. He saw the Painted Hall at Greenwich as a superb opportunity to advertise his talents as a history painter, and did not seek to be paid for the labour until it was finished. (This inevitably led to a dispute over how much he deserved to be paid, the price eventually being calculated by the square yard: £3 for the ceiling and £1 for the walls.) Begun in 1708, his ceiling took him nineteen years to complete. Afterwards he was knighted – the first British-born painter to be so – and amassed sufficient wealth to be able to purchase the old seat of his family at Thornhill in Dorset and become a Member of Parliament.

Thornhill did not enjoy an entirely happy reputation among contemporaries. Vanbrugh belittled his attempt, in 1719, to obtain the office of Royal Architect:

Twou'd be a pleasant Joke to the World, to See a Painter made Surveyor of the Works, in Order to Save money; When all the Small knowledge or tast they ever have of it, is only in the Great expensive part, as Collumns, Arches, Bas reliefs &c which they just learn enough of, to help fill up their Pictures. But to think that Such a Volatile Gentleman as Thornhill, Shou'd turn his thoughts & Application to the duty of a Surveyors business, is a Monstruous project.

**Sir James Thornhill's sketch of John Worley, the model for winter in the ceiling of the Painted Hall. Despite his venerable appearance, this ancient seaman could still misbehave, being put in the 'confining house' for swearing and getting drunk at the age of ninety-six.**

Vanbrugh died in 1726. His place at Greenwich was taken by the neo-Palladian Colen Campbell, a Scot who had several rich and influential patrons, including the now Prime Minister Sir Robert Walpole. But the familiar problem returned, and the year after Campbell's appointment lack of money caused work to stop altogether. On Campbell's death in 1729 Walpole put in place his protégé, Thomas Ripley. It was patronage of this kind that had enabled Ripley to rise to a position of some prominence in the eyes of his contemporaries, though not of esteem. His origins had been so poor that he is supposed to have walked to London from his

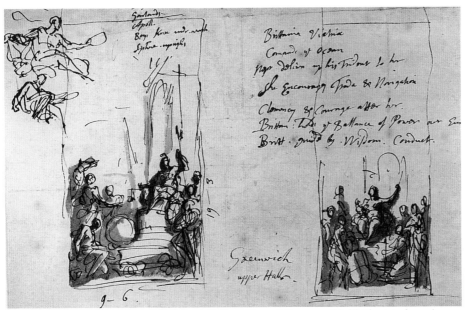

*Above:* 'Brittania Victoria Commands ye Ocean. Nep. delivers up his Trident to her…'
Preparatory sketch by Thornhill for the Painted Hall, with jottings of the iconography.

*Below:* A portrait of Thornhill attributed to his assistant Dietrich André, from the Painted Hall.

(Which is a bit rich, considering that Vanbrugh began life as a soldier and playwright.)

From 1708 Thornhill's work caused pensioners' meals to be permanently moved to kitchen level in the vaults below. Later they were also served in the under-Chapel. The Painted Hall was given over to the many visitors who flocked to see it, buying a printed description, supplied by Thornhill, from the hall-keeper. Later it became a picture gallery. It never resumed its function as a dining-room during the time of the Seamen's Hospital.

native Yorkshire to seek his fortune. Once there, he seems quickly to have established himself as a carpenter, being admitted to the Carpenters' Company at the age of eighteen in 1705. These humble beginnings could not be concealed by later pretension. When in 1721 Vanbrugh saw his name in a newspaper, followed by the honorific Esquire, 'such a Laugh came upon me, I had like to Beshit my Self'. His association with Walpole had been cemented by marriage to one of his servants, and the flagrant political jobbery by which his career progressed – the summit of which was the unfortunate portico that he added to the Admiralty

building in Whitehall – caused derision at the hands, and pens, of those who aligned themselves against the administration. Pope had a go, not just once but three times. The anti-Ripley passion came on him at six-yearly intervals. Thus in the *Epistle to the Earl of Burlington* of 1731:

> Heav'n visits with a taste the wealthy fool,
> And needs no rod but Ripley with a rule.

In the Imitations of Horace of 1737:
> Who builds a bridge that never drove a pile?
> (Should Ripley venture, all the world would smile).

And in the Dunciad of 1743:
> See under Ripley rise a new White-hall,
> While Jones' and Boyle's united labours fall.

In view of such an onslaught, it is satisfactory to see that Ripley's Surveyorship at Greenwich was something of a success. He may not have been much of an architect, but he was a capable organiser and businessman. In the year that he assumed the position, Parliament granted £10,000 a year for continuing the work. Hawksmoor, so loyal to Greenwich, so badly used by Ripley's appointment, resigned three years later. But nothing would now stop the progress of building. With the windfall of the Derwentwater estates, the Hospital fairly sailed forward to completion. Queen Mary's Block arose as almost a mirror to King William's, with only the east side being altered by Ripley to give more accommodation. Finally, fifty-five years after the foundation stone had been laid, the Hospital was finished. Beneath the domes, behind the columns, pilasters and porticos, moved the blue-coated figures of seventeen hundred pensioners, for whose accommodation this masterpiece of English architecture had been achieved.

\* \* \*

'The English say that their palaces are like hospitals, and their hospitals like palaces; and the exterior of St James's and of Greenwich justifies this saying.' Ostensibly the author of these words was Don Manuel Alvarez Espriella; in reality the Don's *Letters from England*, 1807, were written by the poet Robert Southey, who sheltered behind an exotic pseudonym in order to reflect freely upon the customs of his fellow countrymen. In the case of Greenwich, though, his observation was something of a commonplace. The Hospital was quite obviously much grander than any of the palaces owned by the royal family; the contrast with the beautifully proportioned but nevertheless miniature Queen's House, which *was* a palace, only emphasised the point. It is unlikely that Southey read James

*Opposite:* **The Painted Hall. The central oval of the ceiling shows William III and Queen Mary giving peace and liberty to Europe; they are attended by appropriate allegorical figures, along with ships, trophies and astronomers, all in a rich architectural setting. On the west wall George I and his family are shown in front of the dome of St Paul's. Other scenes on the general theme of British maritime power occupy the other walls, coves and vestibule.**

Bramston's *The Man of Taste*, published more than seventy years before *Letters from England*: Bramston was scarcely Southey's kind of a poet. But Bramston made just the same point:

To lofty *Chelsea* or to Greenwich *Dome*,
Soldiers and sailors all are welcom'd home.
Her poor to palaces *Britannia* brings,
St. *James*'s hospital may serve for Kings ...

It was the sort of paradox of which a Briton could be proud.

It was also regarded as one up on the French: Greenwich was thought to be at least as splendid as Les Invalides, probably more so. Thus Valentine Green, in *A Review of the Polite Arts in France ... Compared with their Present State in England* of 1782: 'L'Hotel Royal des Invalides, at Paris, may exult in its beautiful dome, and glory in the munificence of its foundation, without hurting our feelings, while

the Royal Hospital of Greenwich can vie with their Palaces in magnificence ...'
'Magnificence' again. But where did this leave the men who inhabited the
Hospital? One of them was John Worley. This nonagenarian looked so venerable,
with his white hair and patriarchal beard, that Thornhill made him the model for a
depiction of winter on his great ceiling. He had spent seventy years at sea.
Seafaring did not, however, inculcate the best drawing-room manners, and at the
age of ninety-six he could still misbehave, using foul language and getting drunk.
His punishment was to be 'put in the confining house for four days and each meal
to be exposed on the elevated place in the hall, and to live on bread and water for
a week, and to wear the badge for swearing, to lose two sennights' allowance
money, and not to go out of the Hospital for one month from that date'. There
was no lash; otherwise naval discipline was maintained, with naval severity.

\* \* \*

Rigaud's view of Greenwich from Castle Hill, about 1750. In the foreground are some of the visitors for whom the Royal Observatory was an excursion. Below the hill, the trees planted by Charles II are reaching maturity.

*Opposite:* **Ballad of 'The Greenwich Pensioner', written and composed by Mr Charles Dibdin. After an adventurous career at sea, the Pensioner can still participate in life – 'Altho' I'm quite disabled, And lie in Greenwich tier.'**

*Below:* **Admiral Sir Thomas ('Kismet') Hardy, shown as a captain in 1807. Buried at Greenwich, he lends his name to the Admiral Hardy pub.**

The naval feeling was continued, more acceptably perhaps, in their dress and lodgings. The pensioners of Greenwich Hospital had a uniform before even the navy itself: first grey, then brown, finally blue. Originally the coat was accompanied by knee-breeches but these were replaced by trousers in the 1830s, during the governorship of Sir Thomas Hardy. (This was the Hardy who had been Nelson's flag-captain at Trafalgar, immortalised as the recipient of his famous dying words. By the time he became Governor of Greenwich Hospital in 1834 he was First Sea Lord and soon to become a vice-admiral. In popular prints the pensioners are invariably depicted as peg-legged, missing arms or blind. 'Do all Englishmen have only one arm or one leg?' inquired the future Queen Caroline, with typically misplaced humour, on disembarking at Greenwich in 1795. She perhaps deserved Lady Jersey's tart reply: 'No persiflage, Madame, if you please' – though the latter's asperity owed more to her position as the Prince of Wales's mistress (he had unaccountably dispatched her to meet his bride) than to sensitivity towards the gallant seamen. The wars against France had increased the numbers of *mutilés de guerre*; but there were also many destitute pensioners who were simply too old or feeble to go back to sea.

The four courts of the Hospital were divided into wards that perpetuated the names of great warships and admirals. In 1700 J. How described a visit to the King Charles Court, still unfinished but nevertheless full of pensioners – 'a means,' as he observed satirically, 'to Encourage others hereafter to venture their Limbs in the Nations Service, to be rewarded with a Lazy Life, no Money, and short Commons'. Every pensioner was 'design'd a distinct Cabbin to himself, and was allotted a little more room than he is like to Enjoy in the Church-Yard'. For all How's mockery, he cannot conceal the fact that, by the standards of the poor of the day, Greenwich afforded a high level of privacy. Later, the principle of separate cabins was not universally maintained, and some berths were provided in small dormitories. This may not have been anathema to the inhabitants: at Chelsea Hospital a similar seventeenth-century arrangement has to this day been preserved by the general wish of the pensioners, who appreciate the sense of camaraderie that it generates. The German visitor Sophie

The GREENWICH PENSIONER.
By Mr. DIBDIN.

'Twas in the good ship Rover,
    I sail'd the World around,
And for three years and over,
    I ne'er touch'd British ground.
At last in England landed,
    I left the roaring main;
Found all relations stranded,
    And went to Sea again.

That time bound strait to Portugal,
    Right fore and aft we bore;
But, when we made Cape Ortugal,
    A gale blew off the shore,
She lay, so it did shock her,
    A log upon the main,
Till saved from Davy's locker,
    We put to Sea again.

Next in a Frigate sailing
    Upon a squally night,
Thunder and lightening hailing
    The horrors of the fight,
My precious limb was lopped off,
    I, when they'd eased my pain,
Thanked God I was not popped off,
    And went to Sea again.

Yet still I am enabled
    To bring up in life's rear,
Altho' I'm quite disabled,
    And lie in Greenwich tier,
The King, God bless his royalty,
    Who saved me from the main;
I'll praise with love and loyalty,
    But ne'er to Sea again.

Published by N. Carpenter, 60 Spencer St London.

von la Roche was favourably impressed when she visited in 1786, recording an attractive account in her diary:

All shipshape: a pensioner's cabin, from the *Illustrated London News*, 1865. The peg-legged veteran is surrounded by mementoes of his travels. Reading was one of the few diversions available to pensioners.

Their dormitories are very pleasant: large, light and lofty, with cubicles containing glass windows on the side, where each has his own bed, small table, chair, wardrobe, tea and smoking outfit which he can lock up. No humanitarian with a philosophical turn of mind could be indifferent to the way in which they decorate their cubicles: a number of them have sea and land charts, with the voyages they have made marked out on them, or spots where storms have been overcome or battles fought, where they have lost an arm or a leg, or conquered an enemy ship, and so on; others have stuck figures of every nationality on cardboard, others of strange beasts in foreign lands, while a number have collected books in several languages with which they amuse themselves.

The corridors are wide enough to admit of eight people walking abreast. It is all beautifully panelled and the floor is covered with rugs. In the centre of each passage there stands a large fireplace around which a crowd of men were sitting; two of them had a bench in the corridor, where they sat astride, leaning up against each other at play; and beneath it was a chamber (in good old English fashion) for their mutual use, so as they should not have to leave their labours.

Everything is spotless. Each man has two white shirts weekly, and a hundred and four women are employed to do the laundry and keep the place clean.

In contrast to the men's shipshape little cabins, the Governor occupied a pavilion containing twenty-two bedrooms.

So far from being the 'short Commons' cited by How, the pensioners' diet seems remarkable for its abundance, certainly as regards meat. Every man was allowed a pound of beef or mutton (generally boiled, sometimes roast) on each of five days of the week. On the pease pottage days of Wednesday and Friday they were given a double ration of cheese (half a pound). There was not much in the way of vegetables, and the shrinkage of cheese when it was stored caused much controversy: what would have been half a pound when it arrived at the Hospital sometimes weighed rather less by the time it was served. Still, whatever gripes the pensioners had generally seem to have concerned quality of preparation rather than quantity of supply. They were served by some of their own number who earned pocket-money by doing so. The officers ate at their own tables. The minutes of the Directors' meeting provide an interesting footnote on the history of dining habits: 'Tablecloths belonging to the Officers' Tables to be enlarged so as to be used without Napkins and more to be bought so as to be clean each day.'

Originally, there was no provision for recreation of any kind. It was not until 1828 that a library and reading-room were created. Boredom must have been one reason why pensioners – such as ancient John Worley – fell victim to the temptations of the town. Those who misbehaved were compelled to wear yellow uniforms which gave them the name of canaries.

Remembering Nelson: Trafalgar Day, 1835, by S. P. Denning, after John Burnet. Most of the pensioners here served with Nelson, including his servant Tom Allen (left, with portrait).

'And for the Sustenation of the Widows and the Maintenance and Education of the Children of Seamen happening to be slain or disabled …' So read the words of the original charter. Eventually the Hospital did employ a teacher, whose first classes seem to have been in 1715. Out of this developed a regular Hospital school. But the needs of widows were never adequately met. Some found employment in the Hospital as nurses: six of them to every hundred men. Typically, great attention was paid to the design of the uniforms, though when a stock of them arrived they were found to be too tight. (As Philip Newell comments in his history of Greenwich Hospital, 'this in itself was a testimonial to the catering'.) But in general women were scarcely more welcome within the precincts of Greenwich Hospital – welcome, that is, by the authorities who ran it – than they were on board ship. There were, for example, no wives. As a result, many pensioners preferred to take their food allowance as a cash payment, which enabled them to help support their families in the town rather than live in the Hospital itself. Eventually this practice became more and more popular, until payment replaced the residential functioning of the Hospital altogether.

For all that, the American Nathaniel Hawthorne, to whom the pensioners were a common sight when he lived on Blackheath, delivered a positive verdict in *Our Old Home*. It is all the more striking because he viewed many British institutions and practices sourly. But the Hospital was one that he believed could be emulated in the

**The Painted Hall in the Victorian period. Following George IV's gift of thirty portraits of naval commanders, it became one of the first public art galleries in London.**

## Morden College

In 1669 Sir John Morden, a merchant trading in Turkey and the Levant, bought an estate in Greenwich, and twenty-six years later founded Morden College as an almshouse for 'decayed Turkey merchants'. By this time Morden was one of the Commissioners for the Naval Hospital, so the architect may well have been Wren. There is nothing to prove this; however, the mason was Edward Stone, whom Wren favoured. Certainly the building is a successful essay in the Wren style, with warm red brick, stone dressings, and enough classical detail to give dignity but not so much as to overwhelm this relatively small edifice. The double-hung sash windows are an early example of a form that would become standard for London houses for two centuries. There is a little decorative cupola over the pediment. Inside, the 'decayed' merchants each had a bedroom, sitting room and the shared use of a bath-room and kitchen. The object, according to Daniel Defoe, was that they should be able to live as gentlemen, though money dictated that the scale on which they could do so was rather more constricted than originally hoped.

**Johannes Kip's bird's-eye view of Morden College, about 1710.**

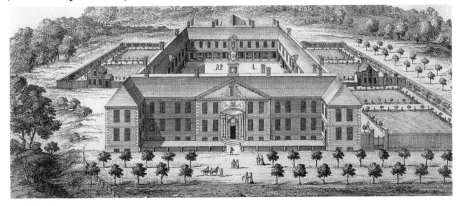

United States. He saw it shortly before its closure in 1865. 'It seemed to me that the Greenwich pensioners,' he recalled in *Our Old Home*, 'are the petted children of the nation, and that the government is their dry-nurse, and that the old men themselves have a childlike consciousness of their position. Very likely, a better sort of life might have been arranged, and a wiser care bestowed on them; but, such as it is, it enables them to spend a sluggish careless, comfortable old age, grumbling, growling, gruff, as if all the foul weather of their past years were pent up within them, yet not much more discontented than such weather-beaten and battle-battered fragments of human-kind must inevitably be.' He concluded: 'Their chief discomfort is probably for lack of something to do or think about.'

# 'Athenian' Stuart's Chapel

In the early morning of 2 January 1779, a fire broke out at Greenwich Hospital which, according to the *Annual Register*, 'burned most furiously'. The water tanks on top of the building were, as bad luck would have it, almost empty, so pensioners formed themselves into a human chain to pass buckets of water from the Thames. It was no good. 'At ten o'clock, the Chapel (the most beautiful in the kingdom), the dome on the south-east quarter of the building, and the great dining-hall, were entirely consumed.' Several of the wards were destroyed, and for a time the Painted Hall was in danger. At eleven o'clock some fire engines arrived from London. But the fire blazed until evening. 'The damage done is immense, and it will cost a very large sum to restore that part of the Hospital to its former beauty and elegance.'

A new chapel was built to the designs of James Stuart, the Hospital's Surveyor. The son of a Scottish seaman, he first trained as a fan painter, but his life changed after he made the journey, largely on foot, to Rome. With one of the English *dilettanti* there, Nicholas Revett, he formed a plan to record and publish *The Antiquities of Athens*.

**Fire consumes the chapel in 1779.**

When the Hospital finally moved, its buildings were left empty until occupied by the Royal Naval College in 1873, filling the great spaces with young cadets from the other end of the naval age spectrum. In 1997 that in turn closed, in a government attempt to save money – which could turn out to be much more expensive than the old arrangements – to concentrate navy, army and air-force training in a new Joint-Services College. The new occupants will be Greenwich

The new chapel designed by Athenian Stuart and William Newton, engraved after Thomas Malton about 1790.

Unlike Rome, Athens was then little visited by foreigners and virtually unknown at home. The resulting volumes caused great excitement among people of taste, offering the promise of a new grammar of ornament to gentlemen and their architects, as well as new prototypes for their buildings (initially follies). The Chapel at Greenwich is one of the few complete Greek Revival interiors to have been created. 'It is to be observed,' wrote William Newton, Stuart's Clerk of Works, 'that the greater part of the aforesaid works are of a kind & in a Style not in common use So that every thing was to be Studied & Invented, not only the Designs of the Several parts & Members, but even in many Cases the Methods of executing them.' Stuart, temperamentally indolent and now at the end of his life, left much of this detail to Newton.

Benjamin West painted an appropriately nautical altarpiece in *The Preservation of St Paul after Shipwreck at Malta*. But generally one has to look twice to spot the chapel's Christian imagery, amid so much Grecian ornament.

University (formerly the Polytechnic of East London) and the National Maritime Museum. We have yet to see whether the University, which is the principal tenant of a new management trust, the Greenwich Foundation for the Royal Naval College, will maintain the naval tradition of shipshape smartness preserved throughout the three-hundred-year history of these great buildings.

Greenwich was the place where many important foreign visitors first put to shore in England. It was also one of the sights that tourists made a point of seeing. Jeanne-Marie Roland, wife of the French Minister of the Interior, was typical in her approval of both the architecture and the charitable purpose behind it. 'We reached Greenwich,' she wrote in 1784, 'the largest and finest edifice that I have yet seen in this country. Two superb ranges of buildings with great colonnades of the Doric order, form the mass of it; the common halls are extensive and magnificent; the small apartments are agreeable, and very airy; cleanliness, order and attention give life to the whole ... How much is the soul elevated and softened, when we see these magnificent establishments formed by the will of the citizens, offering their fortunes towards the relief of their defenders!' (Her Republican sympathies did not prevent her from losing her head during the Terror some years afterwards.)

*London from Greenwich Park* by J. M. W. Turner, exhibited in 1809. The domes of the hospital find an echo in St Paul's.

*Top: **Woolwich Naval Dockyard**, 1790.*

*Left: **HMS** Buckingham on the stocks at Deptford.*

During the Napoleonic Wars, the dockyards of Chatham, Portsmouth and Plymouth overtook those of Woolwich and Deptford. Nevertheless, the latter remained a major naval presence and were large employers. They continued as building yards long after the increased draught of warships made it impossible for them to take on stores so far up the Thames.

# SIR JOHN VANBRUGH PLAYS AT CASTLES

O NE OF THE MANY PEOPLE who crowded into the last chapter as Greenwich Hospital was being built was John Vanbrugh. As the Surveyor who succeeded Christopher Wren, he did not leave much impression on the architecture of the Hospital; but he did embellish another area of Greenwich – Maze Hill, just to the east of the Park. He built at least five houses there, one of them for himself. In some ways they were an idiosyncratic ensemble. But they also represented a revolution in taste. So remarkable were they that it is worth digressing on the subject of Vanbrugh's early life in order to understand this contribution to Greenwich.

Vanbrugh, nearly forty, had turned to architecture only three or four years before being made a Director of Greenwich Hospital in 1703. His appointment is evidence of the speed with which this dazzling man established himself as an authority on architecture and taste. He had already had several careers. The only unsuccessful one had been his first. The son of a Chester linen merchant, his unusual surname reflecting the origins of his family in Flanders, the young John Vanbrugh tried his hand at soldiering – in his case, the resort of a twenty-two-year-old who did not have much idea of what to do. He may have come to it by accident, having approached Lord Huntingdon, a kinsman, to see if he would give him a job. As Vanbrugh's biographer, Kerry Downes, observes, he can hardly have expected that the result of his request would be the offer of a commission as ensign in Huntingdon's newly formed regiment. Vanbrugh took it, but, for once, does not seem to have shone.

Vanbrugh's late twenties were spent languishing in a series of French jails, following his arrest at Calais for lack of the correct papers. France was going to war with Holland, and he appeared to bear a Dutch name. Once he was incarcerated, the French formed the opinion that he was a valuable property (those noble connections) and sought to trade him for a Frenchman imprisoned in London. But poor Vanbrugh was not, at that stage, of much interest to anyone. He was twenty-nine when he was released, having wasted four or five years behind bars. Within a few years, however, he had written a witty, worldly, to some people scandalous play called *The Relapse, or Virtue in Danger*. It was his first attempt for the theatre: he claimed to have written it in six weeks. From the moment the curtain went up on Boxing Day 1696, the London audience relished its urbane saltiness. Vanbrugh was a celebrity.

Sir John Vanbrugh, soldier, playwright, herald and architect, painted by Thomas Murray in 1718. He built a mock castle for himself, as well as other buildings for his family, next to Greenwich Park.

175

His career as an author continued, his greatest hit being his second play, *The Provok'd Wife*. His natural conviviality now had the outlet that had been denied it during his incarceration in France. In 1701 he built a house, rather miniature, in one of the grandest and most prominent locations in London: the grounds of the old Palace of Whitehall. The poet and satirist Jonathan Swift likened Vanbrugh's building to 'a Goose-pie', and it was known as Goose-pie House ever after. There is some doubt as to what exactly constituted a goose pie in the first years of the eighteenth century. The dish was probably known for its curious shape and ingredients. We can be sure that Swift meant no compliment. And Goose-pie House (long demolished) must have seemed very odd, with its recession and projection, its bold rusticated stonework in the centre contrasting with plain ashlar to either side, and its contrast of height between wings and centre block. The house was novel, baroque and, considering its small size, full of architectural content. This was the first of the three houses Vanbrugh would build for himself, the last being started seventeen years later on Maze Hill at Greenwich. The Greenwich house would be equally idiosyncratic.

Goose-pie House came only two years after Vanbrugh made his debut in architecture by ousting the establishment architect, William Talman, from the favour of Lord Carlisle, for the new house, almost a palace, he was building in Yorkshire. In Renaissance Italy, great artists sometimes became architects, without much preparation or training. But they could at least draw. For someone without any previously demonstrated artistic or craft skill to design a great architectural project such as Castle Howard – and supervise its execution – is virtually without parallel. At this stage, Vanbrugh had almost no skill as a draughtsman. His client had to be persuaded of his ideas through the construction of a wooden model. In his lampoon on the Whitehall house, written in 1706, Swift drew attention to his lack of experience:

Van's genius without Thought or Lecture
Is hugely turn'd to architecture.

Scholars have puzzled over whether this comment was literally true. Surely some 'thought or lecture' – that is to say, study of architecture – must have preceded his first essay. But no: there is no evidence of his having worked with an architect, or even having read many books on architecture, before Castle Howard. He had become friendly with Sir Christopher Wren, who had similarly embarked on architecture as a comparatively understandable extension of his work as a mathematician. That would have been, of course, a considerable advantage. But we do not know of much else.

Castle Howard was vastly bigger than Goose-pie House, but the idiom was not dissimilar. It was rich and flamboyant, with an entrance hall rising into a great dome. But in the grounds of this immense baroque pile he would, later, build ramparts and fortifications that evoke the castle element of the name.

While building Blenheim Palace for the Duke of Marlborough, Vanbrugh developed an interest in the old Manor of Woodstock which lay in its grounds. This interest was not purely academic: he set about rehabilitating it as a residence for himself. Since this was done without authority from the Duke, he found himself in the position of having to explain his actions when Marlborough's implacably Vanbrugh-hating Duchess, Sarah, realised what he was at. Thinking on his feet, but also exploring a revolutionary aesthetic idea, he wrote a 'Memorandum' on the restoration of Woodstock Manor. In it, he sketched a philosophy that would come to colour the way in which many British people have regarded buildings ever since. Architecture, in the sense of mass, proportion and ornament, was not the only attribute by which they should be judged. Old structures should also be valued, he argued, for the associations that they aroused in the mind. As Vanbrugh put it, 'they move more lively and pleasing Reflections (than History without their aid can do) on the Persons who have inhabited them; on the remarkable things which have been transacted in them, or the extraordinary occasions of erecting them'. He also argued that they might form pleasing episodes in a landscape, enhancing, say, a gentleman's park rather than detracting from its appeal.

It is difficult to appreciate the originality of this approach today. But Vanbrugh was writing in an age when form seemed everything in architecture; it was difficult and costly to construct any building, let alone a great one: so people preferred structures that were solid, new and swanky to ancient ruins. It is difficult to imagine that Vanbrugh's Memorandum was very widely read after it had served its purpose with the Duchess; it was a battle that she won, and Woodstock Manor is no more. But its content prefigures such pervasive and particularly British responses as the Picturesque Movement in the eighteenth century, the writings of John Ruskin in the nineteenth century and the conservation crusade in the twentieth century. Greenwich was to see the idea of the Picturesque, including a preference for asymmetry, applied to Vanbrugh's development on Maze Hill.

Vanbrugh's architecture is, for obvious reasons, often characterised as dramatic – too often, indeed. But his appreciation of Woodstock Manor can truly be said to have an attribute of drama, since it was based more upon the Manor's ability to move the mind than, in a conventional sense, to please the eye. He carried this notion over into his own architecture, when, for example, he remodelled Kimbolton Castle near Huntingdon. Kimbolton was an old house built round a courtyard, where the latest phase of work had been carried out by a provincial architect in the 1690s. But in 1707 the south front collapsed, and Vanbrugh rushed to the scene. 'As to the Outside,' he wrote to Kimbolton's owner Lord Manchester, 'I thought 'twas absolutely best, to give it Something of the Castle Air, tho' at the Same time to make it regular.' In Vanbrugh's œuvre, the 'Castle Air' is less familiar than the formal baroque manner, laden with columns and carved stone, of Castle Howard and Blenheim. Architecturally, the ingredients were simple. There were no columns, only rather plain volumes of masonry perhaps alleviated by rustication. Battlements break the skyline. Vanbrugh, of course, was no Victorian Gothic Revivalist: as his observation to Lord Manchester indicates, he did not seek to abandon the cardinal principle of symmetry. It was enough that battlements and a general impression of bulk should raise the appropriate associations in the mind. Nevertheless, the importance of the 'Castle Air' to him should not be minimised. He used it for his own house at Greenwich.

Vanbrugh had already rented a house at Greenwich for a year or two before building his new one, to be known as Vanbrugh's Castle. A friend referred to it as his 'country morsell', for Greenwich was still rural in 1717. But it was not isolated: a couple of Vanbrugh's friends already lived nearby. Various prosperous houses had been built in Greenwich in the previous century. As years went on, they reflected the change that overcame the area after the Civil War. No longer were the houses for the luminaries of the court, but for successful merchants, City men and sailors – with one or two owners, like Vanbrugh, who defy categorisation. In the 1630s, the Duke of Buckingham's secretary, Dr Robert Mason, had built a little red brick Dutch 'Hermitage', in the manner of the innovative Dutch House at Kew. 'The house is a wretched one,' judged John Evelyn, who had been invited over from Deptford. However, that was twenty or so years after its construction, and he liked the view. Views, or prospects, were important in an age when, as here, special belvederes or other provision were made to take them. In

**Vanbrugh Castle, sketched by the antiquarian William Stukeley in 1721. Vanbrugh's fascination with military architecture has been associated with the years that he spent as a young man incarcerated in French jails, as a political hostage. His own castle is a very early example of medieval revivalism.**

the middle of the eighteenth century, Lord Chesterfield described the views from his bow windows in his house on Crooms Hill – on the other side of the Park from Maze Hill – as 'the finest prospects in the world'. The panorama from the top of Maze Hill must have been one of its attractions to Vanbrugh, since he gave his Castle a roof of lead flats that could be walked upon.

The glass engraver Laurence Whistler, who wrote a biography of Vanbrugh in 1954, evokes the vista that could be enjoyed.

> In the middle distance, then, lay London in the hollow of green hills, still cupped like jewellery in the palm of a hand, and more like jewellery than ever before or ever again. For even in the ordinary kind light of this country, the grey and usual, its many new steeples might be told in the smokeless air, with the whitish lantern of St Paul's high above them, as yet unweathered. Closer at hand rose Greenwich Hospital, with only one cupola silhouetted against the shine of the river, crawling with masts, and beyond the grey-green water-meadows, were the inconspicuous hills of Essex. Nothing much moved in that emptiness, except the gulls, and a row of windmills that for much of the year would be turned to receive the west wind, all moving together like toys.

Whistler may have exaggerated the clarity of the air over London, but it is easy to see why the panorama that he describes, with its combination of pastoral landscape and fine architecture, would have delighted Vanbrugh.

It is an intriguing irony that Vanbrugh's family should have originated from Ghent, given that the manor of Greenwich was for so many years owned by the Abbey of Ghent. Naturally, Vanbrugh already knew the area from his association with the Hospital, where he was now Surveyor (Wren had retired from the position in 1716). But it was not only work that persuaded him of the need for a country house. In January 1719, at the age of fifty-four, he got married.

It was an episode that allowed Vanbrugh's contemporaries some humour at his expense. Early in the courtship, when he was but forty-nine, Lady Mary Wortley Montagu reported from York (Vanbrugh had been staying at Castle Howard) to a friend: 'His Inclination to Ruins has given him a fancy for Mrs Yarborrough. He sighs and ogles that it would do your heart good to see him.' One would hardly know it from the disparaging reference to 'Ruins', but 'Mrs Yarborrough' was in fact unmarried (it was relatively common for women who were past girlhood to be styled as 'Mrs') and just the same age as Lady Mary Wortley Montagu herself – twenty-four. The old, or oldish, man who takes a much younger wife has been an object of other people's mirth since at least the days of Chaucer's *Merchant's Tale*. Vanbrugh was, furthermore, a wit. Some, then and since, have suggested he was a roué, though only from his having written mildly improper plays. He therefore

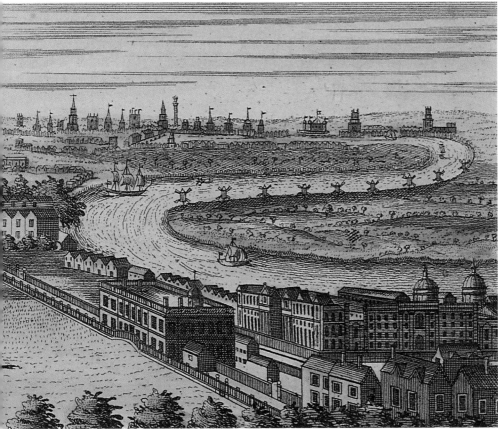

*Top:* The Vanbrugh estate, viewed from the west. This stylised drawing of 1790 shows the sequence of structures that visitors would have encountered after passing through the gateway on the right. First comes a low building which was probably a stable or outhouses. It is followed by one of the tall pair of White Towers. Between the White Towers, partly obscured by trees, is The Nunnery. Vanbrugh House, or Mince-pie House, is reached after the White Towers. The next substantial building, Red House, was not designed by Vanbrugh, having been constructed in 1736, after his death. Finally, on the far left, stands the castle itself.

*Bottom:* View over Greenwich Park towards Deptford, with London on the skyline and the windmills of the Isle of Dogs on the right. The view was one of the principal attractions of Greenwich: Vanbrugh gave his castle a roof of lead flats from which it could be enjoyed.

Vanbrugh Castle, in an engraving of 1798. As castles go, it was not large. As Vanbrugh wrote to a friend, 'one may find a great deal of Pleasure, in building a Palace for another, when one shou'd find very little living in't ones Self'.

made a particularly satisfying object of ridicule. The Vanbrughs' domestic contentment seems to have been quite unaffected by it. There may have been thirty-five years between them, but everything suggests that their marriage was happy.

The new house was begun seven months before the knot was tied – perhaps even before he knew that he would marry. It still stands on Maze Hill, though the yellow London stock bricks have darkened to their usual grimy colour and it is now hemmed in by other buildings. When Vanbrugh acquired his lease of 'a Field and other Grounds' – a triangle of twelve acres carved from the Westcombe estate (once the property of the antiquarian William Lambarde) – it was still in the country, with just a few other houses round about. The Vanbrughs moved into their new home in 1720. The year before, Vanbrugh heard that, while he had been away, the Duke of Newcastle 'was pleas'd to Storm my Castle'. Nor could there be any doubting it was indeed a castle – original though the conceit must have seemed. From the Dover Road visitors to Vanbrugh Castle had first to penetrate a defensive ring of walls, bastions and gatehouse – a miniature version of the mock fortifications built at Castle Howard. Then, there was another gateway, just in front of the Castle, on the Greenwich side. The Castle itself comprised a four-square keep, with two square towers at the corners of the south façade (overlooking the field) and a circular one in the centre. The circular tower gave every floor a bow window, to take advantage of the view. There are battlements, a string course and a kind of scalloped corbel-table – all very medieval. The etiolated proportions do not suggest any great strength, but the relative height (it rises four storeys) gives a fairy-tale character – in the late twentieth century, reminiscent of Disney. Vanbrugh Castle might be called a revival for revival's sake. It is difficult to estimate its influence, but it must have struck contemporaries as unprecedented. It can claim a place at the very beginning of the Gothic Revival that so delighted Horace Walpole and swept Victorian architects off their feet.

Despite its military bearing, this remarkable house is not large; nor are the rooms within it. As he wrote to 'old Jacob' Tonson, the publisher who had also been secretary of the Whiggish Kit-Cat Club, much frequented by Vanbrugh at one time: 'one may find a great deal of Pleasure, in building a Palace for another, when one shou'd find very little living in't ones Self.'

The Mince-pie House, which Vanbrugh constructed for his brother Charles. Vanbrugh's own residence at Whitehall had been lampooned as Goose-pie House.

Mince-pie House (more formally known as Vanbrugh House) from the south about 1830. William Stukeley had called it *Castellulum Vanbrugiense*, or little Vanbrugh castle. This view shows it after the addition of an attic storey.

By 1722 Vanbrugh could report that he was 'now two Boys Strong in the Nursery'. He adored his children, in the way that older fathers do. Their own arrival necessitated expansion, with the building of new wings. Whereas the original castle had been fanciful in style, but symmetrical in form, symmetry was now thrown to the winds, in favour of Picturesque irregularity. It was not something that Vanbrugh ever tried in one of his larger commissions, but he could do it at home.

Nor was that all. Very soon after he acquired the lease of Maze Hill, Vanbrugh set about gathering other members of his family around him. Almost as soon as he began his own Castle, work started on another house on the site, probably for his youngest brother Philip, a captain in the navy and recently widowed. From earliest days, the house was called the Nunnery – which must have meant something to the Vanbrughs, though we can only guess at its significance now. In the next century it would have been called a bungalow: a spreading single-storey structure, with a little tower over the middle of it. Then came the *Castellulum Vanbrugiense* (little Vanbrugh Castle) for his 32-year-old brother Charles, already prosperous from a faintly shady career at sea and subsequent investments. It was called Mince-pie

House – an echo of the Goose-pie House at Whitehall. There is not much that is obviously a mincepie about it. But it was a colourful conception, with a square centrepiece of five bays, a rusticated doorcase and circular side towers, again rusticated (on second thoughts the crenellated tops do suggest a piecrust). Like Vanbrugh Castle itself, these sibling mansions were built of London stock brick. Two further houses, the White Towers, were constructed out of patented white bricks supplied by a Fulham brickmaker to whom Vanbrugh had given financial backing. Altogether there were five houses on the estate. Each in a different idiom, they were dotted about the site in a thoroughly Picturesque manner.

They seem to have delighted Vanbrugh's older son Charles, which may have been part of the point (sadly, the younger of the two boys in the nursery, John, died at the age of a year). To Vanbrugh, one imagines that the sensations that passed through his breast as he went under the gateway included family warmth, amusement at his own architectural conceit, a sense of entering a self-contained world of his own making, relief after the externally imposed artifice of the town, and pride in his achievement.

He had half a dozen years to enjoy it, before his death of a quinsy in 1726. With his death the heart went out of the quirky assemblage of houses on Maze Hill – a family compound, as it would have been called later in the United States. Today only his own house survives.

Vanbrugh in Woolwich. Many of the buildings for the Royal Ordnance, erected hurriedly after the Jacobite rising of 1715, are in the Vanbrugh manner, including the Royal Foundry shown in this engraving of 1779. It would have been convenient for Vanbrugh to reach Woolwich from Maze Hill.

185

# As Much Honour and Delight as This World Can Give

*On Thames's bank in silent thought we stood*
*Where Greenwich smiles upon the silver flood.*
Samuel Johnson, who lived in Greenwich in 1737

MUCH OF THE GREENWICH which Vanbrugh knew was a poverty-stricken slum. 'I took notice of several good houses on the left hand [of the church] which looked like habitations fit for Christians to live in,' writes the author of a newspaper account of a journey through Greenwich to Charlton Fair in 1700. 'But in some parts of the town the huts were not bigger than wigwams, scarce big enough for a man to lye at length in without putting his head or his heels in the chimney corner.' Nevertheless the place was acquiring an overlay of gentility. Daniel Defoe, author of *Robinson Crusoe* and supplier of bricks for the Seamen's Hospital, wrote of the 'lustre of its inhabitants' when describing Greenwich in his *Tour through England and Wales*, published in 1724-6: 'there is a kind of collection of gentlemen, rather than citizens, and of persons of quality and fashion, different from most, if not all, the villages in this part of England.' There was a special Greenwich flavour to this gentility: a salty, leathery, gunpowdery note which came from the number of retired officers, from both army and navy, who resided there. As Defoe puts it:

> Here several of the most active and useful gentlemen of the late armies, after having grown old in the service of their country, and cover'd with the honours of the field, are retired to enjoy the remainder of their time, and reflect with pleasure upon the dangers they have gone thro', and the faithful services they have perform'd both abroad and at home.
>
> Several generals, and several of the inferior officers, I say, having thus chosen this calm retreat, live here in as much honour and delight as this world can give.

In addition to these retirees were the serving officers employed in the dockyards and arsenal. Altogether there was such a demand for good houses that 'the town of Greenwich begins to out-swell its bounds'. New streets were planned, the population grew, the new church, built only a dozen years ago, was already beginning to look small.

Princess Caroline of Brunswick, painted by Sir Thomas Lawrence in 1804. One of the Princess's accomplishments was that of sculpting, hence the modelling tool in her hand. It was said that Lawrence became her lover in the course of painting the portrait.

It was not only naval officers who had connections with the sea. Sir Ambrose Crowley had purchased what was to become Crowley House – the house built by Sir Andrew Cogan just before the Civil War and finished by the regicide Member of Parliament Gregory Clement – in 1704, and reconstructed it. 'Very great manufacturers of iron anchors, etc.,' was how Horace Walpole's antiquarian correspondent, N. Hillier, described the Crowley family in 1780. Thomas Pennant found the grounds of Crowley House littered with 'all kinds of iron manufactures'.

Greenwich was also becoming fashionable among people who had no connection with shipping and the sea. Lord Egremont, who lived at Charlton House, records the visits that he made to people in nearby Greenwich and Blackheath in his diary. In August 1731, he returned 'Mr Signoret's visit'. Mr Signoret was a merchant, and as such worked in the City; but he could spend 'much of his time at Greenwich, where he has a pretty house and garden, and a fine study of books. He married a daughter of the famous Dr Allix, French minister: a handsome woman and of great merit.' Later that month he 'returned the visits of Lord Pomphret, Sir Archibald Grant, and Mr Kellet, all on Blackheath'. The advent of Sir John Vanbrugh is evidence enough of the area's growing elegance; and as we have seen, some of his friends lived in the area already. The two white towers that he built on his fields were an early example of speculative building, having been constructed without a specific occupant in mind. They were not quite the first of this kind. For half a century there had been a demand for substantial houses, homes of the prosperous newcomers who were settling here; and where a demand exists, there will soon be speculators to take advantage of it.

Defoe had noted that in the 1720s Greenwich was extending itself 'to the top of the heath, by the way call'd Crum-Hill'. Building on Crooms Hill had begun nearly a century before: externally, the oldest surviving house, now called Heath Gate House, appears to have been erected about 1630 by William Smith, hereditary Sergeant-at-Arms to the King. Smith comes down in Greenwich history as the founder of the Ship tavern. He was, therefore, a man of some enterprise, and Heath Gate House seems to have been a speculation. It was in the newly fashionable Dutch style, seen at Kew and elsewhere, well calculated to catch the eye of courtiers in need of lodging. Originally, Crooms Hill had been part of the gardens and orchards belonging to a house that lay near the river, built by the courtier family of Compton. Much of this land had been acquired by Sir Thomas Lake, who eventually succeeded Robert Cecil as Secretary of State. Lake was not an attractive figure: limited of talent, venal and and unscrupulous. These qualities were not, in other people, a disadvantage at the Jacobean court, but in Lake's case they seem to have been, since his tenure of office was not only inglorious but brief.

But his grandson Lancelot, who was knighted at the Restoration of Charles II, deserves to be remembered locally as one of the earliest of Greenwich's developers. His activities were not confined to Crooms Hill; he seems to have built several houses round about, using his cousin Richard Ryder, who was the King's master carpenter, as architect. Sir Lancelot lived on Crooms Hill, in an old house called the Grange: it may once have been part of Paternoster Croft, a house that had belonged to the Abbey of Ghent. More recently it had been home to Edmund Chapman, Queen Elizabeth's chief joiner, and then the Lanier family of musicians. Lake remodelled this building, as well as erecting the house that is now numbers 16–18 on Crooms Hill. It may have been at the Grange that Sir William Boreman lived while he was replanting Greenwich Park. In 1662 the Grange was acquired by Sir William Hooker, a member of the Grocers' Company who would rise to be Lord Mayor of London. Alderman Hooker had been one of a group of leading citizens in his parish who had consulted with Pepys about plague measures. Pepys had no great opinion of him: 'a plain ordinary silly man I think he is, but rich.' Furthermore, he found that he kept 'the poorest mean dirty table, in a dirty house, that ever I did see any sheriff of London'. That was in Eastcheap North, in

*Doc. Sutton's house on Crooms Hill, Greenwich, 1808.* It was built about 1630, in the newly fashionable Dutch style, by William Smith, hereditary Sergeant-at-Arms to the King. Smith was also the founder of the Ship tavern at Greenwich.

189

the City of London. No wonder Hooker felt he needed a change of abode. In the garden of the Grange he employed Robert Hooke, the associate of Christopher Wren whose instruments caused poor Flamsteed such grief at the Observatory, to build a gazebo.

An engraving by Francis Place, made in about 1700, shows Crooms Hill from the Park. In this can be seen the house built originally by Robert Osboldston which Pepys, visiting Mark Cottle, had found 'very pretty'; it no longer exists. Cottle built 'five fair tenements' on the east side of the hill in 1702. A couple of years after Vanbrugh brought his wife to his Castle, a terrace went up at the foot of Crooms Hill, apparently a private venture to house captains of the Hospital. The architect John James built and lived in Park Hall, on Crooms Hill. It is to James that we owe the design of the steeple of St Alfege's Church. The original steeple had survived the collapse of the old church and had not been demolished: hence its exclusion from Hawksmoor's design. Alas, James's rather too dainty steeple does not possess the monumentality of the body of the church. Another resident was Sir James Thornhill, who worked for nineteen years on the Painted Hall at the Royal Hospital, and lived at 64 Crooms Hill from 1722 to 1724.

Crooms Hill about 1700, seen from Greenwich Park in a detail of the engraving on pages 118–19. The house with the cupola is The Belvedere, built by Erasmus Snetting, who sold a lease of it to Robert Osboldston in 1640. It was later occupied by Pepys's friend Mark Cottle. 'A very pretty house,' wrote Pepys, who praised its view. It had a tiled barn, a banqueting house, a walled orchard, a mount (a miniature hill) and various arbours.

At the southern end of Crooms Hill lies what is now Chesterfield Walk, in the area of which Andrew Snape, the King's sergeant farrier, built three houses, in somewhat suspicious circumstances, given that the lease on the land had not actually been granted to him when work began. Snape belonged to a family whom Evelyn mentions as having been sergeant farriers to the sovereign for three hundred years. He published a book called *The Anatomy of an Horse* in 1683. But he was equally 'a man full of projects' and builder of the new tavern by the bowling green at Blackheath. If Snape hoped that the area would increase in fashionability because of the association with royalty, he must have been disappointed to discover that William and Mary, coming to the throne in 1688, had little interest in Greenwich for their own occupation. But this did not deter others from erecting four-square, quite stylish residences, such as Macartney House. Built in 1694, this was bought by the parents of General James Wolfe of Quebec, when he was twelve years old. Wolfe, educated in Greenwich, lived here when he was not soldiering,

General James Wolfe, the conqueror of Quebec, 1727-59. Brought up and educated in Greenwich, it was from there that he left for his last expedition to Canada, dying in the hour of victory on the Plains of Abraham.

and it was from Greenwich that he left on his last expedition to Canada, in September 1759. After his death on the Plains of Abraham, his remains were brought home and buried in a vault below St Alfege's Church.

Next to Macartney House is the Ranger's House, built somewhat after its neighbour for Captain, later Admiral, Francis Hosier. Hosier was the son of a Deptford storekeeper, who had done well from victualling the royal ships (Pepys, as Secretary to the Navy, had contact with him). The young Francis went to sea at twelve or thirteen, and was a captain ten years later. At the brow of the hill, the house even now enjoys a fine view of the Thames: this prospect must have been ravishing before the banks of the river were developed. No doubt it was particularly pleasing to the eye of a sailor, though Hosier's choice of the site may also have been determined by a desire to get on in society; there were aristocrats like the 2nd Duke of Richmond living nearby. He furnished his house in walnut, with one or two mahogany pieces and what must have seemed the princely extravagance of a suite of silver furniture in the dining room. Seven or eight servants kept the place going. Hosier was one of four thousand seamen to die of yellow fever while blockading Spanish treasure ships into the port of Porto Bello, in central America, in 1725 and is best remembered by Richard Glover's political ballad of some years later, 'Admiral Hosier's Ghost'.

View of Crooms Hill from Blackheath, painted by
Thomas Hofland, 1777–1843, an artist famous for
the accuracy of his depictions. Still a sylvan scene,
despite the development that had taken place since
the seventeenth century.

There was a lengthy court case after Hosier's death, but the house was eventually bought by John Stanhope, younger brother of the Earl of Chesterfield. He was appointed a Commissioner of the Admiralty in 1748 – perhaps the naval connections of Greenwich had appealed to him. He appears to have spent large sums on improving the house. But in 1748 he died, leaving the house to Lord Chesterfield.

To begin with Chesterfield found the Blackheath property something of a burden. For one thing, while Greenwich was adequately fashionable, it was not nearly fashionable enough for Lord Chesterfield, who prided himself on knowing all the most glittering people in Europe. He would much rather his villa had been at Twickenham or Richmond, where Alexander Pope, the Countess of Suffolk and others added intellectual and social lustre. But within a few years he had fallen for

*The Ranger's House, overlooking Blackheath. Originally built about 1700 for Admiral Francis Hosier, who had made a fortune from victualling the King's ships, it became the property of the supremely urbane Lord Chesterfield in 1748.*

the place. As deafness encroached, shutting him off from easy conversation with his contemporaries, it may have suited him to be geographically remote from society. And he had a fashionable house in Mayfair, built for him by the Palladian architect Isaac Ware. He referred to the Blackheath house on one occasion as his 'petite Chartreuse' (a monastery of the worldly Carthusian order) and on another as 'my hermitage'. He continued: 'This, I find, is my proper place; and I know it, which people seldom do. I converse with my equals, my vegetables, which I found in a flourishing condition.' As this letter suggests, he was seized by the *furor hortensis*, as he described it, 'and my acre of ground here affords me more pleasure than kingdoms do to kings'. Already on 23 December 1748 – the year that he acquired the house – he wrote to his friend Solomon Dayrolles, asking for 'seeds of the right Cantelupe melons. It is for Blackheath that I want it.' He was proud of the results, writing a few months later: 'I shall keep a little room for you at Blackheath, where I will refresh you with the best ananas and melons in England.'

By Chesterfield's standards, the house was not big. He made a joke of it to the Marquise de Monconseil, whose

The 4th Earl of Chesterfield, 1694–1773, statesman, man of letters and cynic. The three bow-windows in the gallery, which he attached to his house on Blackheath (now Ranger's House), gave him 'three different, and the finest prospects in the world'. The name Ranger's House derives from the period during which it was the official residence of the Ranger of Greenwich Park.

lodge in the Bois de Boulogne in Paris was called Bagatelle, or trifle. His own 'very small house' five miles from London 'I would have called Bagatelle had not I felt such a respect for yours; so I call it Babiole [meaning a bauble]'. In 1750 he went some way towards rectifying the defect of size by adding a large gallery on the south side, designed by Ware, running the full depth of the house, of one storey with no fewer than three bow windows – one for each of the external walls. 'Blackheath,' he wrote to Dayrolles, 'is now in great beauty. The shell of my gallery is finished,' and the three bow windows gave him 'three different, and the finest prospects in the world'. There were now eighteen servants to look after the house and its solitary owner. To the outside world, Chesterfield in his 'hermitage' presented a sage-like picture:

> By wisdom purify'd, by age inspir'd,
> For twice nine years in Greenwich groves retir'd,

as a verse in the *Gentleman's Magazine* expresses it. He himself did not feel that age was so very inspiring. 'Retirement was my choice seven years ago,' he wrote; 'it is now become my necessary refuge. Blackheath, and a quiet conscience, are the only objects of my cares. My little garden, the park, reading and writing, kill time there tolerably; and time is now my enemy.'

195

Woodlands House, the country villa built by John Julius Angerstein in 1774. When this engraving was published in the 1790s, Greenwich and Blackheath were still surrounded by country estates, whose proximity to London made them attractive for both busy and fashionable people. Angerstein was the insurance underwriter whose art collection formed the basis of the National Gallery.

It was part of the Chesterfield code that he never intentionally committed the vulgar act of laughing. Nevertheless, a smile was permitted, and he was celebrated for his wit. When someone asked after Lord Tyrawley, who had taken the lease of Vanbrugh Castle from Sir John's widow, Chesterfield replied: 'Tyrawley and I have been dead these two years but we do not choose to have it known.' After Chesterfield's death, without legitimate issue, his house was inherited by his rackety godson, a distant cousin who became 5th Earl of Chesterfield. His period is remembered for a drunken dinner, with the future George IV present, when a ferocious dog called Towzer was released and savaged a footman, before being clubbed into submission by one of the party. In the mêlée Lord Chesterfield tumbled down the front steps, badly hurting his head. Early in the next century, Chesterfield House became the Ranger's House, the official residence of the Ranger of the Park. Beyond it lay the house owned by the Duke of Montague that became known as Montague House (see below).

William Lambarde's 'poore cabben' of Westcombe (not so poor as all that) was replaced by Captain Galfridus Walpole's new residence in the early eighteenth century. By 1739 it was occupied by the 9th Earl of Pembroke, and criticised by Sarah, Duchess of Marlborough, who thought it was 'the most ridiculous thing I ever saw', built by 'somebody that is mad'. The lease passed to the Duke of Bolton, who made himself an enemy of the theatre-going public by depriving them of the popular young Lavinia Fenton, playing Polly Peachum in the *Beggar's Opera*; he made her his mistress and after just sixty-one nights as Polly she left the boards. In 1779, when the latest of Westcombe's noble occupants was the Marchioness of Lothian, it took pride of place as the first plate in W. Watts's *Seats of the Nobility and Gentry*. On 'an agreeable Eminence', it was praised for the 'many picturesque Views' that it commanded. 'The Variety of floating Objects beheld (from the Front of the House) upon the *Thames* at a considerable Distance off (and those, from its serpentine Course, rendered much more brilliant and enlivening) must necessarily claim our Attention, especially if we include a Multitude of Cattle continually grazing on each side of the River's verdant Banks.' The house itself was judged to be neat and elegant, surrounded by gardens of such taste 'as to render them a perfect scene of rural Simplicity'. Judged by the estate agent's three determinants of property value – location, location and location – Westcombe (and Greenwich) could hardly have been bettered: 'Notwithstanding the Vicinity of this Seat to the Metropolis, yet from the Advantage of *Greenwich* Park on the Left, *Charlton* on the Right, and *Blackheath* to complete the Whole, we may, without Hesitation, pronounce it one of the most desirable Spots in *England*.'

A few years before this description was published Westcombe acquired a new neighbour. This was Woodlands, the country villa built in 1774 by the insurance underwriter John Julius Angerstein. Then thirty-nine years old, Angerstein's rise to a position of fortune had been meteoric. Born in St Petersburg, he had been apprenticed in a London counting-house at the age of fifteen before entering Lloyd's Coffee House. He quickly became the leading man in the industry, moving what was to become Lloyd's of London from the coffee house and becoming its first chairman. He was a man of method. He dressed always in the same uniform of blue coat, striped waistcoat, drab cloth breeches and buckled shoes. He talked little, often went to sleep during dinner, might well go to bed when a rout was taking place in his house, and insisted on his meals being served punctually, with no waiting for late arrivals. 'Now comes the unpleasant part of

Children of the Angerstein family at Woodlands. This drawing by Caroline, granddaughter of John Julius Angerstein, is from an album she made for her mother, Amelia.

197

This engraving of Westcombe House in 1779, after Paul Sandby, shows it during the period when it was owned by the Marchioness of Lothian, and surrounded by gardens of such taste 'as to render them a perfect scene of rural Simplicity', according to William Watts's *Seats of the Nobility and Gentry*. It lay to the east of Greenwich Park.

my letter, viz.: that I fear I shall be prevented from dining at Woodlands tomorrow,' wrote the portrait painter Sir Thomas Lawrence to Mrs Angerstein on one occasion.

The Duke of York sits to me in the morning, and after him (an apointment made in the presence of His Majesty) Lady Elizabeth Cunningham. She comes at two but is not usually punctual to the hour. Now, if I could bribe Mr. Angerstein's cook to delay dinner a quarter of an hour [it was invariably served at 6.30pm], and gain over his Clocks to the conspiracy, I might possibly keep my appointment with the Lady, and yet enjoy the company of my kind Friends. Will you, my dear Madam, assist me and be chief Conspirator in the project? As it is now however, too late to wait for your answer to decide me, I will trust my fortune and take my chance of coming in for the soup or for that stage of the dessert that may preserve to me my rightful and long established station at the dining room door …

Lawrence was not the only artist attracted to Woodlands. Angerstein's picture collection was purchased by the government after his death in 1823 and forms the basis of the National Gallery. He is buried in St Alfege's at Greenwich.

It is surprising that a man of such taste did not seek out a more distinguished architect than the one he employed: George Gibson. Gibson, the son of another architect of the same name, had local connections, and built himself a house on the other side of Blackheath, on Loampit Hill, in Lewisham. In this he deposited the collections of 'curiosities in Art' that he had gathered while travelling in Italy. The effect of the ensemble was indicated by the name of the 'Comical House' by which the dwelling came to be known. Gibson, according to an account quoted in Howard Colvin's *Biographical Dictionary of British Architects*, was too gentle-manly in his tastes to care much about building sites. 'He would rather sip his claret, drink his Madeira, chat about Art and Music, and take snuff with a gusto, than ascend ladders, tramp scaffolds to see how Briklayers filled in their work, or try the scantlings of wall plates and bond timbers … [like] the practical men of Sir Robert Taylor's working school.' It may have been a recommendation that George Gibson senior was employed by the future Queen Caroline, who was a friend of the Angersteins.

'The Princess is grown very coarse and … she dresses very ill, shewing too much of her naked person,' grumbled the antiquary Samuel Lysons, after one of Princess Caroline's frequent appearances at a Woodlands party. 'A Mrs. Weddel,

View of Charlton in 1775, after Paul Sandby. It was to Charlton that Princess Caroline came after her estrangement from the future George IV; she later moved to Blackheath. In this engraving, a turret of Charlton House can be seen on the far right.

199

**Montague House, Blackheath. In 1798 the lease was taken by the Prince of Wales for his estranged wife Princess Caroline, to provide a salubrious upbringing for their daughter, Princess Charlotte. However, the goings on there became the subject of the Delicate Investigation into Princess Caroline's morality, being resurrected by the Secret Committee of the House of Lords before her trial for adultery.**

who is large and unwieldy, came to the rout and was followed into the room by a little man of the name of Parrot. The Princess said "she should have brought him on her finger".' The humour of that sally was dissipated by her standing 'with her back to a table the whole time, which prevented every other person from sitting, this being the etiquette'. On another occasion she teased the artist Fuseli, who was staying at Woodlands, to such an extent that he left the next morning.

Friends such as the Angersteins must have viewed the Princess's arrival in the area – first at Charlton, then at Blackheath – with trepidation. The daughter of George III's sister, Augusta, and the Duke of Brunswick, she had a robust sense of humour, boisterous manners, slatternly habits and little regard for what any-one thought of her behaviour. Two of her brothers were weak in the head, and she herself was, by the conventions of Georgian England, more than a little odd. She was in an odd position. Before she married the Prince of Wales, he had con-tracted an invalid marriage to the Catholic Mrs Fitzherbert, and on her first arrival in Greenwich the Prince had made so little attempt to conceal his subse-quent mistress, Lady Jersey, that he actually sent her to greet his bride. The Prince and Princess managed to produce a daughter, Princess Charlotte, but after that led separate lives, the Prince being free to consort with whom he chose, the Princess, not yet thirty, expected to deport herself as though still conventionally married to her errant husband. It was not in the Princess's nature to conform.

In the summer of 1798 she moved to Montague House, the lease of which her husband had taken from the Duchess of Buccleuch to provide a salubrious home for the little Princess Charlotte. The Duchess had written: 'I am afraid it is not in very good order, having been very long uninhabited. The situation, however, I flatter myself will make it agreeable to the Princess of Wales.' It lay next to Lord Chesterfield's old house, and had been built about the same time. In comparison to the palaces occupied by her building-mad husband, Princess Caroline's accommodation was rather modest, though it had the advantage of a second house at the end of the garden, built against the wall of the Park. This took its name of the Round Tower from a circular projection looking over the Park, whose rooms must have enjoyed panoramic views. It was useful as a lodging for a lady-in-waiting, her husband and a servant – or as a place of intrigue for Princess Caroline. The main house itself was distinguished by its greenhouse or conservatory – a very Regency feature – reached directly from the Blue Room, the principal room in the house. Stables, kitchen gardens and outhouses were all located some five hundred yards from Montague House, next to a building called, from its Chinese roof, the Pagoda. This still stands in Pagoda Road, Blackheath.

To some, Montague House had, on first acquaintance, a rather melancholy appearance, partly because it was so well shaded by trees. The Princess did what she could to banish any such impression. It may seem that, with her romps, noisiness and 'pandemonium games', kissing games, Caroline was an unlikely friend for such a dry stick as John Julius Angerstein. With her 'very short neck, low stature, large and, as she dresses, not only prominent but ascending posterior', and her comical English ('Are you not glad to see me with my head upon my rump,' she once said, meaning 'on my shoulders'; *Rumpf* in German translates as 'body' or 'trunk'), she was an easy object of fun – and even friends, such as Lord Glenbervie whose words I have quoted, did not scruple to laugh at her. (Lord Glenbervie's wife was Caroline's mistress of the robes.) But for all of that, she had artistic tastes. She was skilled at such ladies' work as marbling paper, painting in watercolours and ornamenting tabletops by arranging dried flowers under glass. A portrait by Lawrence shows her wielding a modelling tool: very unusually for the age, she was an amateur sculptress.

Naturally she was much occupied by the decoration and, after three or four years, enlargement of the house. In this she could hardly compete with her husband's opulent, fantastic and ruinously expensive works at Carlton House, Brighton Pavilion and Buckingham Palace. But she did her best, employing, in the words of Miss Hayman, the long-suffering keeper of her privy purse who occupied the Round Tower, 'ten thousand workmen smelling of the humble humanity and stupid as posts and slow as snails'. She added a Gothic dining room, a new library and created a tented room, *à la turque*. The last would have appealed to her husband, if he had ever seen it. The inspiration came from the brilliant and heroic Sir Sidney Smith, whose picaresque naval career culminated in an action at St Jean d'Acre in which he captured all the French siege artillery at sea, mounted on the walls of Acre and, with a motley band of British and Levantine troops, repulsed Napoleon's siege. Sir Sidney, she wrote, 'furnished me with a pattern for [the room], in a drawing of the tent of Murat Bey, which he had brought over with him from Egypt. And he taught me how to draw Egyptian arabesques, which were necessary for the ornament of the ceiling.' To some people this sort of thing seemed flashy and gimcrack. 'All glitter and glare and trick, tinsel and trumpery, altogether like a bad dream,' concluded Horace Walpole's protégée Mary Berry. 'The dining room, *à la Gothique*, very pretty but the rest of the house in abominable taste.' But even she found the 'drawing room which opens into the greenhouse, a very warm and comfortable room'. And to the romantic Sir Walter Scott, probably introduced to the Princess by his friend the Duke of Buccleuch, Caroline was 'an enchanting princess who dwells in an enchanted palace'.

The enchanting princess amused her friends by organising novel entertainments for them, such as an alfresco breakfast. Lord Minto found it 'extremely agreeable', despite 'a slight shower, which drove the white muslins for a few minutes into the house'. But the Princess's disregard for the norms of society went beyond open-air breakfasts. It was her practice, of an evening, to single out a man to share her conversation, and often the two of them would retire from the party, into a separate room or the garden. This invited comment; and the comment was not always without foundation. Her intimacy with Sir Sidney Smith went far beyond a discussion of tented ceilings. And he was but one of the many naval figures which Greenwich society could supply for her parties. Captain Thomas Manby was fitting out a frigate at Deptford in 1802: Sir Sidney was mortified to spot them playing footsie under the table one evening. Another intimate was Henry Hood, son of the naval hero Viscount Hood who was Governor of the Naval Hospital. But even ship's officers could find Princess Caroline's behaviour rather too much. According to Lady Hester Stanhope, her sometime lady-in-waiting, one of the rooms at Montague House contained a Chinese automaton which performed obscene movements. 'How the sea-captains used to colour up when she [the Princess] danced about, exposing herself like an opera girl; and then she gartered below the knee: she was so low, so vulgar!' In 1806 a public enquiry, or 'Delicate Investigation' into her life after her separation from the Prince of Wales was conducted, and the evidence, in so far as it reflected her general behaviour, was damning. We cannot be sure that the painter Lawrence became her lover when staying at Montague House – against convention – while painting two portraits. It hardly matters; there were so many others.

But Caroline was more than a rackety, over-boisterous vulgarian. There was a warmth and humanity to her, expressed in a love of children. This was much more than a Rousseau-esque affectation. At the Pagoda, she established a small nursery for orphans, winning the approval of the German educationalist Joachim Heinrich Campe when he visited in 1802. He described the garden and the Pagoda in his journal:

> I admired the beautiful order and the careful cultivation of even the most insignificant spot; the judicious combination of the useful with the agreeable, which appeared so delightful wherever I cast my eyes. I was charmed with the neat borders of flowers between which we passed, and was doubly rejoiced to find them so small; because, as the Princess remarked, too much room ought not to be taken from the useful vegetables.

The Round Tower of Montague House, useful for lodging Princess Caroline's lady-in-waiting – and as a place of intrigue for the princess herself.

I was transported with the elegance, taste and convenience displayed in the Pavilion, in which the dignified owner, who furnished the plan and the directions for every part of it, had solved the problem, how a building of but two floors, on a surface of about eighteen feet square, could be constructed and arranged in such a manner that a small family, capable of limiting its desires, might find in it a habitation equally beautiful, tasteful and commodious. The manner in which this has been effected deserves, in my opinion, the notice and admiration of professed architects.

The Princess directed the education of the children at the Pagoda and came to talk to them every day. They were 'clothed in the cleanest but at the same time in the simplest manner, just as the children of country people are in general dressed'. The children were evidently fond of her, and she did not strive to promote them

*Anticipations for the Pillory.* In this caricature of 1813, the pillory has been set up outside Montague House, where Princess Caroline appears at a window. The figure being led to the stocks is Lady Douglas who had asserted that a boy whom the Princess had adopted was in fact her own child.

into an impossibly exalted station in life: 'The boys are destined to become expert seamen; and the girls skilful, sensible, industrious housewives – nothing more.'

In the case of one act of charity, she went rather further. In the autumn of 1802, allowed only a weekly visit to her daughter Princess Charlotte, she asked her servants to keep an eye open for a baby that she could take into the house. As it happened, one was to present itself that very October, in the shape of a three-month-old boy called Willie Austin. His father had recently been discharged from Deptford dockyard, as part of the economies that followed the Treaty of Amiens, bringing temporary peace with France. His mother hoped that the Princess could be persuaded to use her influence to reinstate him. She did not gain admittance to Princess Caroline, but her page offered Mr Austin employment in his wife's Pimlico laundry and, to ease the family's finances, the little boy was adopted.

From this distance in history, it seems an act of compassion; to her contemporaries a 'strange whim', if not necessarily a malign one. But the last judgement depended upon the extent to which they regarded Caroline as a potential political nuisance. If she were to claim the baby as her own and legitimate, the boy could one day claim the throne. Hence the Delicate Investigation into the Princess's conduct at Blackheath.

George III, with whom she had been popular, made her Ranger of Blackheath, as a means of clearing some of her debts (it enabled her to let Chesterfield House). The findings of the Delicate Investigation killed the sympathy that he had felt for her. Caroline came to spend less and less time at Blackheath, forsaking her gallant sea-captains for the *bon ton* of the West End. On one of her later visits, in 1811, she arrived to find that the upstairs ante-room had been graced, as Lord Glenbervie wrote, by 'a fine bust of the Duke of Cumberland, which before their rupture she ordered of Tonerelli, and which had lately been sent home'. The Duke was one of George IV's many brothers, and the rupture had apparently been over his disapproval of her adoption of Willie Austin. It stood on a bracket too high for her to reach, but she nevertheless assailed it with a poker, blackening the lower part but not breaking it. She was interrupted by a servant, whom she asked to take down the bust. 'This being done, and the servant gone, she again took the poker, and with hatred and fury in her eyes broke the bust by repeated blows into a thousand pieces, which she made Miss Hayman throw out of the window.'

Eventually, in 1814, she left England altogether. Montague House was demolished the next year. But she was remembered by her friends around Greenwich. When John Julius Angerstein's mother-in-law Mrs Lock visited Woodlands at the time of Queen Caroline's trial for adultery in 1820, her maidservants attended a concert of religious music held at the Green Man, the tavern that used to stand at the top of Blackheath Hill. Many ladies in the audience were seen to be wearing white bows in their hair as a symbol of the Queen's innocence.

\* \* \*

While the royal soap opera at Montague House had been playing under the footlights of national publicity, Greenwich and Blackheath had both been making every effort to transform themselves from an impoverished fishing village (in Greenwich's case) and bare fields (in Blackheath's) into neat little suburbs. At the beginning of the eighteenth century, the Seamen's Hospital was edged by a surf of higgledy-piggledy timber-fronted houses, tumbling into mean streets and around odd little courts and inlets, bearing such richly prosaic names as Bugg's Pond, Fubb's Yacht (a beer house), Stocks Lane, Assiter's Yard, Barber's Court, Leach's Alley, Maiden Row and Graham's Passage. Romney Road, separating the Queen's House from Greenwich Park, had, alas, been built; but it ended in the Market

Square, so that traffic heading for London from the east had to take a tortuous route through the town. As the Hospital itself came within sight of completion, the Commissioners turned their thoughts towards pushing back this tide of flotsam and jetsam which rose almost to their doors. To begin with, they did little more than erect handsome gates to the west of the site. This involved purchasing and clearing the intervening land to give Wren's architecture a little breathing space. Their main campaign of civic improvement came later. But this first blow was enough to make other concerns in Greenwich look to their laurels. Buildings such as the coaching inn the Spread Eagle smartened themselves up: it was rebuilt with stabling for sixty horses, a malt kiln and the stone archway to what used to be the coaching yard in 1780. The shops still identified themselves with pictorial signs – banned in the City of London since 1762 – such as 'The Yellow Boot, opposite the Church', to quote one letterhead. But developers were striking out into the pastureland that lay back from the river, imposing order and geometry on what had been fields. They emulated Bath, Buxton and the other great schemes of Georgian town-planning, but on a miniature scale.

In Greenwich the one attempt at grandeur is Gloucester Circus, designed by Michael Searles in 1790. Searles was a local man, the son of a surveyor, and it was as a surveyor that he first practised. He proved himself to be an architect of ability. The Circus, just off Crooms Hill, was intended to be exactly that: two crescents

One of Michael Searles's drawings for the Paragon on Blackheath. Searles, the son of a Greenwich surveyor, worked mostly on small domestic developments in south-east London. The Paragon was his most ambitious undertaking.

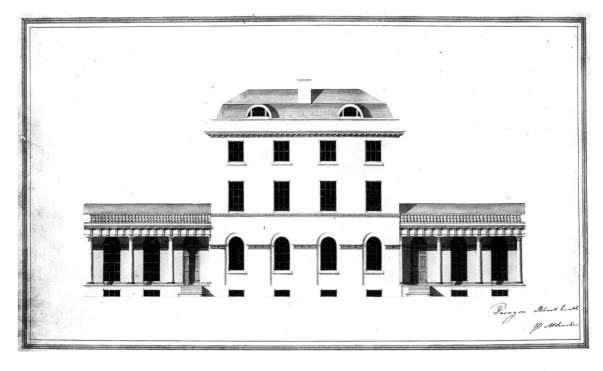

The Paragon, Blackheath, in 1852. This crescent of semi-detached houses, linked by colonnades, was begun by the architect Michael Searles in the 1790s. Each house had a nine-acre garden that could provide milk and vegetables.

enclosing a central circle. But the development never took off sufficiently for the second of the crescents to be built. Even the single sweep of twenty-one houses that now exists took until 1809 to complete. There were plenty of crescents and circuses being built in Britain during these years, but these developments were pitched at the grandest end of society. The Greenwich Circus aspired to be nothing more than middle class. What is more, it broke away from the blandness of form that had characterised previous crescents and circuses (like most of its forebears, it was not a true circus, which would have been circular, but an oval). Elements recede and project in a somewhat syncopated rhythm (though the feeble little pediments at the ends are a weakness). So architecturally it had much to recommend it; but as a speculation, less so. Nevertheless, the experience gave Searles sufficient confidence to project a development in association with the landowner John Cator to the south of Blackheath: the semi-circle of fourteen houses which was named, with estate agent's bravado, the Paragon.

It was less than twenty years before that John Julius Angerstein had built Woodlands. Now the trend was not to create new little country estates, but to butcher the land that went with the big houses around Greenwich into manageable joints, to be cooked by developers and served up, with appropriate garnishes, in slices to the superior middle classes. The Paragon occupied part of the estate belonging to Wricklemarsh House, where Colonel Blount had nurtured his vine-yard and developed his inventions. Later Wricklemarsh had been owned by Sir John Morden, the merchant who founded Morden College. About 1725 John James rebuilt it as a handsome box, its entrance shaded by a giant portico, for Sir Gregory Page, son of a dracoman (or interpreter) who had risen to become a director of the East India Company and a baronet. Page lived there in state: according to his contemporary Sir Henry Dryden, 'the princely magnificence of his residence, his Park and his domesticks surpassed everything in point of grandeur that had been exhibited by a citizen of London since the days of the munificent Sir Thomas Gresham and almost equally the Italian merchants of the ducal house of Medicis.' He was by nature a generous man, but his life of opu-lence did not always sit easily upon his shoulders. In 1736 he tried to hang him-self, being cut down 'while warm' by his servants. Depression may have overcome him from having nothing to do. For all the money that his father had left him, he had little education and, in the words of his neighbour Lord Egremont, at Charlton House, 'knew no way to amuse himself but by walking out of one room into another and ordering the dust to be swept from corners, grates to be scoured, his shirts pleated and the like'. A few days later he tried to shoot himself. For all that, he survived at Wricklemarsh for half a century, dying in 1775.

Eight years later the estate was purchased by Cator. Brought up in Bromley, only a few miles away, he came from a prosperous family and was himself a shrewd businessman. He ran a profitable timber business from Mould Strand Wharf, on the site of what is now Bankside Power Station. A political opponent referred to him as 'a damned carpenter'. Clearly he was more than that. He became a Member of Parliament and knew, or was known by, various literary figures, the most prominent of them being Samuel Johnson. Johnson held Cator in esteem; he was the sort of no-nonsense individual who appealed to him. Johnson's friend Mrs Thrale found the carpenter in need of sanding and polishing. 'It is possible to gain great information from keeping him company; but his voice is so loud and his manners so rough that disgust gets the better of curiosity.' He had no use for the Hall, already having two other houses to live in, so he took the roof off and even-tually demolished it. He may not have had any immediate thought of developing his land, but he was too good a businessman to pass up the occasion when it arose in 1793.

There had been, or would be, other Paragons. Searles himself had erected a terrace on what is now the New Kent Road bearing that appellation. Others can be found in Bristol and Richmond. But the Paragon at Blackheath is the one that most justifies the boast.

A semi-circle of seven pairs of houses, each entered at the side, the ground-floor windows set into arches; each pair linked to the next by a single-storey Tuscan colonnade – it is a handsome composition, which makes one wish that Searles had enjoyed more opportunities in architecture. Searles not only designed the scheme; he was the developer who took the risk. These houses sold more quickly than those in Gloucester Circus, and the development was complete by the time that Nelson's funeral cortège left the Royal Hospital in 1806. They were 'substantially built' dwellings, in the words of an advertisement for number 1 the Paragon which appeared in *The Times* in 1801 (the original occupant had lived there only a year):

> The family apartments consist of two handsome drawing rooms, fitted up with great taste; a spacious eating parlour, a gentleman's room, library and boudoir; and excellent entrance hall and light staircase; eight family bedchambers, dressing rooms, water closets; and admirable nursery and store rooms complete. The servants' apartments are suitable and the domestic offices are of every description with good cellaring and dairy. The outdoor offices are laundry, men's room, stabling, coach house, attached farm yard, with every requisite for pleasure and economy.

These houses, for all their urbanity, still had a whiff of the country about them. Each came with nine acres, and the outside attractions extended beyond 'pleasant views in every direction, with lawn pleasure ground, cold bath, etc.' to include a productive operation that would supply the family with food. 'The kitchen garden is well stocked and in most excellent heart and the pasture land is immediately attached and in high condition for produce.' In an age when difficulties of transportation of food meant that it often arrived in poor condition, if not actually contaminated, growing vegetables and keeping cows were of more interest than just a hobby. Some of the houses had the benefit of fish ponds.

The Paragon, as its name suggests, is the nonpareil of Blackheath development, but it was not alone. It typifies the dismemberment of the country estates that proceeded with dignity in the Regency and early Victorian periods, and with rather less decorum thereafter. The Wricklemarsh estate became developed as the prestigious Blackheath Park in the first half of the nineteenth century. The character of the place was captured by the American novelist Nathaniel Hawthorne in *Our Old Home* (published in 1863 but recalling time spent in England in the 1850s). 'We were dwelling in one of those oases that have grown up (in comparatively recent years, I believe) on the wide waste of Blackheath, which otherwise offers a vast extent of unoccupied ground in singular proximity to the metropolis.' The look of the streets, with their 'villas or boxes' occupied by businessmen, seemed more American than English.

The scene is semi-rural. Ornamental trees overshadow the sidewalks, and grassy margins border the wheel-tracks. The houses, to be sure, have certain points of difference from those of an American design, though seldom of individual taste; and, as far as possible, they stand aloof from the street, and separated each from its neighbor by hedge or fence, in accordance with the careful exclusiveness of the English character, which impels the occupant, moreover, to cover the front of his dwelling with as much concealment of shrubbery as his limits will allow. Through the interstices, you catch glimpses of well-kept lawns, generally ornamented with flowers, and with what the English call rock-work, being heaps of ivy-grown stones and fossils, designed for romantic effect in a small way. Two or three of such village streets as are here described take a collective name, – as, for instance, Blackheath Park, – and constitute a kind of community of residents, with gateways, kept by a policeman, and a semi-privacy, stepping beyond which you find yourself on the breezy heath.

Given that Hawthorne was not, to say the least, an unthinking anglophile, it is a benign judgement.

Whatever foundations survive of Wricklemarsh House itself lie under the crossroads of Blackheath Park, Pond Road and Foxes Dale. Galfridus Walpole's Westcombe was pulled down in 1854 – nobody wanted a house of that size in what was now an area of suburban streets. John Julius Angerstein's Woodlands survives, but it stands not in parkland but on Mycenae Road, developed in the 1870s and named after Heinrich Schliemann's excavations in Greece, taking place at that time. The last estate in the area to be developed, the Earls of St German's estate at Kidbrooke, was purely agricultural. It had never had a country house on it. Perhaps that accounts for its survival, given the liability that country houses so close to London had become. Most of Kidbrooke was still fields in the 1920s.

As these developments were being effected around Blackheath, the centre of Greenwich had been receiving attention. While the Commissioners of the Hospital had managed to erase the worst of the slums that lay around their building, the streets that lay immediately beyond the gates remained unwashed by the tide of taste. To the kindly eye of the painter, they might be considered picturesque. It was here that the poor of the town lived, and the lanes and courts had something of a Neapolitan air, the buildings crumbling, the alleyways festooned with washing, the inhabitants of the houses sitting on doorsteps. Charming in their way, but also malodorous, disease-ridden and squalid. The Commissioners bought them up, and drafted a Greenwich Improvement Bill to lay out roads and improve the approaches to the Hospital. It was passed as an Act in 1831, and Joseph Kay, the Surveyor to Greenwich Hospital, created Nelson Street, King William Street and Clarence Street (now College Approach). A new wing to the Hospital Infirmary, the Helpless Ward, was built over the ancient market-place, so a new market had to be erected. Assiter's Yard, Barber's Court and the others disappeared, along with Friars Road, Tavern Row, Taylor's Rents, Stagg Court and a host of other hovel-lined alleys. And in 1823-4 the neo-classical architect George Basevi built the new church of St Mary, to supply the need which Daniel Defoe had identified a century before, by the north gate of the Park. Henry H. Richardson, writing his guidebook to Greenwich of 1834, called it 'a neat edifice in the Grecian style of architecture … The interior is decorated in a style of elegance and chasteness superior to most new Churches.' It was demolished in 1935. Samuel Nixon's 1844 statue of William IV, 'the Sailor-King', now stands on the site.

*Opposite:* Greenwich pensioners in Fisher Alley, with the old Ship tavern and Greenwich Hospital beyond. The area had been demolished before Clarkson Stanfield painted it in 1848. Captain Marryat's novel *Poor Jack*, published in 1841, is partly set in the old Greenwich of narrow lanes, alleyways and yards. He comments on the transformation of the town since the beginning of the century. 'Narrow streets have been pulled down, handsome buildings erected – new hotels in lieu of small inns – gay shops have now usurped those which were furnished only with articles necessary for the outfit of the seamen.'

# Arcadian Life Among the Cockneys

THE OPEN SPACE of Blackheath was used for many things in the Georgian age. Various local militia regiments, such as the Blackheath Rangers, the Loyal Greenwich Volunteers, the Blackheath Volunteer Cavalry and the private army of five hundred men raised by Sir Gregory Page of Wricklemarsh House, exercised on the heath. In 1683 John Evelyn visited the first of the agricultural fairs that were held each year until the 1860s. He thought they were more London than country affairs, and he was right. In his book *The Heath*, the local historian Neil Rhind quotes an advertisement for a booth at an early fair. 'This is to give notice to all gentlemen, ladies and others, that there is to be seen from eight in the morning till nine at night, at the end of the great booth on Blackheath, a West of England woman 38 years of age, alive, with two heads, one above the other, having no hands, fingers, nor toes; yet she can dress or undress, knit, sew, read, sing. She has had the honour to be seen by Sir Hans Sloane, and several of the Royal Society. *N.B. Gentlemen and ladies may see her at their own houses if they please. This great wonder never was shown in England before this, the 13th day of May 1741.* Vivat Rex!'

GEORGE WILSON.
The Blackheath Pedestrian.

Holiday gambols in Greenwich Park. The scene, depicted on a linen handkerchief of c.1770, includes music, country dancing and the joys of 'tumbling', as men and women join hands to run down Castle Hill.

George Wilson on the morning of 19 September 1815, attempting his thousand-mile walk.

Feats of athleticism aroused great interest. Various races were run in May 1717, including one between two wenches with the prize of a holland smock. An officer was so exasperated when a maltster on a horse blocked his view that he drew his sword; but the maltster broke his Toledo, bloodied his nose and generally proved the superiority of plain John Bull to arrogance in uniform. George Wilson's prowess as the 'Blackheath Pedestrian' attracted huge numbers of spectators, sideshows and even a small herd of elephants. He set out to walk a thousand miles in a thousand hours, and would have done it, if the authorities, known as the Black Beaks of Blackheath, had not arrested him, fearing a riot. The charge of walking for money on a Sunday did not stick, but he was not given the opportunity to complete his thousand miles. Another endurance sport on Blackheath was prize fighting.

215

TO THE SOCIETY OF GOLFERS AT BLACKHEATH.

Nothing, though, can compare to the golf played on Blackheath. Blackheath Golf Club is the oldest outside Scotland. In the eighteenth century, it was played principally by Scots, and it is possible that the association of the place and the game dates from the era of that Scot and golfer James I. The earliest written records of the Club date from 1784. It possesses a silver club dated 1766. Earlier golfers sometimes wore uniforms, such as the scarlet jackets and white waistcoats of the London Scots Society. Greenwich pensioners served as caddies. The wearing of red jackets became a club rule in the mid-nineteenth century when the other members of the public had to be made aware of the golfers' approach. Caddies walked in advance, carrying flags. The pressure on the heath required the Club to introduce local rules to meet sometimes difficult circumstances. Balls that fell on the cricket or football pitches had to be regarded as unplayable. 'Golfers must wait for people and conveyances to pass out of their way before playing.' There was even a rule covering balls that got stuck in a gas lamp.

\* \* \*

William Innes, Captain of the Society of Golfers, in 1792, from a painting by Lemuel Abbott. Blackheath Golf Club moved to Eltham, about three miles from Blackheath, in 1923.

The Georgian architecture of Greenwich, with its decorous villas and neatly geometrical streets, might suggest that the earthiness associated with the Pepys era had been thoroughly tamed by politeness. This was certainly the image that P. Russell wanted to put across in *England Displayed*, 1769, when he described the town as 'one of the genteelest and pleasantest in England'. This opinion was repeated by Edward Hasted in his *History of Kent*, 1778, with the addition:

> The dryness and salubrity of the soil, the convenience of the park, the
> general pleasantness of the adjoining country, and its near neighbourhood
> to the metropolis, contribute to make it a most desirable residence for
> people of fashion.

There was an element of wishful thinking in this emphasis on the polite qualities of the place. Blackheath retained an air of primitive wildness, and the well-to-do must have felt relieved to cross it without incident. There are many newspaper accounts of highwaymen. One of them, known as Jack of the Green, robbed three gentlemen's coaches in the summer of 1759. After he had galloped away, one of the victims ordered his coachman to unhitch the horses from the coach, and together they set off in pursuit. Jack of the Green was not a master of concealment. They found him at a drinking booth in Dartford. 'On searching him they found a brace of pistols, loaded each with a brace of balls, a hat and a piece of stocking sewed to it for a mask, a watch, eleven guineas, some silver, a pair of silver buckles, and two Spanish pieces.' He turned out to be a sailor called Sam Walker belonging to the *Blenheim* man of war. Even Greenwich Park was not perfectly safe. One Saturday in June 1774, four footpads entered it by the north, south, east and west gates and systematically robbed all the ladies taking their exercise there. Nathaniel Hawthorne rejoiced in Blackheath's lawless reputation when he lived there in the mid-nineteenth century. 'Even now, for aught I know, the Western prairie may still compare favourably with it as a safe region to go astray in.'

In 1774 the *Gentleman's Magazine* records a Greenwich riot after some sailors, who had been pilfering from local gardens, were locked up in the watch house. There was another riot in 1811, when four hundred Irishmen 'assembled and knocked down every person in the streets they met with'. They stopped the service in the church, and assaulted the congregation as it left. These were some of the usual afflictions of port areas into which arriving ships would suddenly discharge large numbers of sailors. Another concomitant was smuggling. One of the officers of the Queen's yacht lying off Greenwich seemed to have grown suddenly corpulent after a voyage in 1744; on being searched, he was found to have a quantity of lace concealed around his body. In the same year a man at Lee was charged with smuggling goods to the value of £15,000 – showing that it was a significant trade.

The highwayman William Davis, nicknamed the Golden Farmer, robs a tinker on Blackheath.

Troops on Blackheath being reviewed by George III in 1787.

View of London about 1838. In the distance, the London and Greenwich Railway can be seen. The woman milking a cow in the foreground indicates how countrified the district remained, even in the early Victorian period.

## Blackheath Caverns

Dainty versus debauched – both these characteristics of Greenwich and its environs can be seen in the seventy years during which the Blackheath Caverns were exposed to view. They consisted of four chambers, hewn out of the chalk. From the moment they were discovered wild theories were advanced as to their origin and history. One of the least fanciful is that they were dug by the Anglo-Saxon inhabitants of the area, wishing to hide from the Danes. But they were in fact created as recently as the fifteenth century, when chalk was quarried from the area. There had been other caves under Blackheath, causing alarm as subsidence swallowed up elm trees or horses.

Whatever the origin of the Caverns, they filled impressionable minds with the romance of remote ages. Sensibilities attuned to Edmund Burke's theory of the Sublime found them gratifyingly horrific. Elizabeth Helme, in her Regency volume *Instructive Rambles in London and the Adjacent Villages,* subtitled *Designed to Amuse the Mind, and Improve the Understanding of Youth,* made them one of the edifying destinations to which the fictional children in the work were brought. 'Charles and Mary were not soon weary of exploring this cavern: but Mr Richardson observing the latter shuddered, and complained of extreme cold, desired the guide to lead the way out,' she writes. ' "How amazingly curious!" said Mary, as they reached the top of the stairs, and again beheld the ray of the sun which was setting as splendidly as possible, for the last of October, "yet how gladly do I again see the cheerful light!" '

Greenwich Park, for all its avenues, Observatory and elegant adjacent streets, was still, perhaps, haunted by the pagan deities whom the Romans had found here. That at least is the impression given by some of the activities for which the Park was used. Then as now, it was not only the preserve of the prosperous families for whom Gloucester Circus, the Paragon and Blackheath Park were developed. It was somewhere that their servants and tradesmen, not to mention seamen, dockyard workers and artisans, could take their relaxation too. There was much clicking of tongues on the part of the genteel element at the lack of propriety evident in some of the demotic pastimes, such as tumbling down the Giant's Steps. To do this, men and women joined hands and ran down the bank from the top of Castle Hill. Inevitably they fell over and ended up in a highly immodest tangle of arms and legs. Women's dress was disarrayed, and undergarments – if worn – were put on view. Contemporary prints suggest that some lubricious individuals haunted the spot, simply to observe this display of feminine indecorum. Tumbling may have been vulgar, but it was invigorating. A piece of doggerel attached to a print entitled *Greenwich Hill or Holiday Gambols* urges the polite society of the West End to give it a try:

Not all the activities that took place there were so decorous. Candles were fitted up; balls and dances were arranged. The impresario who organised the 'Grand Bal Masque' in 1850, a Mr J. Sleaman, boasted of the wonderful effect of the music at two hundred and eighty feet below ground. The penumbral lighting, combined with the generally thrilling air of the place, caused censure: anything might be happening in the shadows. Eventually, when somebody (or lack of oxygen) doused the lights completely during a masked dance and panic ensued, it was felt that enough was enough. The caverns were closed in the mid-1850s, a few years before Greenwich Fair.

**Blackheath Caverns, in a wood engraving of 1833. Note the chandelier: dances were held here until they became too indecorous for the Victorians.**

Ye sweet scented Sirs who are sick of the Sport
And the stale languid follies of Ballroom or Court,
For a Change leave the Mall and to Greenwich resort:
There heightened with Raptures which never can pall
You'l own, the Delights of Assembly and Ball
Are as dull as Yourselves, and just nothing at all.

But tumbling was a risk sport. There were accidents, as on a Tuesday on 4 April 1730, when, according to the *Daily Journal*, crowds of Londoners 'diverted themselves' by running down the hill beneath the Observatory: 'one of them, a young woman, broke her Neck, another ran against one of the Trees with such Violence that she broke her Jaw-bone and a third broke her leg.'

Twice a year, probably from the beginning of the eighteenth century, the boisterousness of tumbling swelled into the organised mayhem of Greenwich Fair. This was one of the events of the London year. Even the French philosopher Voltaire visited it, entranced by what he took to be 'people of fashion' – who turned out to be only the servant girls, apprentices and other townspeople of Greenwich dressed in their best for the fair.

Caricature entitled *Spys Taken at Greenwich on Easter Monday.* **A bishop and a duke are apprehended for spying on the young women tumbling down the hill in Greenwich Park.**

That was in 1726. Then there was a racetrack, for the use of both equines and humans, but the scale of the fair was still manageable and the atmosphere generally sedate. Respectable people went to meet each other, dine in specially erected booths, listen to music and dance quadrilles. But in the second half of the century the crowds coming to the fair were so great that they could not easily get through the entrances into the Park. The tone degenerated. What might be described as the tumbling classes got the better of the solid citizens, who stayed away, locking their windows and doors. An account in *The Gazetteer* describes how, in May 1776, the road from London was lined with every sort of conveyance, containing

*Holiday Gambols on Greenwich Hill*, 1761. On the left a fiddler plays to a sailor (wearing 'slops', in the form of a divided skirt) with his lass. Men and women tumble down the hill behind, their clothes awry.

**Greenwich Park on Easter Monday, 1804. The scene shows working people enjoying themselves, with dancing (to the fiddle of a one-legged lad, presumably a cabin boy at Greenwich Hospital) and canoodling.**

pickpockets and disreputable women. Once the Greenwich Railway had opened in the next century, as many as two hundred thousand people poured into the fair. Some of the fairground entertainments were innocent enough. The atmosphere is conveyed in the slightly tortuous mock-Caroline prose of *Pips' Diary*, written by Percival Leigh in 1849 – a late account of an occasion that in some respects stayed remarkably the same:

> The passage most insufferably crammed; and we having to force our way between walls hung with dolls and gilt gingerbread. The stalls and booths crowded also, and the tobacco smoke rising from the drinking places like a fog. Young prentice-blades and shop-boys pushing about with large masquerade noses …

Needless to say, Dickens, describing the fair in the *Evening Chronicle* in 1835, loved it. 'If the Parks be the "lungs of London" we wonder what Greenwich fair is – a periodical breaking out we suppose, a sort of spring-rash; a three days fever which cools the blood for six months afterwards, and at the expiration of which London is restored to its old habits of plodding industry.'

Posing as distinctly older than his twenty-three years, Dickens evoked the rack-ety conveyances into which Londoners – himself included – crowded to visit the Fair, and return from it, supposedly in his 'earlier days'.

We cannot conscientiously deny the charge of having once made the passage in a spring van accompanied by thirteen gentlemen, fourteen ladies, an unlimited number of children, and a barrel of beer; and we have a vague recollection of having, in later days, found ourself the eighth outside, on the top of a hackney coach, at something past four o'clock in the morning, with a rather confused idea of our own name, or place of residence. We have grown older since then, and quiet, and steady …

In the thick of the fair, the weight of humanity compressed fair-goers into a single, unified mass, assaulted on all sides by, and contributing to, a cacophony of sound.

Imagine yourself in an extremely dense crowd, which swings you to and fro, and in and out, and every way but the right one; add to this the screams of women, the shouts of boys, the clanging of gongs, the firing of pistols, the ringing of bells, the bellowings of speaking trumpets, the squeaking of penny dittoes, the noise of a dozen bands, with three drums in each, all playing different tunes at the same time, the hallooing of showmen, and an occasional roar from the wild beast shows; and you are in the very centre and heart of the fair.

George Cruikshank's depiction of the heady delights of tumbling in 1836. As the group in the left foreground indicates, it could be a dangerous as well as indecorous pastime; occasionally necks were broken.

Greenwich Fair: a pensioner charges for views through his telescope, probably pointed at Execution Dock on the Isle of Dogs.

Adding to the hubbub would be the boom of preachers decrying the licentiousness of the event. There were plenty of others who shared their view.

The chief amusement, mentioned time and again, was scratching. The trick was to buy a little serrated wheel, made of wood, at the end of a wooden stick. You then came up behind someone and ran it over his or her back. The noise was supposed to make the victim believe that his clothes had been torn. Scratchers were such a feature of the fair that one can hardly imagine that there were many people innocent enough to be caught out. Still, it was all part of the general hilarity. A more sedate pleasure was to look through the telescopes set up by Greenwich pensioners on the top of Castle Hill, offering views of the other bank of the river for a halfpenny. The principal feature of interest, in the previous century, was the gibbet on the Isle of Dogs, where the bodies of pirates swung in their chains. Naturally, great quantities of rum, brandy and gin were consumed and the public houses were thronged, fuelling the sort of misbehaviour that culminated in a riot of drunken soldiery in 1850; it was subdued by a combined force of policemen and mounted militia.

It was at Greenwich that the first 'Voyage Volante', or rising and descending roundabout, was brought before the public, in 1835. Two men underneath the machine turned a central mast, from which four boats hung on beams. The famous Wombwell's menagerie was there, with its elephants, freak shows, 'Intelligent Pig' and Wallace, the first lion to be born in captivity in Britain (born in Edinburgh, it was named after William Wallace, the Scottish patriot). 'No one probably has done so much to forward practically the study of natural history amongst the masses,' pronounced *The Times* in the obituary that followed Wombwell's death in 1850. John Ruskin, having suffered a childhood drained of almost any stimulating experience, confessed in *Fors Clavigera* that: 'One of the nearest approaches to insubordination which I was ever tempted into as a child was a passionate effort to get leave to play with the lion cubs in Wombwell's menagerie.' At Greenwich, Wombwell was not allowed undisputed mastery of the animal shows; his great rival Hilton would also bring his menagerie, its lion tamer being a black man and former sailor called Macomo. Likewise Saunders came with his Royal Circus, performing equestrian stunts. 'The dwarfs are also objects of great curiosity,' wrote Dickens, 'and as a dwarf, a giantess, a living skeleton, a wild Indian, "a young lady of singular beauty, with perfectly white hair and pink eyes", and two or three other natural curiosities, are usually exhibited together for the small charge of a penny, they attract very numerous audiences.' Perhaps an even greater attraction was Richardson's Theatre. At one time it may have been set up in the Park, but its more familiar location was an immense booth beside Creek Bridge, a confection of canvas, red serge draperies and brass ornaments, all lit by thousands of glittering candle-flames behind different coloured shades. There might be an overture, melodrama, three murders and a ghost, a pantomime and a comic song – not bad for twenty-five minutes. How did they manage it? To judge from the depictions, several of the varied offerings took place on stage simultaneously. There was considerable interaction with the audience, who blew pennywhistles and trumpets. 'But the best of the fun,' according to Percival Leigh, took place outside the booth, between performances, when the company would parade about 'with the Beefeaters' band playing and the show-girls in their spangles and paint dancing and the clowns grimacing and flinging somersaults, and the robber Chief standing in a brave posture in the cornerstone of fat ladies, wonderful pigs, giants and dwarfs to see, and conjurors in plenty, specially in the crowd, conjuring handkerchiefs out of pockets.'

It was all rather too uproarious for the more established citizens of Greenwich. They began their campaign to close the fair in 1825, but the showmen, stallholders and crowds kept coming. Eventually, the forces of Victorian propriety proved too much for the fair, and it was shut down in 1857. By then, Richardson, Wombwell and most of the other principals of the big shows were dead. Their entertainments were passing out of favour, as travelling theatres gave way to permanent ones and the public was less easily taken in by talking pigs and lion-headed ladies. 'The spirit of public enquiry which marks the age has been fatal with regard to the wonders of Greenwich Fair,' opined the *Illustrated London News* in 1850. Though the crowds do not seem to have diminished much in the last years, there was now less need for a great popular jamboree to take place so close to London, since the railways had made it possible for holiday crowds to reach seaside towns such as Margate and Brighton.

Nathaniel Hawthorne, living in Blackheath Park, witnessed the very last of the Greenwich Fairs, finding it distasteful and malodorous. Writing about it later, he could recall

little more than a confusion of unwashed and shabbily dressed people, intermixed with some smarter figures, but, on the whole, presenting a mobbish appearance such as we never see in our own country. It taught me to understand why Shakespeare, in speaking of a crowd, so often alludes to its attribute of evil odor. The common people of England, I am afraid, have no daily familiarity with even so necessary a thing as a washbowl, not to mention a bathing-tub.

**Holiday crowds at Greenwich Fair. On the right, a tipsy pensioner knocks over a basket of fruit; left of centre an urchin picks a pocket. Behind can be seen Richardson's Theatre and the entrance to Wombwell's Menagerie.**

The seething, whistle-tooting, brandy-quaffing, shouting, familiar, malodorous press of people, which Dickens enjoyed with gusto, was barely endurable to Hawthorne's fastidious temperament.

But that was not Hawthorne's last word. His general asperity in his comments about English life make his appreciation of the daily scene in Greenwich Park, with its crowds of forthright, open, gutsy Londoners, an even greater accolade than they would be from another writer.

They adhere closer to the original simplicity in which mankind was created than we ourselves do; they love, quarrel, laugh, cry, and turn their actual selves inside out with greater freedom than any class of Americans would consider decorous. It was often so with these holiday folks in Greenwich Park; and, ridiculous as it may sound, I fancy myself to have caught very satisfactory glimpses of Arcadian life among the Cockneys there, hardly beyond the scope of Bow-Bells, picnicking in the grass, uncouthly gambolling on the broad slopes, or straying in motley groups or by single pairs of love-making youths and maidens, along the sun-streaked avenues. Even the omnipresent policemen or park-keepers could not disturb the beatific impression on my mind. One feature, at all events, of the Golden Age was to be seen in the herds of deer that encountered you in the somewhat remoter recesses of the park, and were readily prevailed upon to nibble a bit of bread out of your hand.

It is a novel definition of Arcadia, but Arcadia all the same.

# ALL HONOUR
# TO THE ENDERBYS

FOR FOUR HUNDRED YEARS, the kings and queens who had stayed here, built palaces, laid out gardens, received dignitaries, alighted on the steps by the river, or extended their patronage towards the Observatory and the Naval Hospital, made Greenwich shine beneath the lustre of their presence. With the departure of Princess Caroline, Greenwich lost its connection with royalty. But that only freed it to participate more fully in the dynamic developments and ideas that gave shape to the nineteenth century. Almost every one of them finds at least an echo, sometimes a shout, at Greenwich. Engineering, through the industries that came into being on what was once thought of as the manor of Old Court, but would become a river-edged promontory hectic with industrial activity, before its present incarnation as the site of the Millennium Dome; empire, because of Greenwich's continuing association with the sea and everything to do with it; railways, as a result of the very first railway line in the metropolis – indeed, the first suburban line in the world – being built between London Bridge and Greenwich. For eleven years the Borough's Member of Parliament was no less a figure than William Gladstone, the Prime Minister. Thanks to the Royal Observatory, Greenwich was indelibly associated with the standardisation of time, which separates the fast-moving, industrialised, modern world from the haphazard, agriculturally based one that preceded it. And through it all, in this heroically energetic age, moved the river, always the river, as fundamental to the identity of Greenwich as it had been at the time of the Romans ...

\* \* \*

If you bought tea in nineteenth-century London, it might have come wrapped in a puzzle paper. The puzzle was a sort of pictorial riddle, enchanting to look at if not always easy to solve. One of them, a great favourite, shows Napoleon III being carried to France on the back of an enormous crow. This was an allusion to Captain M. Crow, whose fishing smack transported the future Emperor back to his homeland, once the Revolution of 1848 made it safe for him to return. Captain Crow was one of the fishermen who worked out of Greenwich. 'On retir-

View of the Seamen's Hospital, with the Yacht Tavern (with flagpoles), by John O'Connor, 1830–89. The Yacht was next to the Trafalgar Tavern. Its premises are used by the Curlew Rowing Club, established 1873.

229

ing from the sea he opened a fish shop in Turpin Lane, and sold very fine fish,' reminisced Mrs Thomas Norledge in 1915. 'I remember him well.'

Captain Crow and the other Greenwich fishermen were the inheritors of a tradition which stretched back for centuries to Greenwich's first settlers. The Greenwich parishioners who petitioned Parliament in 1710 for a new church, after the collapse of the old St Alfege's, could claim that nine-tenths of the population were seamen – an exaggeration in which there lay a kernel of truth. Their successors sailed in the navy, in merchant ships and on the lighters that distributed the huge quantities of goods arriving in the Port of London from around the world. The fishing fleet clung at first to the Thames, its estuary and the coastal waters around its mouth; but when the method of fishing the seabed with a trawl was developed in the early nineteenth century, they roamed as far as Iceland and the Faroes in their fishing smacks. A rich hunting ground was the Dogger Bank, east of Yorkshire. The Greenwich fishermen were so well known in the ports that lay nearest to it that they were asked to help develop one of them. A new dock had been built at Grimsby; before it opened in 1845, the directors of the company which owned it met a party of Greenwich captains, in the hope of persuading them to make it their local base. They even made one of the first fishing smacks to be powered by steam, the *John Ellis*, available to them as an inducement. They accepted the invitation, as well as the *John Ellis*. (The new-fangled *John Ellis* was not a success as a steamer; thinking that the noise of the engines disturbed the fish, the Greenwich sailors had it converted to old-fashioned sail.) For years the Greenwich men jealously guarded their right to precede all other boats out of the harbour. 'When the dock gates opened, Captain McBride, the first dockmaster, could be heard shouting, "Greenwich men first",' remembered Mrs Norledge, whose husband was an official of the company. 'I have seen the dock crowded with smacks, ready for sea, which would draw in close to make a waterway for a few Greenwich smacks to pass first. Compliments were very plentiful, which the Greenwich men would receive with a bow; and the old captain – eye steady, hand on tiller, hat raised and a smile of triumph on his lips – would make for the open sea.' The Greenwich men would ply between home and Grimsby, until home actually became Grimsby and they forgot Greenwich altogether.

Before the defection of the fleet, the fish landed at Greenwich included shoals of tiny sprat-like whitebait. They were much prized by the Victorians, and fuelled an appetite for whitebait suppers, served, most famously, at the Ship Hotel and Trafalgar Tavern on the waterfront. These whitebait feasts became a great London tradition. The whole Cabinet, Liberal or Tory, would assemble in an upper room of one of these pubs (the Trafalgar for Liberals, the Ship for Conservatives) to enjoy them. They were also popular with writers and artists. Dickens was fêted at the Trafalgar Tavern after his return from his first American visit in 1842. 'There is

230

no next morning hangover like that which follows a Greenwich dinner,' he moaned. And it was to Greenwich that Bella, heroine of his *Our Mutual Friend*, insisted that her Pa should take her out to dinner, after she had bought him a new outfit and provided him with money for the outing.

> The little expedition down the river was delightful, and the little room overlooking the river into which they were shown for dinner was delightful. Everything was delightful. The park was delightful, the punch was delightful, the dishes of fish were delightful, the wine was delightful … And then, as they sat looking at the ships and steamboats making their way to the sea with the tide that was running down, the lovely woman imagined all sorts of voyages for herself and Pa.

To judge from contemporary illustrations – and it says something for the fame of these dinners that they were recorded pictorially – the atmosphere of these whitebait dinners was relaxed, convivial of course, the mood owing something to the almost seaside nature of the fishing port. The whitebait had to be served fresh. So fresh, in fact, that they were kept alive in water, fished out with a skimmer, then rolled around in a large napkin containing flour, and tossed into a cauldron of

*The Greenwich Dinner. A Convivial Moment.* **This *Punch* cartoon depicts gentlemen 'under the influence of whitebait'.**

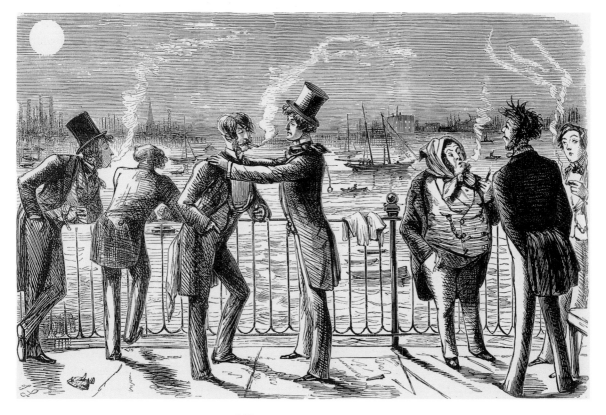

bubbling lard. Just two minutes' cooking, never more. 'The rapidity of the cooking process is of the utmost importance and if it be not attended to, the fish will lose their crispness,' opined John Timbs in *Club Life of London*, with reference to the Trafalgar's whitebait dinners. 'At table, lemon juice is squeezed over them and they are seasoned with cayenne pepper; brown bread and butter is substituted for plain bread and they are eaten with iced champagne or punch.' Who could resist them?

The architecture of the Trafalgar, designed by Joseph Kay in the year of Queen Victoria's accession, 1837, echoed this mood of relaxation, with its canopies and loggia, and general air of taking a liberty with the classical conventions. Men sprawled across chairs, threw their arms around each other in camaraderie, drank too much. Women do not seem to have featured very much. The Ship staggered on as an inn until 1941, when it sustained a direct hit by a German bomb; the site is now occupied by the dock containing the *Cutty Sark*. The Trafalgar still operates, its popularity drawing a veil over a period after 1890 when it ceased to function as an inn, becoming variously the Royal Alfred Aged Merchant Seamen's Institution, a working men's club and a block of flats. When it closed (temporarily) in 1890, a valediction was published in the *Kentish Mercury*. 'There are few of us of middle age who do not know something of the enjoyment of the exquisite dinners that were served in its public and private rooms of a balmy summer evening as the breezes from the Thames on the spring tide brought the refreshing flavour of sea salt,' wrote the *Mercury*. Was every evening balmy? Was a tang of salt really detectable above the other odours of the Victorian river? The jaunty architecture of the Trafalgar seems to tell us yes.

In size, whitebait are among the smaller fry to be harvested from the sea. Greenwich men went after not only them, but the very largest creatures of the deep – whales. And sometimes, the whales came to Greenwich. This was the case in 1273 when a whale, described as twelve 'toises' in length and five in girth (a toise being a length of very nearly two metres), was captured at Greenwich, and taken to London Bridge to be cut up. Another whale appeared at Greenwich in late 1658. Not only was it so extraordinary an arrival that people thought it must be an omen presaging Oliver Cromwell's death, but a pamphlet was published recording the event in graphic terms. The title alone unburdens a quantity of fact: *London's Wonder. Being a most true and positive relation of the taking and killing of a great Whale neer to Greenwich the said Whale being fifty eight foot in length, twelve foot high, fourteen foot broad, and two foot between the Eyes …* The whale was first spotted by a boy, who was frightened to see 'such a Monstrous fish'. The boy told some watermen, who immediately armed themselves with harpoons, hatchets, billhooks and anything else they could lay their hands on. Then, 'stripping off their Doublets and Breeches, [they] went only in their Shirts and Drawers to be light

## Greenwich Inns

From S. Shoberl, *A Summer's Day at Greenwich*, 1840:

There is ample accommodation at Greenwich to supply all the wants of the visiter [sic], be he rich or poor. Among the largest hotels are the Trafalgar and the Crown and Sceptre, both situated to the east of the Hospital, to which successive whitebait parties resort throughout the season. At either of these he may obtain an excellent dinner, tea, or other refreshments.

Should, however, his means not justify him in resorting to the aforesaid inns, he will do well to direct his steps southward to the Admiral Hardy tavern, which he will find in the second street on the right from the New Pier. Here he may obtain all he can desire on the most economical terms, everything being of the best quality; a good dinner, wine of course *not* included, for about half-a-crown, or excellent tea for one shilling.

To the more humble almost every street in Greenwich also offers a facility for obtaining the refreshing beverage last mentioned at a charge of little more than they might procure the same for at home. Decently attired females appear at their doors, ready to welcome the stranger into a snug little parlour, or into some little arbour in the garden, where he may for once enjoy the China fluid in the open air.

**Balconies of the Ship Hotel, which stood on the site of the dock that now holds the *Cutty Sark*. This wood engraving suggests the charm of dining at Greenwich, which brought many visitors – including entire Cabinets – from London.**

and nimble at their worke'. The harpoons stuck into her, but came out again; the watermen stabbed her with spears, someone fired a couple of bullets into her, various anchors were flung at her, and eventually a fisherman lodged a little anchor in her nostril, which stuck fast. 'Whilst she was in this extasie and danger of death she would sometimes bounce above the water as high as a house, and down she would sinck into the Thames again, then up again leaping and tossing her body above the water, sometimes eight or nine foot high.' When, after further gory stratagems, she was killed, she became an instant marvel, with all London wanting portions of

The Greenwich waterfront in 1835. The majestic hospital rises serenely above the bustling wharves and river life.

her flesh as souvenirs. 'Some bought peeces as big as a man's middle, and some took lesser peeces to shew to their neighbours, friends and acquaintance, that what is reported concerning this hugeous whaile, is an absolute truth; and as a monument of Remembrance, they do both safely and securely lock it up, esteeming more rarely of it, than a dish of Anchovis, Salmon, or Lobsters, that is a present for a Lady, for although a Whale be not good to eate, it is novelty, and very strange and much more stranger to be cacht in the River of Thames so neere to London bridge.'

For all the commerce on the nineteenth-century river, and the pollution inside it, the spout of confused whales was a spectacle that once or twice astounded Greenwich residents in the Victorian era. Perhaps it reflects the skills that local people had in whaling that, when one appeared off Deptford in 1842, it was quickly despatched by five watermen. Measuring fourteen foot six inches, it was thought to have gone 'blind in the river while in pursuit of herrings' – though whales only eat plankton. A much larger whale, all of sixty-six feet seven inches, was chased aground at Woolwich in November 1899. At first a wonder, the huge animal soon presented problems of disposal, which became increasingly acute as decomposition set in. (When the body of the whale burst, it revealed two calves, still just alive.) Curiously, another whale beached itself at Woolwich a few days later. According to a report in *The People*: 'About two o'clock the crew of the steam tug Empress fastened a rope to it, dragged it off the beach, and took it in tow with the intention of consulting the Thames Conservancy as to what was to be done with the monster.'

Whaling vessels had been sailing from the Thames since the eighteenth century. Some time in the first years of the nineteenth century the whaling firm of Samuel Enderby and Sons established a rope and sail manufactory on the west of the peninsula of East Greenwich, the tongue of land looped by the Thames at the top of which the Millennium Dome has arisen. Enderbys had been trading in whale oil for years. Originally they had simply bought it from the Nantucket men, and it was the latter who incurred all the terrible risks of the hunt. This trade was disrupted by the American Revolution: the vessels from which East India Company tea was thrown into Boston Harbour in 1773 belonged to Enderby – the tea was to have been their return cargo. This may have spurred the company to investigate alternative sources of supply. They began to test the southern hemisphere for whales. They found them, and a flotilla of Enderby ships set off to reap the reward. This time the outward cargo was made up of convicts, destined for Australia. These ships sailed far into the Antarctic. Their presence is commemorated in the name of Enderby Land given to a black outcrop of mountain rising out of the icefloes. One Enderby ship, the *Britannia*, had Thomas Melville of

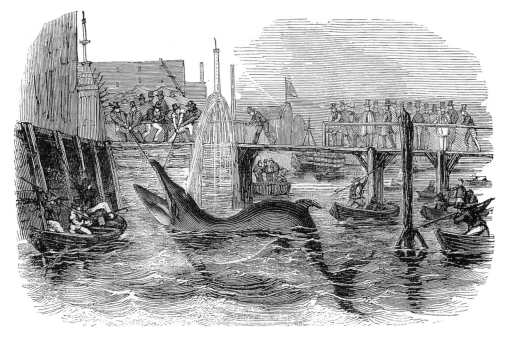

Catching a whale off Deptford pier in 1842.

## W. E. Gladstone

Greenwich was one of the five constituencies represented by the Liberal Prime Minister William Gladstone during his sixty-two and a half years in Parliament. But during his eleven years as Greenwich's Member of Parliament he rarely visited the place. Occasionally he would heroically address open air meetings, as in 1871 when he spoke for two and a half hours on Blackheath in defence of his government's policies. His next visit was during the general election campaign of 1874. In 1876 he again appeared on Blackheath, his theme being the 'Bulgarian Horrors' perpetrated by the Turkish. A crowd of ten thousand heard him, despite heavy rain. Top hats on heads, dozens of reporters took down his words from beneath the rostrum from which the Grand Old Man was thundering. Queen Victoria's offer of a grace and favour house at Greenwich to enable him to discharge his constituency duties was declined, presumably because those duties occupied so little of his time. 'Greenwich was a thoroughly unfortunate constituency for him,' comments Gladstone's biographer, Roy Jenkins, bleakly. 'It aroused neither his affection nor his interest.'

**W. E. Gladstone, MP for Greenwich, speaking on Blackheath during a rare visit to his constituency in 1876. Below him, top-hatted reporters record every word.**

Boston as its captain. His grandson, Herman, would be the author of *Moby-Dick*. 'All honour to the Enderbys,' wrote Melville in that great work. The narrator of the book, Ishmael, believed that the house of Enderby, 'in my poor whaleman's opinion, comes not far behind the united royal houses of the Tudors and Bourbons, in point of real historical interest'.

On the other side of Greenwich, at Deptford, the dockyard continued as a building yard, long after the draught of the warships made it impossible for them to be fitted out there. Naval stores such as timber, pitch, tar and hemp could be bought at good prices there, since the ships bringing them from overseas could be sure of collecting another cargo from the London docks. River-built ships enjoyed a premium in the eyes of sailors. There were boat-building yards on the peninsula: the National Company for Boat Building by Machinery declared its purpose in its title, though it seems not to have prospered, being taken over by the more famous firm of Maudslay, Son and Field, from Lambeth, in 1865. Maudslay's continued building quite sizeable ships at Greenwich until 1872, before the yard was converted into a boiler-making works. In between boilers they managed also to build the Great Wheel for Earl's Court in the 1890s. The works closed in 1900. Then there was John Penn and Company, makers of marine engines, who were later absorbed by the Thames Ironworks and Shipbuilding Company. In 1911 the latter were responsible for constructing the last battleship to be built on the London river, the *Thunderer*; the yard where this took place lay at Bow Creek opposite Greenwich, on the north bank of the river. It was near the spot where Isambard Kingdom Brunel's immense leviathan, or rather white elephant, the *Great Eastern*, was constructed, no doubt with Greenwich men supplying labour. It must have made an extraordinary sight, dwarfing all other boats on the river, marooned after completion for several months while the great engineer worked out the means of launching it.

More modestly, East Greenwich also supplied many of the barges that, with their ochre-coloured sails, used to make such a picturesque sight on the river. To the men who owned them, the appeal of the barges was that they could go almost anywhere, because their draught was so shallow, and with their flat bottoms they could sit upright on a beach or on mud when the tide was out. There could be as many as eight thousand barges working the Thames at any one time. They carried every kind of cargo, including hay from the Essex countryside into London to feed the enormous numbers of horses in the metropolis, and horse manure back to Essex for the fields. Hay would be built up into towering stacks, upon which stood a mate or boy to tell the skipper – whose view was filled with nothing but hay – how to steer. The firms that built the sailing barges also made the 'dumb barges', or lighters – barges without any independent means of propulsion – which can still be seen snaking their way along the river, in procession, behind tugs.

There was a tarry smell – sometimes literally – about a number of businesses on the peninsula, beyond those that actually built boats. As well as their wharfs,

The Great Wheel for the Earl's Court Exhibition of 1895 was built at the Maudslay, Son and Field works in East Greenwich.

John Penn and Sons, Engine Works, on Blackheath Road, in 1863. The company supplied marine engines to shipbuilders throughout the world. John Penn Jr is first on the right in the foreground.

the Enderbys owned a factory to make rope. When iron cable began to replace hemp, the Camberwell firm of William Kuper and Company opened a works at East Greenwich to produce it. Most of their production was used as rope would have been; but the factory also had the distinction of producing much of the vast length of electric cable, for telegraph, that was laid beneath the Atlantic to link Britain and the United States. Laying this cable was one of the great triumphs of Victorian engineering, and it took four attempts to get it right. For the first two, half of the cable was embarked on each of two ships; in the summer of 1858, on the second try, a telegraph message was sent across the Atlantic. But the euphoria that this caused was short-lived, since within a month the cable had broken and could not be repaired. Nothing daunted, the promoters raised more money and ordered a heavier cable. There were disadvantages in using two ships, so they commissioned the only ship in the world big enough to carry the 22,500 tons of cable: the *Great Eastern*. The ship could not sail until 1865, due to the American Civil War. When it did so, the cable broke and it had to turn back. Yet another cable was made for the same ship, and in 1866 was laid successfully. Not only that, but the 1865 cable was recovered and spliced to one remaining on board; this provided two cables across the Atlantic. Part of the triumph could be ascribed to the Greenwich time signal which was received twice a day by the ship, making it possible to calculate its longitude accurately (see next chapter). The company's subsequent cable-laying ships would be moored off Greenwich.

*A Hay Barge off Greenwich,* **painted by Edward William Cooke in 1835. Barges brought hay from the Essex countryside and bricks from the brickfields into London, the return cargo being horse manure to spread on the fields.**

The hulk of HMS *Dreadnought* being towed down the Thames by a paddle tug. This old man of war was moored off Greenwich as a hospital ship, later bequeathing its name to the Dreadnought Seamen's Hospital. The *Dreadnought*'s 'splendid frame fills up half the river', wrote Captain Marryat in *Poor Jack*, 'and she that was used to deal out death and destruction with her terrible rows of teeth is now dedicated by humanity to succour and relieve.'

This watercolour shows it on its last voyage before being broken up in 1875.

**Reels of cable being covered in rubber for laying beneath the Atlantic. The scene is at Enderbys Wharf.**

The expansion of London Docks, in Britain's heyday as a world power, passed Greenwich by. Perhaps its roads and railways were not good enough to distribute the merchandise as it arrived from overseas. Furthermore, the City, with its merchants, and the East End, with its manufacturers, lay on the north side of the Thames. So when the Royal Dock was built in 1855 and the Royal Albert in 1880, they too were located on the north bank. Greenwich took note, launching its own bid for docks to be constructed on the peninsula in 1858 and 1881 – each time just a little too late, since the big new docks had already absorbed the demand. A Greenwich Dock would have dominated the area. Without it, the peninsula continued to support its brood of motley industries; and besides, though the big ships did not come into East Greenwich, their presence in such numbers just a short distance away provided all the more work for bargees and lightermen, and all the more call for Greenwich-built vessels to deliver cargoes from the Docks to elsewhere.

Not that the peninsula's industries were exclusively to do with ships, the river and the sea; far from it. The marsh, unseen and increasingly unsightly, was the place from which many appetites of the greedy behemoth of London, expanding rapidly, were supplied. There were brickworks, cementworks, works for making the creosote-soaked wood blocks that were used to pave many streets (Bethell's Timber Preserving Works became the Improved Wood Pavement Company). There was a company that crushed foreign seeds to extract oil (the London Seed Crushing Company). It went out of production in about 1900, just at the time that the Greenwich Inland Linoleum Company got underway. The latter was a big name in linoleum during the golden age of that floor covering; it ceased manufacture in 1935. There were businesses supplying ice, candles, soap, oxygen and animal feed. In 1867 a gun factory called the Blakeley Ordnance Works was built on the tip of the peninsula, where the Millennium Dome now stands, but it only lasted a few years. A rather more permanent presence was that of the South Metropolitan Gas Company, which converted mountains of coal, landed from the river from the big new screw-propeller-driven colliers, into the gas that flickered in the homes and streets of Victorian London. Its legacy of pollution caused the whole of the millennium site to be sealed with a membrane before work on the Dome began.

Making coal gas and its by-product, tar, were not traditional river occupations, but, like many of the other activities on the peninsula, they depended upon the river for their supply of raw materials, and it was the existence of the river that determined their location. As though to emphasise the extent to which water was the natural element in these parts, there was even a station for the river police, on a floating pier.

* * *

Just at the time that Britain was celebrating its victory at Waterloo, a new and delightful method of reaching Greenwich made its appearance on the river. With a ring of the bell, a whistle of steam and perhaps a shower of soot, the first paddle-steamer whirred into motion. Soon the *Ariel*, the *Nymph*, the *Naiad*, the *Sylph* and the *Fairy* were all ploughing their cheerful way between Woolwich and Hungerford

EASTER MONDAY ON THE RIVER THAMES.—GOING TO GREENWICH.

*Easter Monday on the River Thames – Going to Greenwich.* This wood engraving of 1847 depicts excursionists on a paddle-steamer, with its plume of black smoke. The *Naiad* is in the background.

A hot-air balloon view from above One Tree Hill in 1845 clearly shows the sweep of the River Thames. Another hot-air balloon is just above the horizon.

Bridge, stopping at Greenwich. Within a few years, another mode of travel was causing a sensation, as the first bout of railway mania convulsed Britain in the early 1820s. The earliest railways were in the north of England. In London, the travelling public may have been fascinated by them, but remained sceptical about their safety. The nervous had their worries about paddle-steamers, whose boilers had been known to explode. But the paddle-steamer, moving decorously along a river that had been sailed, if admittedly not paddled, for centuries, offered a rather less frightening experience to passengers than the steam locomotive running on iron rails.

The Kentish Railway Company was formed in 1824, with the object of opening a line from London to Greenwich and ultimately Dover, but the *Quarterly Review* would have none of it. It would be too expensive to build and too alarming to travel on. As it opined, in somewhat gusty style, in March 1825:

> It is certainly some consolation to those who are to be whirled at the rate of eighteen or twenty miles an hour, by means of a high pressure engine, to be told that they are in no danger of being seasick while on shore; that they are not to be scalded to death, nor drowned by the bursting of the boiler; and that they need not fear being shot by the scattered fragments, or dashed to pieces by the flying off or the breaking of a wheel. But with all these assurances, we should as soon expect the people of Woolwich to suffer themselves to be fired off upon one of Congreve's ricochet rockets, as to trust themselves to the mercy of such a machine going at such a rate. Their property they may, perhaps, trust, but while one of the finest navigable rivers in the world runs parallel to the proposed railroad, we consider that the other twenty per cent which the subscribers are to receive for the conveyance of heavy goods is almost as problematical as that to be derived from the passengers. We will back old Father Thames against the Woolwich rail-way for any sum.

The Kentish Railway Company quietly expired.

Enter George Landmann and George Walter. Landmann had been born in Woolwich and brought up in Blackheath. Having served as a lieutenant-colonel with the Royal Engineers, he sold his army commission in 1824 and set himself up as a civil engineer. He formed a scheme for a line between London and Greenwich that would run ultimately to Dover. Walter, though the son of a clergyman, came from a family of financial risk-takers (one had lost a fortune in the South Sea Bubble). He had been in the navy, knew many people of influence, had experience of promoting railways and was a member of the stock exchange. Between them, Landmann and Walter had exactly the experience necessary to form a railway company. They did so in 1831, and called their proposed line the London and Greenwich Railway. It may have been under four miles in length, but it brought the railway to London.

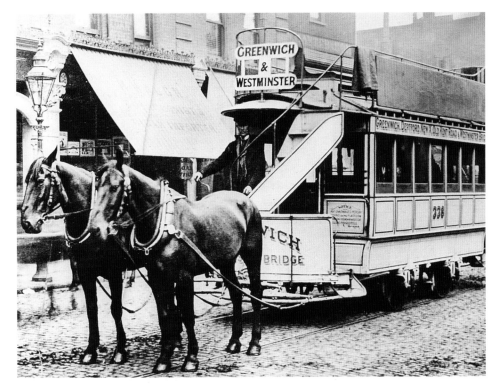

Horse-drawn tram on the route between Greenwich and Westminster in 1885. This operation survived competition from the railways, unlike George Shillibeer's horse-omnibus service of fifty years earlier.

Greenwich at that time had a population of 24,500 people. It had just been made a municipal borough. But it was still a separate entity from London. The wave of Georgian and Regency development, which created Gloucester Circus in Greenwich and the Paragon in Blackheath, had not caused this rock-pool to mingle its waters with those suburbs nearer the metropolis. There were still fields between the crowded little courts of Bermondsey and the now rather old-fashioned town of Deptford. The railway crossed country that was described, in 1835, as 'very rich … almost wholly laid out in vegetable gardens'. The writer added prophetically: 'These will probably disappear ere long before the encroachments of brick and mortar.' There were wharfs along the riverfront at Greenwich, and the stirrings of industry on the marsh. The town itself, dominated by the Seamen's Hospital, was a contrast of large houses, with pretensions to gentility, and a jumble of odd little alleys around the river, next to the Seamen's Hospital, composed of ramshackle wooden buildings.

The Green Man at Greenwich was well known as the first stopping-place of the Dover Mail. The journey there, from Charing Cross, took at least an hour. For all that, a new horse omnibus service was started shortly before the railway came into prospect, its proprietor being the celebrated George Shillibeer. In 1834 Shillibeer gave up the other routes he had been running to concentrate all his twenty vehicles on the London-Greenwich-Woolwich run. It was popularly assumed that this would defeat the railway promoters. Safety was again uppermost in the public mind. The battle became the subject of a music-hall song entitled 'Shillibeer's Original Omnibus versus the Greenwich Railroad':

> These pleasure and comfort with safety combine,
> They will neither blow up nor explode like a mine;
> Those who ride on the railroad might half die with fear,
> You can come to no harm in the safe Shillibeer.

**The London and Greenwich Railway was London's first railway, and the first suburban railway in the world. The viaduct was necessary to preserve an even gradient.**

But the safe Shillibeer could not remain the prosperous Shillibeer, when battle was joined with the railway; before long he had gone out of business.

The railway strode down to Greenwich on arches – nearly a thousand of them. The viaduct, the purpose of which was to keep a steady gradient for the track, was a wonder in itself. 'As a work of art it is undoubtedly very striking, while the minor considerations involved in the plan are novel and interesting,' commented the *Penny Magazine* in January 1836. Even before the first trains were running, the company obtained a modest income from charging the public sixpence to walk down the line. It had been hoped that the arches could be turned into dwellings,

and the *Penny Magazine* reported the optimistic verdict of a couple of families who were trying out two prototypes at Deptford.

> One individual described the passing of a train, while he was within one of the houses, as resembling a distant roll of thunder, which was, however, from the rapidity of the motion, away in an instant; another thought it resembled the sudden passing of a heavily-laden waggon, the noise of which did not at all disturb his comfort. There will be different opinions upon this point, according to the varying sensitiveness of individuals, and no fair opportunity will be afforded of forming a correct judgment until the railway is opened and the traffic on it is begun. The noise will, however, be much less than many persons might be inclined to suppose; the solidity of the arches and the smoothness of the railway will diminish the vibration.

A better use was as storage or workshops: even at a time when the London slums were so overcrowded the idea of living beneath railway arches did not take off.

The first experiments in running trains along sections of track took place in 1835, with the engineer Sir John Rennie; the Astronomer Royal, Professor Sir G.

*Opposite:* **The foot tunnel, built by the London County Council, which connects Greenwich with the Isle of Dogs. When it opened in 1902, regulations forbade the herding of sheep through the tunnel.**

B. Airy; and the mathematician Charles Babbage being among the first passengers. Several Members of Parliament, the Swedish ambassador and the Prince of Orange joined the fashionable ladies making up parties to ride in the carriages. Not everyone was caught up in the enthusiasm, however. Sir Thomas Hardy, Nelson's old friend who was now governor of the Hospital, refused, on the grounds that it was pointless to take an unnecessary risk. And he may have felt vindicated when, on 12 November, the engine broke an axle on a new stretch of track and the train was derailed. The periodical *John Bull*, never a friend to the railways, was scathing:

> The loss of life upon the favourite toy from Liverpool to Manchester has already been terrific. Mr Huskisson was the first martyr to this favourite absurdity; and the last splendid exhibition took place only on Thursday, upon the new Tom-foolery to Greenwich, when in the outset 'by some accident', one of the carriages, in which a party of noodles ventured themselves, was thrown off the rail, but although it ran a vast many yards, no serious accident occurred. How lucky! Nobody killed the first day of trial!

'What have we let come amongst us?' asked a correspondent to a local Greenwich paper, under the signature of 'A Mourner', when the opening of the railway seemed imminent. 'This infernal Greenwich Railway, with all its thundering steam engines and omni*busters*, just ready to open, and destroy our rural town of Greenwich with red-hot cinders and hot water ...' But as the letter-writer admitted, it was too late to complain. In December 1836, with banners flying, bands playing national airs and the bells of parish churches pealing gaily, the first train to Deptford started – an hour and forty minutes late. The line reached Greenwich in 1838. The station was on the site of the present one. It is a short walk to the west of the town, opposite the almshouses founded by the Elizabethan antiquary William Lambarde.

And there it stopped. The intention had been simply to push onwards in a direct line towards Dover, but to do that would have meant crossing the Park. There was a proposal to run the railway on a viaduct between the Queen's House and the Observatory, an aesthetic disaster. It was not something that the people of Greenwich, not specially enamoured of the railway in the first place, would tolerate. Remarkably, in that age of expansion, the directors of the London and Greenwich accepted defeat. They turned to tunnelling instead. Professor Airy objected against the tunnel going under the Park, on the grounds that it would upset his instruments. So the directors adopted the more expensive option of tunnelling beneath the grounds of the Hospital; the result was called College Tunnel. It was not to be built for forty years. The sinking of the line was

*London from Greenwich Hill*, by C. F. Buckley, 1851. By this date, the holiday crowds were rather more seemly than their Regency forebears.

attended by the building of a new station, in 1878. By then it was too late to save East Greenwich's chances of becoming a major industrial centre: heavy ship-building now took place in the North. In view of Greenwich's subsequent development, as largely a residential suburb of London, this may have been just as well.

* * *

Elsewhere in Europe 1848 was the Year of Revolutions. This could hardly be said of Greenwich, but ten years after the railway first arrived, it was undeniably a different place from 1831, when the London and Greenwich Company was founded. The number of people living there had increased by five thousand, to just under thirty thousand inhabitants. The Hospital had introduced various schemes to improve the character of the town, and the building of the new market in 1831 entailed sweeping away some of the worst streets. The old wooden houses were being replaced by brick façades: often no more than façades applied to old struc-

Turner's *View of London from Greenwich*, 1825: a reflection on the gargantuan growth of the metropolis over the previous three centuries.

tures. With their smart shop fronts, they were transforming Church Street into a place of regularity and order. It was still an age of small specialist shops. There were no fewer than twenty-seven straw-hat makers, twenty-two cowkeepers, seventy-seven hotels, inns and taverns, fifty-six beer-houses and, just as surprisingly, twenty-six surgeons and three physicians. Gas was provided by the Phoenix Gas Company, which had been supplying the town – or that section which could afford it – from six gasometers in Bridge Street since 1827. The main streets were now lit by gas. Concerts were held (the librarian was sacked for attempting to charge ten per cent on admissions), and the East Greenwich Madrigal Society met weekly at the Mitre. A Literary Institute had opened in 1837, followed by the Greenwich Society for the Diffusion of Useful Knowledge in 1843. The Temperance Society met monthly and, if we can believe its own verdict, 'accomplished much in ameliorating the condition and elevating the character of some of the most degraded of our fellow countrymen'. The town was overrun with places of worship: two congregational churches, a Baptist chapel, a Wesleyan Methodist chapel, and an English Presbyterian church and the Catholic Our Lady Star of the Sea both rising – all in addition to the Church of England's St Alfege's and St Mary's. For all the front of respectability, there was a seditious undercurrent, with Chartists meeting secretly in their Wat Tyler Club and rallying on Blackheath. The large number of foreigners, who came with the ships and sometimes made Greenwich their home, added a note of colour. In the previous century a society of anti-Gallicans met at the Chocolate House on Blackheath, presumably in response to the many French people living in the area.

'Situated on the banks of a noble river, and adjacent to a beautiful park; the salubrious air, and the charming views from the hills and the high grounds in and around it, render it a delightful place of resort for all classes.' Such was the judgement of *The Stranger's Guide to Greenwich* of 1855. It is no wonder, then, that its population grew and grew, to 46,500 in 1881. This led W. Howarth, author of *Greenwich: Past and Present* of 1885, to comment: 'Perhaps never before have houses been erected to such a great extent as in the last ten or fifteen years. *East* Greenwich, as we term it, has lately felt the hand of change upon it; the fields and meadow lands of a short time ago are now streets of thickly populated houses.'

Such was the reality of Greenwich towards the end of the nineteenth century: an active, developing suburb, with more than its fair share, one would imagine, of awkward, argumentative people, commercially minded and church-going, their English solidity spiced with a sprinkling of foreigners and a tang of the sea. But as the name of Greenwich flew around the world it was associated, not with a tangible, durable and populous neighbourhood beside the Thames, but with that most ethereal and fleeting of concepts – Time.

*Right:* **Pensioners in the Grand Square of the Seamen's Hospital, in the 1840s. The statue of George II was carved by Rysbrack from a single block of marble, captured from a French ship, and erected in 1735.**

*Below:* **The prison hulks *Warrior* and *Unité* moored off Woolwich. They were converted from old Royal Navy ships after American Independence stopped Britain transporting convicts across the Atlantic. The prisoners worked in the Royal Dockyard and Royal Arsenal until the system was discontinued in 1857. After a spell being used as isolation vessels during cholera epidemics, the ships were finally broken up and burnt.**

*Above:* **John Riddle, headmaster of the Royal Hospital School, photographed with a class in the Queen's House, 1855. Founded in 1717, the school was attended by the sons and daughters of seamen. Riddle died after falling off a classroom platform during a lesson.**

*Left:* **Children at the gates of the Royal Hospital School, which occupied the Queen's House during the nineteenth century. The vessel obscuring the view of the Queen's House was appropriately called the block ship.**

*Above:* The thirty-five-ton Woolwich Infant, built at the Royal Arsenal in 1870. There might be fifty such guns under construction at one time. Trials at sea proved disastrous when the prototype Infant exploded, killing many. It was then improved and adapted for use on land.

*Opposite:* Pastoral Greenwich, photographed on 11 August 1858. The view shows Woodlands home farm, Combe Farm and Greenwich Marshes, with the masts of ships on the Thames visible in the distance. In the foreground are the Roberts family who ran Combe Farm as a market garden.

*Right:* Window-mender, King Street, Greenwich, 1885.

# THE WORLD
# SETS ITS WATCH

I N 1833, a curious ritual could be observed at the Royal Observatory. A tall spike supporting a weathervane had been erected on top of one of the turrets. It had been made by Messrs Maudslay, Son and Field (still of Lambeth: they had not yet acquired the National Company for Boat Building by Machinery on Greenwich Marsh) who also constructed, out of sight, a winding apparatus on the floor below the turret. At five minutes to one, a big red ball was hoisted halfway up the spike. At two minutes to one, it rose as far as it could, to the crossbars of the weathervane. At one o'clock exactly, it came plummeting down again. This is said to have been the world's first public time signal. The ball could plainly be seen from the river, and the mariners whose vessels were about to sail down the Thames, out into the estuary and perhaps to far-flung places around the world, knew that it would begin to fall at precisely one o'clock. They could set their watches by it.

Time had been a preoccupation of astronomers working in the Royal Observatory since it was founded. Without an accurate idea of what time it was, seafarers were unable to plot their longitudinal position at sea. By the nineteenth century, they had the chronometers that could enable them to do this. But these timepieces, to be accurate, needed to be set to the correct time in the first place. It was difficult, if not impossible, to make the precise lunar observations that would give the time while a ship was at sea. This could be done ashore, but was not very convenient. An observatory clock could be used to adjust a pocket watch, which was then carried to the chronometer on board ship (the chronometer itself was too sensitive to move). This was cumbersome. In short, no method was perfect. Sometimes ships at sea were alerted by means of guns or rockets fired, or flags dipped, but these were not regular occurrences. As an experiment, a timeball was erected at the entrance to Portsmouth Harbour in 1829; and in 1833 Captain Robert Wauchope of the Royal Navy, the champion of the timeball, suggested to the Admiralty that one should be set up at Greenwich. John Pond, the Astronomer Royal, was quick to agree. On 28 October, the Lords Commissioners of the Admiralty gave notice that a timeball 'will henceforward be dropped … By observing the first instant to its downward movement, all vessels in the adjacent

The timeball falls on the Royal Observatory at one o'clock precisely. The purpose of the timeball, instituted in 1833, was to allow mariners to take an accurate time reading, based on observations of the sun made by the Greenwich astronomers. This was of critical importance to the calculation of longitude by sea. By the end of the century, Greenwich time had been adopted as standard time almost throughout the whole world.

reaches of the river as well as in most of the docks, will thereby have an opportunity of regulating and rating their chronometers.' Noon might have seemed a more obvious time to choose than one o'clock; but noon was the moment when the astronomers were making the observations to find the time in the first place.

Soon, however, it would not only be mariners who wanted to keep the exact time. Following the railway's arrival in Greenwich in 1838, by the middle of the century, the whole of the country had been cross-hatched with iron lines. The guards waving off the trains would look importantly at their official timepieces, to keep the service running precisely to time. But whose time was it? Because of the curvature of the earth's surface, the sun rises and sets at a slightly different time in each part of Britain. Before the railways, time did not have the same importance that it was to assume in a busier age. There were few public clocks, and not all of them were accurate. Those that were carefully regulated – the clocks on town halls, for example – were set to local time. The local time in Bristol, to the west of London, was sixteen minutes behind that of the capital. That did not matter when those places were a world away from each other. But once they had been joined by the railway, and not only joined to each other but to dozens of other towns and cities, so that the possibilities of the system became more and more complex, there was no room for local variations in time. Fortunately, just as the railways provided the need for a standard time, they also provided them with the means by which it could be distributed.

The idea of introducing a standard time throughout Britain was not absolutely new. It had been advocated by one of the Commissioners for Longitude, Captain Basil Hall, as well as Abraham Follett Osler. According to a report of a lecture given by Osler to the Birmingham Philosophical Institution, which appeared in the very first issue of the *Illustrated London News* (14 May 1842), Osler urged it upon the Postmaster General, Rowland Hill, 'as a matter of some importance in connection with the post-office department'. Neither Hall nor Osler was the first to come up with the notion of standard Post Office time; he ascribed the credit for that to Dr William Hyde Wollaston, who died as early as 1828. Hyde proposed that all post-office clocks throughout the United Kingdom should be regulated 'by means of the time brought from London by the mail-coach chronometers; and he had no doubt that, ere long, all the town clocks, and, eventually, all the clocks and watches of private persons, would fall into the same course of regulation; so that only one expression of time would prevail over the country, and every clock and watch indicate by its hands the same hour and minute at the same moment of absolute time'. For this purpose, time was like any other commodity, to be distributed around the country physically. The idea was sound but there was as yet no urgent reason to adopt it. The means of implementation – carrying clocks around the country by coach – may seem impractical; yet that was pretty much how time was delivered to chronometer makers around London until the 1930s. Miss Ruth Belville, the daughter of one of the Observatory assistants, visited the Observatory every Monday, checked her personal timepiece (a 'warming pan' of a silver watch made by John Arnold and Son), then made the rounds of the major clock-makers in London.

Parliament was slow on the uptake: it rejected petitions for introducing a standard time. But the railways had to get on with it. In 1840 the Great Western Railway ordered that London time would apply throughout its network, and one after another the other railway companies followed suit. The Post Office fell in with them. Before long, the public clocks in major provincial cities such as Manchester showed London time. This was not, strictly speaking, Greenwich time, but the body co-ordinating railway operations between the companies officially adopted Greenwich time in 1847. It was therefore in place before the Great Exhibition of 1851 caused an enormous movement of people around the country, with some six million people making the journey to Crystal Palace, the vast majority of them by train.

Greenwich time would sometimes still be distributed by the physical transportation of timepieces, long after the advent of the electric telegraph. Until the 1930s, Miss Ruth Belville called at the Observatory every Monday to check her pocket chronometer before carrying it, and the correct time, around the watch- and clock-makers of London.

The Astronomer Royal, George Airy, believed that it was the 'very proper duty of the National Observatory to promote by utilitarian aid the dissemination of a knowledge of accurate time which is now really a matter of very great importance'. Fortunately, just as demand was arising for a standard time throughout Britain, science provided a method by which a signal could be sent instantaneously to any part of the kingdom, and the railways were supplying the wires along which it would be transmitted. Electricity (or, as it was then known, galvanism) could be used to regulate all the clocks throughout the Observatory. More than that, as Airy reported to his Board of Visitors in June 1849:

> The same means will probably by employed to increase the general utility of
> the Observatory, by the extensive dissemination throughout the Kingdom
> of accurate time-signals, moved by an original clock at the Royal
> Observatory; and I have already entered into correspondence with the
> authorities of the South Eastern Railway (whose line of galvanic
> communication will shortly pass within nine furlongs of the Observatory) in
> reference to this subject …

Telegraph lines were laid from the Observatory to Lewisham station in 1852. From Lewisham the signal would flash to London Bridge station, and from there around the other stations of the South Eastern Railway. More importantly, it went also to the distribution centre of the Electric Telegraph Company in the City of London; this was connected with offices all over the country. Since 1851 there had even been a cable beneath the English Channel, so that Greenwich time could be bestowed on the Continent. It was not without mechanical difficulties. The underground wire to Lewisham failed in 1859, so overhead wires were constructed to the Electric Telegraph Company. Other wires were constructed to Greenwich station, for the benefit of the South Eastern Railway; this signal operated a timeball – one of half a dozen hoisted around the country – at Deal, in Kent. To Airy, reviewing the achievement in 1865, it was a blessing that Britain enjoyed above other countries. 'The practical result of the system will be acknowledged by all those who have travelled abroad. We can, on an English railway, always obtain correct time, but not so on a French or German railway, where the clocks are often found considerably in error.' Oh, the hopelessness of foreigners, to the Victorian mind!

But there was one respect in which the British way was less than perfect. While the whole of the country operated according to Greenwich time, the legal system did not recognise it. In theory, this could have serious consequences: there might be confusion as to, say, whether an insurance policy was in effect if a man died close to midnight. As it turned out, the muddle seems to have been restricted to different parties in court cases arriving at different times (Greenwich and local), and pedantic officials being uncertain when officially to open and close polling booths during general elections. The anomaly was put right by Act of Parliament in 1880, when Greenwich time was adopted for purposes of law.

So much for Britain. But time knows no national boundaries; ships pass from one national jurisdiction to another; even before the age of radio and telephone it was recognised that for different countries to keep different times was inconvenient. Since 1870 scientists and geographers had been bending their minds towards the question of a prime meridian: that is, a line of longi-

tude which everyone acknowledged as zero. Early astronomers, from the Ancients onwards, took their observatories as the meridian. Thus for Hipparchos, the first astronomer to perceive longitude, it was Rhodes. To early royal astronomers in France, it was Paris. But the prime meridian that was most widely used happened to be Greenwich. The explanation for this lies in the British *Nautical Almanac* first published in 1767. This supplied the information from which seafarers of all nations calculated their positions. And from the late eighteenth century

Greenwich came to be taken as zero longitude on many maps and charts, whether or not they originated in Britain. These included J. F. W. DesBarres's 'Atlantic Neptune' covering the east coast of North America from Labrador to the Gulf of Mexico. Most American charts for the next half century were based on DesBarres, entrenching the Greenwich meridian in the New World.

A move to adopt the Greenwich meridian as the prime meridian of the world was made at the first International Geographical Congress, which took place in Antwerp in 1871. Three years later, an International Meridian Conference was convened at Washington. The Canadian geographer, Sanford Fleming, produced figures on the extent to which shipping followed the different meridians then current. He calculated that the Greenwich meridian 'is used by 72 per cent of the whole floating commerce of the world, while the remaining twenty-eight per cent is divided among ten different initial meridians'. Not everyone agreed that there should be a prime meridian (an unexpected dissenter was Airy, so progressive in establishing a common time), or that the meridian adopted ought to be Greenwich. Some thought it should be based on an island, such as the Azores; or on a mountain, like Tenerife; in a strait, like the Baring Strait; or on some timeless historical monument, such as the Great Pyramid or Temple of Jerusalem. After that were the observatories of Paris, Berlin and Washington. In a masterly, though unsuccessful, negotiation, the French said they would only accept Greenwich as the prime meridian if Great Britain adopted the metric system. The Conference overrode the French objections. They recommended to the different governments from which the delegates came that Greenwich should become the prime meridian. Another resolution proposed that this new, universally recognised zero longitude should also be the legally recognised date line for the world. So it is at Greenwich, at midnight, that one day officially turns into the next. With the exception of New Zealand, every country in the world will take the start of the new millennium as 00h 00m 00s Universal Time (within 0.9 of a second of Greenwich Mean Time). In other words, the millennium begins at Greenwich.

It took a little longer for time around the world to be co-ordinated according to Greenwich Time. But it happened sure enough. With international telegraphy and the radio, a standard time was inevitable. Serbia 1884; Japan 1888; Belgium, Holland, South Africa 1892; Italy, Germany, Austria-Hungary 1893 ... so it went on. Only France continued stubbornly to go its own way, adopting Paris Mean Time as *l'heure nationale* by a law of 1891. Five years later, there was an attempt to persuade the *Chambre des Députés* to substitute Greenwich Mean Time. *Greenwich* Time? That was a little too strong for the patriotic deputies, who proposed that the time adopted should in fact be Paris Mean Time diminished by nine minutes twenty-one seconds (Greenwich Time without the Greenwich). This went up to the Senate, who passed it to a commission. It was only in 1911 that the bill was enacted. That law stayed on the statute book until 1978 when France adopted Universal Time.

Universal Time is co-ordinated from Paris. But it is based not on Paris Time but on Greenwich Time. The discrepancy of nearly a second from Greenwich Time is explained by the development of quartz and atomic clocks, which are more reliable than the globe itself. It is now known that the world does not rotate at an *absolutely* constant speed, and there is an infinitesimal wobble in its orbit. For all that, the prime meridian on which the world's time is based is still that which passes through Greenwich.

# PARASOL ON THE SUNNY STRAND OF THE FUTURE

TIME IS NOT ONLY A MATTER OF SCIENCE, there is an element of magic in it too. Certainly it is capable of wondrous transformation scenes, on a par with those perpetrated by an Inigo Jones masque or Richardson's Theatre at Greenwich Fair. Who could have imagined, surveying Greenwich in 1900, that the twentieth century would go out with such a roar? Its opening was something of a low point in Greenwich development. This was the Greenwich which Joseph Conrad made the turning point of his novel *The Secret Agent* in 1907. In it, an anarchist seeks to blow up the Royal Observatory but the bomb explodes in the hands of his simple-minded brother-in-law instead. It was based on the real life Greenwich Bomb Outrage, which had taken place in 1894. Altogether, a contrast could be drawn between the serene Newtonian rationalism of the Observatory and the chaos of humanity living beside the waterfront. Young officers in the Royal Naval College were held to be at risk from the prostitution to be found there.

Recently, though, the roar of the departing century has been only too literal, at least in the case of the Millennium Dome: on the day that I visited it with the project architect Michael Davies in 1998, the noise from the pile drivers at work in the centre of the building did not allow us to penetrate further than the circumference.

Michael Davies is a colourful figure in the story of Greenwich. Only one colour: red. He wears a red shirt, red trousers, red shoes, a red construction hat and carries a red mobile phone. With a grizzled beard and pony tail contrasting with the tomato hue of his clothing, he looks part hippy environmentalist and part pixie. As he described the building, statistics seemed to tumble over one another in their effort to convey the wonder of it. No man has ever driven a golf ball further than the diameter of the Dome. You could lay the Eiffel Tower down in it and its feet would not stick out. It is the largest such construction in the world. The circumference is the exact size of the Avebury Ring. High above us, tiny figures of men, chosen for their skills in abseiling, moved along swathes of fabric as big as a ski slope – 'it could be Val d'Isère,' he mused. Thousands upon thousands of people will visit it – a little like Nelson's lying-in-state, though rather more cheerful.

Aerial view of the Millennium Dome, built in record time to celebrate the year 2000. The structure resembles an umbrella, with fabric stretched over metal ribs. On what used to be a marsh, it occupies the site of the old Greenwich gas works, one of the largest in the country. This photograph is taken from the north-east, with the Isle of Dogs in the middle.

Michael Davis, the man in red, project architect of the Millennium Dome for Richard Rogers Architects. The Dome has instantly acquired landmark status and will open up the industrial Greenwich peninsula to residential development.

One of the best places from which to see the Dome is the sky. Looking like a crown roast of lamb beside the heaped swede and potatoes of the gravel works and other industrial sites beside the Thames, it has become an unmistakable landmark for visitors arriving at London by plane. On the day that I met Mr Davies, however, he was more interested in a voyage being made through another element: not air but earth. Nearby where we were standing, a drill was boring its way far down below the surface of East Greenwich to form the artesian well that would provide one source of water for the site. Above ground, we seemed to be at the limits of our present age, pushing into the future. But as the bore hole went down and down it nosed its way backwards through time: time that had collapsed to a fine layer of black tilth. 'They have just reached a layer of rotted vegetation,' announced Mr Davies, a man whose imagination is stirred as much by archaeology as architecture. 'They think it dates from the time of the dinosaurs, eighty million years ago.' Just as the parasol of the Dome was opening on the sunny strands of time future, here was a sudden reminder of the dark immensity of time past, which lay literally beneath our feet.

This book has been burrowing down through the strata of history during which man has been associated with the site. Two thousand years – a mere eye blink in comparison with the aeon of time since the mammoths and other prehistoric beasts, whose remains have sometimes been found in the area, roamed these parts. But a time also of rapid change. Originally the peninsula had been nothing but a marsh, too boggy for any practical use. At one time, before the course of the Thames took on a regular outline, it was probably as much part of the river as of the land; it would have been regularly flooded if not permanently under water. Its Tudor landowners dug a system of dykes, ditches and sluices which succeeded in draining part of it. It could now be used to graze animals, and Henry VIII rode out from Placentia to hawk there. The stratum of the Elizabethan age has a particular resonance in the history of Greenwich (or the history of Greenwich's history), since a large portion of the peninsula was owned by the antiquary William Lambarde, otherwise remembered as the builder of Queen Elizabeth's College. He used to be commemorated here through the embankment he erected to prevent flooding, originally called Lambarde Wall and then corrupted to Lombard Wall. Occasionally the river claimed back its own. Sometime before

1600 – perhaps in Lambarde's time – the Thames took a bite out of the peninsula's flank when some of the land was lost permanently to flooding. The unwelcome inlet was known on old maps as the Great Breach or Horse Shoe Breach. In the early seventeenth century the Court of Sewers for East Greenwich was established to regulate the drainage of the marsh. A map of 1745 shows the only buildings on the peninsula to be a watch house and what was called the 'New Magazine'. The latter was a powder magazine, which stood near the site of the future Enderby's Wharf.

Not far away was Execution Dock, moved from Wapping in the eighteenth century. It consisted of a metal cage surrounding a gibbet, where river pirates, hanged, would be left in their chains while three tides passed over them. There were three cottages beside Enderby's Wharf, and some others, as well as the Pilot public house, near Ceylon Wharf, an old landing stage whose name reflected the exotic destinations familiar to Greenwich seamen. The Pilot had been built in 1801. The marsh had been chosen as the site of the powder magazine because almost nobody lived there. (The handful of people that did reside on the peninsula objected to the magazine's dangerous state in a petition of 1759.) The marsh remained sparsely populated, with only modest residential development until the Millennium Village was constructed in the hinterland of the Dome. But this promontory, so close to London, attracted industry, and an ever-shifting band of enterprises – brave ventures, profitable ventures, outposts of concerns based elsewhere, flourishing, closing, being bought by other companies, their fortunes so accurately reflecting the market provided by the Victorian world – sprang into varying degrees of life, for varying lengths of time. Many of them, such as the barge-building yards and rope-factory, were connected with shipping. Others were supplied by the river. Some still prosper, such as the gravel works which piles up mountains of stones beside the Millennium site. Most are ghosts.

By the beginning of the twentieth century industry had got the upper hand in Greenwich. Gentility had largely fled, and with it the shades of the kings and queens, courtiers, sea captains and members of the Royal Society who had in previous ages built houses here. Even Gloucester Circus, which looked so dashing when it had been built a hundred years before, was now a series of shabby tenements, whose occupants worked in East Greenwich or the Docks on the other side of the river. They could now walk to the Isle of Dogs, with its docks and industry, by means of the foot tunnel built by the London County Council in 1902. It replaced the old ferry.

Proximity to the Docks was no blessing during the Second World War. Greenwich suffered heavily from those bombs that missed their intended targets there, and it also contained its own targets of strategic importance. By the river the Ship tavern was reduced to rubble. The bright smile of the Paragon on Blackheath lost four of its teeth, two pairs of houses being blown out by either the Luftwaffe or

flying bombs. Reviving the martial spirit of the Fencibles, the Home Guard exercised on Blackheath, pretending to bomb All Saints Church. Hawksmoor's St Alfege's church was burnt out for real, with the loss of most of the Grinling Gibbons carving. Yet, it would have pleased John Betjeman, who invoked 'friendly bombs' to fall on Slough, to reflect that in some respects recent history had been kind: it had generally spared Greenwich the suburban housing estates which had spread like a rash across other areas of London. Not every twentieth-century building in Greenwich has added to its beauty. There are some big blocks of council housing and a town hall in the Dutch style of Dudok (any lingering rivalry from the Dutch Wars having been forgotten), which one might have thought replaced bomb damage but was in fact constructed, large and alien to the surroundings, before hostilities had broken out, in 1939. After the Second World War, Greenwich was still shabby. Dick Moy, who opened his first antique shop here in 1956, remembers the houses of Croom's Hill as having been divided up, and still with a reputation as bordellos. Gradually the middle classes began to recolonise Greenwich's better streets. The Greenwich Society was founded, battling against 'horrific road schemes' and winning for Greenwich the first three conservation areas to be designated in London. Even today, the centre of Greenwich, around St Alfege's church, does not live up to the smartness that has undeniably visited Crooms Hill. The pleasure of strolling along Church Street is diminished by the volume of traffic. Still, the groups of school children, who come from all over the world to visit the *Cutty Sark*, seem to enjoy the experience. And Greenwich has been lucky in one respect. Since the attempt to drive a railway line across the Park in the nineteenth century was repulsed, most of Greenwich's great monuments have been regarded as untouchable. There was no wholesale demolition to widen the roads. Greenwich may, like so many other places, suffer from too many cars, but it has retained its Georgian scale. It is an asset that can only appreciate with time.

And for the past half-century Greenwich has been setting its sails towards a new destiny. This is the topmost layer of its history, to which more seems to be added day by day. Much of it is associated with other layers, for the optimism with which it is facing its future is inseparable from the interpretation of its past. A symbol of this endeavour is the *Cutty Sark*. It is now such an inseparable part of the Greenwich scene, so much one of the monuments that could never be demolished, that it takes some effort of imagination to think of the time before the ship came to its home next to the Greenwich landing stage. Its rescue dates from the years immediately after the Second World War, when decisions had to be taken about the last of the wooden vessels to survive from Britain's nineteenth-century maritime supremacy. Previously, all too many of these decisions had gone against restoring the ships. One December day in 1949, HMS *Implacable*, a seventy-four-gun 'wooden wall' that had fought at Trafalgar, was loaded with ballast and blown up off the south coast. 'I watched as she

*Opposite:* **View of the Isle of Dogs and (bottom right) Greenwich, 1940, taken from a German bomber. Proximity to the Docks did Greenwich no favours: many bombs intended for more important targets instead hit such monuments as St Alfege's church, the Paragon and the Ship tavern.**

*Following page:*
'The people are sooner or later the legitimate inheritors of whatever beauty kings and queens create,' wrote Nathaniel Hawthorne in 1863. This photograph shows the royal park with the old Royal Observatory, the Queen's House and the Seamen's Hospital – the heart of Greenwich for the visiting public. Maze Hill can be seen on the far left. The white quadrangle on the right of this view is the former Dreadnought Seamen's Hospital, originally by Athenian Stuart but rebuilt after a fire in 1810–11. The long red building above it is Sir Edwin Cooper's Devonport House, 1929, on the site of what used to be the hospital cemetery.

was towed to her death. I marvelled at the beautiful way in which her lovely hull slid through the water, causing scarcely a ripple; I wept when she sank,' wrote the Director of the National Maritime Museum, Frank Carr. The arrival of the *Cutty Sark* at Greenwich as her permanent home in 1954 was the result of a determination on the part of many people who loved ships – not least Frank Carr – never to let such a thing happen again. As the *Cutty Sark*'s rigging rose beside the Thames, Greenwich itself seemed to recapture some of its old confidence and identity.

The focus of the new Greenwich, so to speak, has been the National Maritime Museum, occupying Inigo Jones's Queen's House and the wings that were added to it in the nineteenth century, when it served as the Royal Hospital School. (The school moved to Suffolk in 1933.) The Museum is no johnny-come-lately in the history of Greenwich: it has emerged from deeper layers of the town's past. From the time of Nelson's funeral the Seamen's Hospital contained relics of naval interest. The Painted Hall, almost from the moment of its creation, ceased to fulfil its original purpose as a dining-room, serving instead as a national achievement that could be shown to visitors. Pensioners collected useful amounts of money for the Hospital – as well as emoluments for themselves – by acting as guides. Athenian

## Cutty Sark

The *Cutty Sark* (seen opposite) was one of the most beautiful ships of the nineteenth century, and is now a rare survival from the last great days of sail. It was built as a tea clipper, in an age when enormous prestige was attached to the ship which could perform the journey to China in the least time. The first master of the *Cutty Sark* had a high opinion of her. 'I never sailed a finer ship,' he declared. 'At 10 or 12 knots she did not disturb the water at all. She was the fastest ship of her day, a grand ship, and a ship that will last forever.'

But when the *Cutty Sark* was launched in 1869 steam had already begun to replace sail. She carried her last cargo of tea in 1877. But then she discovered a new career in the wool trade to Australia, and in the late 1880s and early 1890s made the fastest passage home several times.

The *Cutty Sark* was exhibited in a mooring off Greenwich as part of the 1951 Festival of Britain. Afterwards, HRH the Duke of Edinburgh was prominent in the campaign to have her permanently docked there, that object being achieved in 1954.

The ship's name is derived from Robert Burns's poem 'Tam O'Shanter', in which Tam is pursued by witches as he rides drunkenly home. The fastest of the witches, young and beautiful, wore only a short linen shift, or 'cutty sark'. She managed to grasp the tail of Tam's mare as they galloped to safety over the river Doon. Sailors used to make a grey mare's tail from an old end of rope and put it in the outstretched hand of the ship's figurehead.

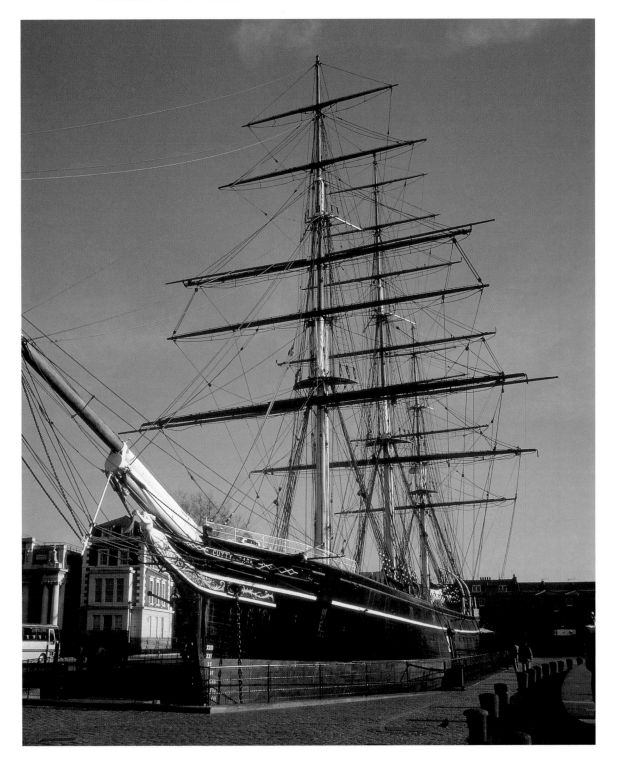

Stuart's new chapel provided another attraction. By the mid-1790s, when the wars on the Continent gave domestic tourism a fillip, the Hospital was taking over £570 a year from visitors. In the 1820s, the collection of John Julius Angerstein – whose country house, it will be remembered, was Woodlands – was bought by the nation to form the nucleus of the National Gallery. At the same time George IV gave thirty portraits of naval commanders to the Seamen's Hospital to augment, very substantially, the modest number of paintings that it possessed. The Painted Hall was turned into a gallery – the National Gallery of Naval Art – to show them. It was then one of only three public galleries in London (the others being the Dulwich Picture Gallery and the incipient National Gallery, then displayed in Angerstein's house in Pall Mall), and became one of the sights that people of all classes wanted to visit. Models of famous ships were added to the collection, which numbered three hundred by the end of the century. They all formed the basis of the Royal Naval Museum, established at Greenwich Hospital in 1873.

In time the Royal Naval Museum evolved into the National Maritime Museum, which opened in 1937. Perhaps appropriately, the opening day inspired a recrudescence of the boisterous behaviour associated with Greenwich Fair: despite free entry, some of the five thousand people who visited the Museum climbed over the railings, all the soap and towels in the lavatories were pocketed and men used the fireplaces in the Queen's House to urinate. It would not have happened in the National Gallery, the Victoria and Albert Museum or the Science Museum; somehow Greenwich, and the public it attracted, were different. Soon Britain was at war. Inevitably, therefore, it was the naval aspect of the 'Maritime' which dominated the Museum's early life. But it also participated in the surge of national redefinition associated with the Festival of Britain (under a Labour government) in 1951 and the coronation of Queen Elizabeth II (under the Conservatives) two years later. When the Royal Observatory, finding that the skies of London were too polluted for observations still to be made from Greenwich, moved its telescopes to Herstmonceux Castle in Sussex in 1948, the National Maritime Museum assumed responsibility for the old building. Flamsteed House and the Octagon Room first opened to the public shortly after the Festival of Britain. In 1951 Her Majesty the Queen opened the east wing of the Museum.

Not everything in the Museum's history has been plain sailing: the recent restoration of the Queen's House, which followed a long period of closure, caused a squall among scholars when it was reopened in 1990. It was not an easy building to display, because of the difficulty of deciding which periods of construction should be the inspiration for the recreated interiors, very little of the original furniture or decoration having survived; but the approach taken was given a mauling by the critics. But this controversy was soon left behind, as fair winds carried the Museum onwards towards the millennium. Money from the National Lottery has made possible a project to remove what was originally the school gymnasium and roof over the courtyard that it occupied to form the Neptune Court. This will provide some twenty new galleries and display spaces. In addition, the status of the old Royal Observatory is set to develop. In the future, it will not only continue to be a museum which the public can visit to experience something of the past history of astronomical endeavour: it will be charged with interpreting the present state of man's knowledge of the cosmos to the public. There is exciting talk of a simultaneous video link with a proposed new telescope in Hawaii, which could be operated remotely from Greenwich: since the skies over Hawaii would be dark during what is daytime for Greenwich, this would enable visitors to explore the heavens for themselves.

There is a brave new future for buildings of the Seamen's Hospital, otherwise the Royal Naval College, too. Three centuries of occupation by the Royal Navy have ended. Very nearly ended, that is: one of the unexpected and somewhat unwelcome layers of Greenwich history to have been brought to general attention recently has been the existence of a nuclear reactor on the site. The reactor (endearingly known as Jason) was installed by the Royal Naval College to give officers the opportunity to study nuclear power as related to submarines. The Ministry of Defence failed to take its existence into account when planning the navy's retreat from Greenwich, which has as a result taken longer than originally expected. But soon Wren's colonnades will shelter the University of Greenwich. Meanwhile, the cultural significance both of this complex and the Park has been recognised by UNESCO, who have declared Greenwich to be a World Heritage Site.

This accolade reflects the extent to which Greenwich embodies values that are perhaps appreciated above all others in the modern age. Greenwich is a place of history and the study of history; it will soon also be a place of more modern learning. One only has to glimpse the masts of the Millennium Dome to see that it is as up to the minute as anywhere in Europe; and yet its ability to keep pace with the future has not been at the expense of its great past. The age of the automobile, now waning, may not, in all respects, have treated Greenwich kindly: there has been too much traffic congestion and it has come to seem far more remote from the centre of London than its geographical separation of only four or five miles would suggest. But it has survived into an era in which the motor car will be less dominant with its human scale and green spaces intact. Now that underground trains are about to reach Greenwich, with the extension of the Jubilee Line, along with the Docklands Light Railway, there is every reason for Greenwich residents to smile. They are living in a town which has both a deep past, rich in its many strata, as this book has sought to show. And a future that leaps up to the sky.

# FURTHER READING

By far the richest source of material on Greenwich is Edward Hasted's *Hundred of Blackheath*, a history based on two manuscript collections, and in turn edited by Henry H. Drake, 1886. It is a cornucopia of references, but in the manner of cornucopias, the organising principle appears to be rich profusion rather than conventional orderliness. An enormous amount is contained in it if you look. Contemporary sources for which I give no other reference will generally be found in Hasted. The antiquarian background is painted in the three Kent volumes of the *Victoria Country History*, 1908, 1926 and 1932. A synopsis of Greenwich's architectural monuments is provided by the *London South* volume of Bridget Cherry and Nikolaus Pevsner's *Buildings of England*, 1983. H. M. Colvin's *Biographical Dictionary of British Architects* is the first place to search for information on any Greenwich (or other) architect. The building of Bella Court, Placentia, the Queen's House and Charles II's palace can be traced in the first five volumes of H. M. Colvin (ed), *The History of the King's Works*, 1963, 1975 and 1976. There have been a number of general books about Greenwich over the years. In the same year that Hasted's monumental volume appeared, 1886, A. G. L'Estrange's *The Palace and the Hospital, or Chronicles of Greenwich* was published. More recently, Olive and Neil Hamilton produced their illustrated *Royal Greenwich* (Greenwich, 1969). Beryl Platts's *A History of Greenwich*, Newton Abbot, 1973, provides a narrative history, particularly strong on the early centuries, if sometimes touched by romanticism. Felix Barker's admirable *Greenwich and Blackheath Past*, with pictures accompanying a rather spare text, came out in 1993. The history of Blackheath is comprehensively detailed in *Blackheath Village and Environs, 1790–1990*, 2 vols, Blackheath, 1976 and 1983, by Neil Rhind. Many papers on Greenwich history have been published in the *Transactions of the Greenwich and Lewisham Antiquarian Society* since the beginning of the twentieth century. The Society and its *Transactions* still flourish. Beyond that, the best starting point for research on Greenwich is the subject catalogue of the Society of Antiquaries, with its many references to topographical works in the Society's collections. Moreover, Greenwich is blessed with a first-rate local history library in what used to be the Angerstein country house of Woodlands, in Mycenae Road.

# PRINCIPAL SOURCES

(All books published in London unless otherwise stated.)

## PROLOGUE
*Fairburn's Edition of the Funeral of Admiral Lord Nelson*, 1806. *A Complete Account of the Procession and Ceremony Observed at the Funeral of Lord Nelson, Thursday, January 9, 1806* (reprinted Eugene, Oregon, 1991).
*The Times* and the *Naval Chronicle* for 1805 and 1806.
Frederick Locker-Lampson, *My Confidences*, 1896.

## CHAPTER ONE
National Sites and Monuments Record, Greater London (computerised record of archaeological finds), kept by English Heritage, London Division.
Reg Rigden, *The Romans in the Greenwich District*, Greenwich, 1974.
Harvey Sheldon and Brian Yule, 'Excavations in Greenwich Park, 1978–79', reprinted from the *London Archaeologist*, 1979.
Arthur D. Sharp, 'St Alfege', *Transactions of the Greenwich and Lewisham Antiquarian Society*, vol.4, 1936, pp 6–16.
*Britannia Sancta: or, the Lives of the Most Celebrated British, English, Scottish and Irish Saints*, 1745.

N. A. M. Rodger, *The Safeguard of the Sea: A Naval History of Britain, 600–1612*, 1997.
Kerry Downes, *Hawksmoor*, 1959.
H. M. Colvin, 'Fifty New Churches', *Architectural Review*, March 1950.
RCHME, *Greenwich Park, An Archaeological Survey*, 1994.

## CHAPTER TWO
Beryl Platts, op. cit.
K. H. Vickers, *Humphrey Duke of Gloucester*, 1907.
Hasted, op. cit.
G. Kriehn, *The English Rising of 1450*, 1892.
Mary Clive, *This Sun of York*, 1973.
Simon Thurley in *The Royal Palaces of Tudor England*, 1993.

## CHAPTER THREE
Van Cleave Alexander, *The First of the Tudors*, 1981.
Thurley, op. cit.
An English translation of the letters from the Venetian embassy can be found at the Public Record Office, Kew (*The Calendars of the State Papers: Venetian*, 19 vols). It is presented as a calendar; that is to say, a precis of the original documents, though sometimes the trans-

lation appears to be direct (I have quoted it as such in the text). Extracts from the papers are quoted in John M. Stone, 'Greenwich History as Told by Venetian Records', *Transactions of the Greenwich and Lewisham Antiquarian Society*, c. 1912.

Philip Dixon, *Excavations at Greenwich Palace, 1970–71*, 1971.

Francis Henry Cripps-Day, *Fragmenta Armamentaria*, vol. 1, part II, 'An Introduction to the Study of Grenwich Armour'.

M. Oppenheim, *A History of the Administration of the Royal Navy*, 1896.

N. A. M. Rodger, op. cit.

John Gough Nichols (ed), *Literary Remains of King Edward the Sixth*, vol. 2.

J. W. Kirby, 'Alfonso Ferrabosco of Greenwich (1573?–1627) Court Musician', *Transactions of the Greenwich and Lewisham Antiquarian Society*, vol. 3, 1924–34, pp. 207–17.

John Kimbell, *An Account of the legacies, gifts and charities for Church and Poor, in tbe Parish of St Alphege, Greenwich*, Greenwich, 1816.

## CHAPTER FOUR

John Summerson, *Inigo Jones*, 1966.

John Harris and Gordon Higgott, *Inigo Jones, Complete Architectural Drawings* (Royal Academy exhibition catalogue), February 1990.

G. H. Chettle in *The Queen's House. Greenwich*, a London Survey Committee monograph, 1937.

J. Charlton, *The Queen's House*, 1976.

Stephen Orgen and Roy Strong's monumental *Inigo Jones, the Theatre of the Stuart Court*, 2 vols, 1973.

G. P. V. Akrigg, *Jacobean Pageant or the Court of King James I*, 1962.

G. P. V, Akrigg, *Letters of King James VI and I*, 1984.

Anne Somerset, *Unnatural Murder*, 1997.

*The Calendars of the State Papers: Venetian*, op. cit.

N. E. McClure (ed), *The Letters of John Chamberlain*, 2 vols, Philadelphia, 1939.

Carola Oman, *Henrietta Maria*, 1951.

## CHAPTER FIVE

W. H. Mandy, 'Notes from the Assize Rolls and Other Documents Relating to the Hundred of Blackheath', *Transactions of the Greenwich and Lewisham Antiquarian Society*, vol. 1, 1913, pp. 300–02

Jane Burkitt, 'Greenwich at the End of the 17th Century', *Transactions of the Greenwich and Lewisham Antiquarian Society*, vol. 8, 1977 (published 1978), pp. 223–33.

John Bold, *John Webb*, Oxford.

Derek Howse, *Francis Place and the Early History of the Greenwich Observatory*, Oxford, 1989.

Richard Ollard, *Pepys*, 1974 (illustrated edition 1990).

R. C. Latham and W. Matthews, *The Diary of Samuel Pepys*, 9 vols, from 1971.

John Summerson, *Sir Christopher Wren*, 1953.

Kerry Downes, *Christopher Wren*, 1971. Wren's buildings, with documents, have all been published in the 20 vols of the Wren Society; the Royal Observatory features in vol. 19, pp. 113–15.

Derek Howse, *Greenwich Time and the Longitude*, 1997 (first published 1980 as *Greenwich Time and the Discovery of the Longitude*).

F. Baily, *An Account of the Rev'd John Flamsteed, the First Astronomer Royal*, 1835.

Eric G. Forbes, Lesley Murdin and Frances Willmoth (ed), *The Correspondence of John Flamsteed, the First Astronomer Royal*, 2 vols, Bristol, 1995 and 1997.

Wren and London's estimate of damages was published in *Notes and Queries*, 10 May 1856.

## CHAPTER SIX

Jock Haswell, *James II: Soldier, Sailor*, 1972.

Pieter van der Merwe, *'A Refuge for All'. Greenwich Hospital, 1694–1994*, Greenwich, 1994.

John Cooke and John Maule, *An Historical Account of the Royal Hospital for Seamen at Greenwich*, 1789.

Edward Fraser, *Greenwich Hospital and the Royal United Services Museum*, 1910.

Philip Newell, *Greenwich Hospital. A Royal Foundation, 1692–1983*, 1984.

The hospital's architecture is the subject of vol. 6 of the Wren Society. We await what will no doubt prove the definitive study, the survey of London volume edited by John Bold.

David Watkin, *Athenian Stuart, Pioneer of the Greek Revival*, 1982.

Lesley Lewis, 'The Architects of the Chapel at Greenwich Hospital', *Art Bulletin*, vol. 29–30 (1947–8), pp. 260–7.

Jeanne-Marie Philipon Roland, 'A Trip to England', in *The Works ... of Jeanne-Marie Philipon Roland*, translated from the French, 1800.

Clare Williams (ed and trans), *Sophie in London, 1786, being the Diary of Sophie von la Roche*, 1933.

The diary of the First Earl of Egremont is published in vol. 63 of the Historical Manuscript Commission Reports, kept in the British Library.

## CHAPTER SEVEN

Kerry Downes, op. cit.

Kerry Downes, 'The Little Colony on Greenwich Hill', *Country Life*, 27 May 1976, pp. 1406–08.

Neil Rhind, *Blackheath Village and Environs, 1790–1970*, vol. 2, Blackheath, 1983.

H. G. Lovegrove, *London Topographical Record*, iv, 1907.

Laurence Whistler, *The Imagination of Vanbrugh and his Fellow Artists*, 1954, pp. 200–06.

W. E. L. Fletcher, 'The Maze Hill Estate of Sir John Vanbrugh', *Transactions of the Greenwich and Lewisham Antiquarian Society*, vol. 8, 1978, pp. 136–42.

## CHAPTER EIGHT

Neil Rhind, *The Heath*, Blackheath, 1987.

Daniel Defoe, *Tour Through England and Wales*, 1724–6.

Derek Howse, *Francis Place*, op. cit.

Lord Egremont, op. cit.

Cyril Fry, 'The Angersteins of Woodlands', *Transactions of the Greenwich and Lewisham Antiquarian Society*, vol. 7, 1964–72.

Neil Rhind, op. cit.

Charles Alister, 'Montague House, Blackheath', *Transactions of the Greenwich and Lewisham Antiquarian Society*, vol. 8, 1973–8.

Francis Bickley (ed), *The Diaries of Sylvester Douglas (Lord Glenbervie)*, 2 vols, 1928, vol. 2, p. 83.

Flora Fraser, *The Unruly Queen*, 1996.

Nathaniel Hawthorne, *Our Old Home*, 1863.

## CHAPTER NINE

Ronald Longhurst, 'Greenwich Fair', *Transactions of the Greenwich and Lewisham Antiquarian Society*, vol. 7, pp. l98–210.

Percival Leigh, *Mr Pips hys Diary*, 1849.

Charles Dickens in the *Evening Chronicle*, 1835.

Nathaniel Hawthorne, op. cit.

Robert Halliday, 'Beastly Business', *Country Life*, 9 December 1993.

Neil Rhind, op. cit.

*The Pictorial Guide to Greenwich. A Holiday Handbook*, 1884.

William Howarth, *Some Particulars Relating to the Ancient and Royal Borough of Greenwich*, 1882.

*Cruikshank's Trip to Greenwich Fair, a Whimsical Record*, 1830.

## CHAPTER TEN

Mrs Thomas Norledge, 'Greenwich as an Ancient Fishing Port', *Transactions of the Greenwich and Lewisham Antiquarian Society*, vol. 1, 1915, pp. 356–72.

Philip Banbury, *Shipbuilders of the Thames and Medway*, Newton Abbot, 1971.

Alan Pearsall, 'Greenwich and the River in the 19th Century', *Transactions of the Greenwich and Lewisham Antiquarian Society*, vol. 8, 1973–78, pp. 20-26.

V. Bartlett, 'The River and Marsh at East Greenwich', *Transactions of the Greenwich and Lewisham Antiquarian Society*, vol. 7, 1964–72, pp. 68–85.

S. Shoberl, *A Summer's Day at Greenwich*, 1840.

R. H. G. Thomas, *London's First Railway: the London and Greenwich*, 1972.

June Burkitt, 'The Town of Greenwich in 1848', *Transactions of the Greenwich and Lewisham Antiquarian Society*, vol. 9, pp. 7–20.

Alec Holden, 'Early Town-planning in Greenwich', *Transactions of the Greenwich and Lewisham Antiquarian Society*, vol. 7, 1966, pp. 106–15.

The story of the *Cutty Sark* is told in the excellent Pitkin's guide, first published 1994.

## CHAPTER ELEVEN

*Illustrated London News*, 14 May 1842, p. 16.

Derek Howse, *Greenwich Time*, op. cit.

## CHAPTER TWELVE

Kevin Littlewood and Beverley Butler, *Of Ships and Stars, Maritime Heritage and the Founding of the National Maritime Museum*, Greenwich, 1998.

# INDEX